THE DISTINCTIVE IDEAS OF THE OLD TESTAMENT

THE DISTINCTIVE IDEAS OF THE OLD TESTAMENT

NORMAN H. SNAITH

SCHOCKEN BOOKS · NEW YORK

First SCHOCKEN PAPERBACK edition 1964

THIRD PRINTING, 1973

This edition is published by arrangement with
The Epworth Press, London.

Library of Congress Catalog Card No. 64-24013
Manufactured in the United States of America

CONTENTS

PREFACE

In this Fernley-Hartley Lecture I have set forth what I believe to be the distinctive ideas of Old Testament religion. These are different from the ideas of any other religion whatsoever. In particular they are quite distinct from the ideas of the Greek thinkers. The aim of Hebrew religion was *Da'ath Elohim* (the Knowledge of God); the aim of Greek thought was *Gnothi seauton* (Know thyself). Between these two there is a great gulf fixed. We do not see that either admits of any compromise. They are fundamentally different in *a priori* assumption, in method of approach, and in final conclusion.

Traditional Christianity has sought to find a middle way, combining Zion and Greece into what is held to be a harmonious synthesis. The New Testament has been interpreted according to Plato and Aristotle, and the distinctive Old Testament ideas have been left out of account. Here is the cause of the modern neglect of the Old Testament. The 'righteousness' of Aristotle has been substituted for the 'righteousness' of the Old Testament. The *logos spermatikos* of the Stoics has largely transplanted the Holy Spirit. The wholly non-Biblical doctrine of the immortality of the human soul is accepted largely as a characteristic Christian doctrine. Plato is indeed 'divine', and Aristotle 'the master of them that know'.

It may be that traditional Christianity has been divinely guided in thus transferring itself into a dominant Greek environment. In that case let us cease to talk of the Bible as the Word of God. On the other hand, if the Bible really is the Word of God, and the Old Testament an integral part of it, then let us be sure what are those ideas common to both which may properly be regarded as creating the norm by which the Bible is to be interpreted.

This lecture does not claim to be by any means complete in its examination of Christian theology. Its scope is necessarily limited. It deals first with the distinctive ideas of the Old Testament, and last with those same ideas as they are to be seen in the New Testament.

NORMAN H. SNAITH

Chapter I

WHY 'DISTINCTIVE'?

'DISTINCTIVE' IN PREFERENCE TO 'FUNDAMENTAL'

OUR concern in this lecture is with those elements of Old Testament religion which distinguish it from other religions. We recognize the importance of realizing that the Hebrews had many items of belief and practice in common with other peoples of antiquity, but our interest in these common features is, for our present purposes, definitely secondary. We are concerned with them only in so far as the study of them throws into greater and clearer relief the essential differences. Our aim here is, so far as may be, to isolate and to emphasize the distinctive elements of Old Testament religion. We use the word *distinctive* designedly and of set purpose. We use it in preference to the word *fundamental*, because of the general tendency to interpret the latter word as having to do with origins. It is sometimes useful, and doubtless generally interesting, to know what the origins are, but it is necessary, and it may be a matter of life and death, to know what the conclusions are going to be. For us, in this lecture especially, ends matter most, in the sense both of endings as against beginnings, and of purposes as against origin and development.

THE RECENT EMPHASIS ON ORIGINS: THE GAIN AND THE LOSS

A book, indeed, on the origins of Old Testament religion would, in these days, be largely superfluous. There has been in recent times a considerable literature dealing with the origin of Hebrew religion, tracing its beginnings in every type of primitive thought and folklore, and emphasizing its similarities with all religions in general, but in particular with the ancient religions of the Near East, proto-Semitic and Canaanite, Egyptian, Mesopotamian, neo-Babylonian and Persian. All this has been done in the most approved scientific manner. Old Testament scholars have responded, equally with scholars in every other branch of knowledge, to the stimulus of the New Scientific Method promoted in the first instance largely by Herbert Spencer's *Synthetic Philosophy*. They have made full use of such pioneering studies as Sir E. B. Tylor's *Primitive Culture* and Sir J. G. Frazer's two works, his many-volumed *The Golden Bough*, and his three-volumed *The Folklore of the Old Testament*. The result has been a tremendous gain in our understanding of Hebrew religion in its relation to other religions. Particularly, we have grown familiar with the common heritage of Hebrews and Gentiles in their awareness of the Supernatural. This has been a definite gain.

Excellent, however, as this movement has been, there has been another and less satisfactory side to it. It is significant that for the last standard work in English on Old Testament Theology we have to go back to A. B. Davidson's *The Theology of the Old Testament*, which is dated 1901, and is therefore over forty years old. The modern tendency is seen in Oesterley and Robinson's *Hebrew Religion, Its Origin and Development* (2nd ed., 1937). Out of 417 pages of printed text, no less than 121 pages deal with such subjects as animism, *taboo*, and suchlike, items which necessarily occupy a large space in books on primitive religion. The discussion of the work of the canonical prophets begins on p. 222, rather more than halfway through the book, and yet it is agreed by all that the truly distinctive Hebrew contribution to religion begins here. We do not wish these remarks to be taken as criticizing this excellent book. The book does what it sets out to do, and does it admirably. It is designedly concerned with the origin and development of Hebrew religion, and within its own prescribed limits it is most helpful to students. Rather we give these facts to illustrate the modern tendency, which deals with origins and developments in preference to final results, and within that sphere finds itself more interested in origins than in developments.

Or, again, W. Robertson Smith's *The Religion of the Semites* was an epoch-making book in that, as long ago as 1889, it set the religion of the Hebrews in focus with respect to Semitic religion generally. In itself, however, it is inadequate as a picture of Hebrew religion precisely because of this insistence upon the common elements of Semitic religions. This feature is further emphasized by the very considerable additions made by Dr. S. A. Cook in the most recent (third, 1927) edition. From the point of view of primitive and comparative religion this third edition is beyond praise, but from the point of view of Hebrew religion specifically, it needs, even more than before, to be supplemented by W. Robertson Smith's *The Prophets of Israel* (revised edition, 1895).

We are therefore of the firm opinion that it is high time for us to awake out of our semi-hypnosis, induced by the desire for comprehensiveness and broad-mindedness, and by the attractiveness of these studies in early comparative religion and native custom. Such studies of the ways and thoughts of primitive man have a strange fascination. This is partly due to the romanticism with which we colour a long-lost unmechanical and unsophisticated age, partly to a real interest in the doings of our brother-man of whatever period of the world's history, but partly also to the sense of superiority which they give us, whereby we can say, 'There but for the grace of centuries, go I.' However that may be, it is time for us now to be able to view the work of Tylor, Frazer, and their successors in its proper perspective. It has taken two generations for the Graf-Wellhausen theory of the literary structure of the Pentateuch to settle down into a moderately fluid mellowness. At last we have realized that there are limits beyond which literary analysis cannot be pressed without doing more harm than good. Even the good order of J, E, D, and P may corrupt the scholarly world. We have been so very energetic in isolating each from other, and even within each, in separating stratum from stratum, that we have tended to forget that there might be method even in the madness which so thoroughly dovetailed them in together. Perhaps after all that madness was divine. In a similar way, our preoccupation with origins and development has blurred our eyes from seeing whither the development was making, and equally has tied our tongues from asking why this way and no other way. Nay more, we can be accused, and with a considerable measure of justification, of being foolish enough to advance backwards, our faces always turned towards the point of our departure.

In this respect Old Testament scholars have themselves largely to thank for the neglect of the Old Testament in these latter days. We have been lured by the attractiveness of a comprehensive outlook, possibly we have been afraid of being thought narrow and bigoted, and perhaps also we have been enticed, as Andrew Lang would say, by the fascinating devices of the naughty man.

We have been content to allow people to study the Bible as literature, and on occasion ourselves so to speak of it. The Bible certainly is literature, some of it comparable in excellence by any tests with any other literature in the world, but its value for us does not lie here. It is the Word of God, and the Old Testament is an integral part of that Word. The Old Testament is essential to the understanding of the whole Bible, and it cannot be replaced by any other way of thought and life, not even by that of Plato and Aristotle. This replacement of the Hebrew knowledge of God by the results of the speculations of the Greeks has been the characteristic feature of the history of Christian thought. The Reformation was an attempt to restore the religion of the Bible, but some of the reformers themselves were not exempt from the old tendency. Even when this has not been the case, Christians have been tempted to regard the Old Testament as being but one of the many sacred books which the world has known. They have thought therefore that it was of small account for the Christian, who would do well to save his time in a busy, thronging world and begin with the Gospel according to Matthew.

From this attitude we strongly dissent, and still more are we at variance with the attitude which has fostered it. If the Old Testament has, for Jew and Christian, a value which no other book has, then it is essential for us to know and to be very sure what that value is, where it is different from other sacred books, and particularly where it is incomparable. Where we have come from is by this time plain for all to see, but it is of little account in comparison with where we are going to. This is true, not only of nations and men, but of religions, as indeed of everything else. We ought never to have permitted our evolutionary zeal to make us forget that lesson which Aristotle himself taught—namely, that the subsequent stages of growth are at least as important for the understanding of the nature of an organism as are its beginnings. It is the oak that shall be which makes the acorn what it is, and not the acorn the oak.

THE IMPORTANCE OF THE HISTORICALLY LATER

The modern tendency has been to emphasize the importance of the historically prior. This tendency has been so marked as to lead many to suppose that the historically prior is of most importance just because of its historical priority. We quote from the late R. R. Marett: 'That ritual, or in other words a routine of external forms, is historically prior to dogma, was proclaimed years ago by W. Robertson Smith and others; yet Social Anthropology is but to-day beginning to appreciate the psychological implications of this cardinal truth.'[1] This statement was made thirty-four years ago. It was doubtless necessary then to emphasize the importance of the early development of ritual. But much water has flowed under that bridge since those days. Indeed, the priority of ritual has been emphasized to such an extent as to make ritual historically prior to any belief at all, however vaguely stated or confusedly understood. 'Cardinal truth' is a strong phrase. We agree that ritual comes before dogma, if the word 'dogma' is taken to mean the declared and official belief of an organized community, even though that organization be rudimentary. But we do not agree that any rite was ever observed by man without any reasons whatever being given or assumed. There is some sort of intention, however ill-defined or scantily formulated, in even the most elementary of primitive rites. The reasons may belong to the most primitive stage of sympathetic magic. They may be expressed with an indefiniteness of category and a consequent diffuseness of thought which is not only alien to our modern scientific attempts at preciseness, but even offensive to them. They may be hardly intelligible, or almost wholly wrong, but whatever they are, they are none the less reasons, and as such they are the raw material out of which dogma is made.

Or, again, the reasons may belong to a later stage of culture, and may be the first efforts of the primitive speculative philosopher. Whatever they are, they are necessary to the rite as it is then observed. Even supposing that any or all of the extant explanations are shown to be later than the rite, it frequently needs the later 'dogma' to decide which of the earlier factors is sound and must therefore receive special notice. Only thus can the true significance of the rite, even at its earliest known stages, be understood. We may easily know what primitive man was doing better than he himself knew, for the passing of the years makes many things more plain. 'By their fruits ye shall know

[1] *The Birth of Humility*, in *The Threshold of Religion* (4th ed. 1929), p. 181. This particular essay was first published in 1910 as a pamphlet by the Clarendon Press.

them' is a wise saying, capable of extension into all realms of knowledge and experience.

All aitiology is therefore instructive, whether it takes the form of ordinary 'straight' explanation, or that of parable, myth, or dogma. Sometimes the value lies in showing what is excellent and of good report in the historically prior. At other times it makes plain what was of the earth, and on occasion very earthy, and must therefore be consigned to the limbo of dreams gone astray. Whatever the statement may be, and whatever its form, it is worthy of the closest attention. It may be a formal statement such as that of Maimonides or the Creeds of the Christian Church. It may consist only of the upward thrust of the hand of Australian aborigines,[1] or the circular and spiral representations on their bull-roarers, 'a pictorial Bible, the parables of which the old men make it their first duty to expound to the younger members of each totemic congregation'.[2]

Dr. S. A. Cook quotes[3] the epigram, 'The most ancient in religion is the purest, the most recent is the truest.' Epigrams are most dangerous when most they are epigrammatic. Here 'purest' must mean unrelated to any other action or idea, and so undeveloped and un- or ill-explained, for it cannot mean excellent in morals or exact in thought and intention. For the rest, there is no virtue in development *per se*, but often much vice. Nor is there any virtue in lack of development, but usually the folly of the unformed or the stagnation of slimy ponds. Ardent evolutionists and ardent anti-evolutionists are equally in error, their error being proportional to their ardour. The former are in error when they assume that the most recent must necessarily be the truest, the latter when they assert that the most ancient must necessarily be the purest. The most recent may be the falsest, and the most ancient the filthiest. In the epigram cited above, we rather suspect that 'purest' actually means 'most meaningless', especially as it refers to the unrelated. If the epigram be taken as a general warning of the limitations of dogma so far as the first part of it is concerned, and as an appreciation of the value of dogma so far as the latter part is concerned, then it is a

[1] A. W. Howitt, *The Native Tribes of South-east Australia* (1904), p. 734.

[2] R. R. Marett, *Sacraments of Simple Folk* (1933), p. 37.

[3] In W. Robertson Smith, *The Religion of the Semites* (3rd ed., 1927), additional notes, p. 683.

guide to truth. Otherwise it is little more than a caltrop to bring down those whose aim it is to ride forward, whatever and wherever they ride.

FURTHER REASONS FOR THE NEED OF THE STUDY OF THE DISTINCTIVE IDEAS

There are two further reasons why it is necessary to examine the distinctive elements of Christianity, and, as is our purpose here, of that older Hebrew religion out of which, in the fullness of time, Christianity was born.

(*a*) *Distinctiveness is the Sole Justification of Continued Existence*

If there are no distinctive elements in Christianity, then, in the name of whatever gods there then may be, let us be realistic and sensible. Let us dismiss the whole affair to its proper home in the limbo of the dead illusions of mankind. Let us then proceed to look for a further development of the 'religious' ideas and activities of mankind, either along the lines of Dr. Julian Huxley's *Religion without Revelation* (1927), supplemented by the last pages (576 *ff.*) of his more recent *Evolution: a Modern Synthesis* (1942), or, alternatively, in some Theosophy more splendid than hitherto, wherein all the religions of mankind are seen to be but one in essence, any apparent differences being merely other faces of the One God, each relatively true. On the other hand, if Christianity does contain distinctive elements, both in common with Judaism against the rest of religions, and of itself as against Jewry, then, in the Name of the One God, let us examine them, and let us be very sure indeed of what precisely they are. No institution, be it religious or secular, has any right to continue to exist unless it has, and can show in all the market-places of the world, a special and distinct reason for its separate existence. If it cannot do this, then it is cumbering the ground. Worse still, it is leading men astray into a darkness which is none the less real because of its semi-enlightened confusion. Rationalization applies to religions equally with industry.

(*b*) *The Need to meet the Challenge of the Rationalist*

It is time that the challenge of such books as those of Sir J. G. Frazer and his successors was met fairly and squarely. Let us not copy them in that pleasant confusion which is part of their attractiveness. Frazer devoted a long and industrious life to the collection with unflagging zeal of details of customs and native folklore from every corner of the world. He piled Pelion on Ossa, and produced volume after volume, giving instance after instance of apparently similar customs, but always stressing the similarities. One result is that in giving reasons for the customs, and in explaining them, his work fails distressingly, and is the very reverse of scientific. His method does not allow for the fact that apparently similar customs may be due, and indeed we are convinced that they often are due, to completely different causes. For instance, there are pyramids in Egypt, in Mexico, and in Babylonia. But they are all different, and must be treated differently. Those in Egypt are graves which have grown up from the ground, and under no consideration can they be classed with the pyramids of either Mexico or Mesopotamia. These others are altars raised up towards heaven, but again they differ each from other, since those in Mesopotamia were probably artificial sacred mountains, whereas this is most unlikely to be the case in mountainous Mexico. The differences are fundamental, though the results are astonishingly similar.

The aspect of Frazer's work, whereby he neglects or slurs over the differences, has never received the attention which it ought to have had. This has been partly because of the difficulty of tracing back his evidence to its sources. Furthermore, when Frazer does provide explanations and theories of origins, these all depend upon his general assumption of similarity of development of custom and idea throughout the whole world. So great, indeed, is his zeal for equation, comparison, and the isolation of similarities, that he has on occasion omitted that part of the evidence which shows the fundamental difference.

An example of such an omission is to be found in the second edition in three volumes of *The Golden Bough* (1900). On pp. 1–5, Frazer discusses the subject of 'the divine king'. We cite this case, in the first place, because we have checked the sources, and, in the second place, because a very great deal has been built on Frazer's conclusions.[1] It seems to us, from the actual evidence

[1] Notably in connection with the development of Mowinckel's theory of a Coronation Feast in Israel. Cf. *Myth and Ritual* (1933), *The Labyrinth* (1935), ed. S. H. Hooke.

which Frazer himself produces, that the man was killed neither because he was a king, nor because he was divine, 'but that is another story'. The specific example which we instance as a horrid warning, both of the perils of accepting too easily Frazer's method and conclusions, and also of the limitations of the theory of the divine king, is Frazer's statement that Pythagoras inscribed a tomb to Zeus in Crete. The inference which Frazer would have us draw from this is, to judge from his context, that here is an example of the death of even such a Supreme Being as Zeus. For Zeus is essentially a sky-god, as we have learned from Max Müller from the early days of the modern study of the origins of religion.[1] The evidence of Frazer's statement is to be found in Porphyry's Life of Pythagoras (*Vit. Pyth.* 17). Porphyry's actual statement, which Frazer does not quote in full, is 'and he carved an inscription on the tomb, writing "Pythagoras to Zeus", of which the beginning was, "Here died and was buried Zan, whom they call Zeus."' This puts a very different complexion on the matter, especially since the context is Porphyry's account of the initiation of Pythagoras into the mysteries of the cult of the Idaean Zeus on Mount Dikte. The tomb, according to its own witness, was not the grave of Zeus at all, but of a being named Zan, who was identified with Zeus. Frazer's account creates the impression that here is a case of even a sky-god dying. It will be noticed that it is Frazer's neglect of the differences that has led to this impression. Porphyry's statement is of the death of a vegetation god, whose fertility cult was synthesized with the worship of the sky-god. If Frazer had searched further, he would have found a similar case of 'another divine being whose tomb Zeus took over'.[2] In this instance the inscription is: 'Here died Pikos and lies buried, who is also Zeus.' Picus, to use the Latin form, is the woodpecker magician, the medicine king of the aborigines of Italy.[3]

We give this as an example of the kind of conclusion to which a passionate search for similarities can lead. On this basis, if the differences are slurred or omitted, one religion is as good as another. Indeed, J. M. Robertson, adding virulence to zeal, can go still further, and can show, to his own satisfaction at least, that Christianity is rather worse than any other religion. His method

[1] *Lectures on the Science of Language* (2nd series, 2nd ed., 1868), pp. 425 *ff.*

[2] Miss J. E. Harrison, *Themis* (2nd ed., 1927), p. 58.

[3] Cf. also J. Rendel Harris, *Picus Who is also Zeus* (1916).

is that of Frazer, equally effective in confusing the issue, though fraught with a greater determination to reach a specified conclusion. He can reach his conclusion only by neglecting two vital factors. One is by omitting to mention, or perchance by eliminating, the differences. This is what Frazer has done in the case of the Idaean Zeus. No one would dream from Frazer's account that he was dealing with a late mystery cult. The other is by neglecting to inquire what are the aitiological statements by which man justifies his stubborn repetition of rites which long since have lost their original meaning. Man is never so conservative as in doing what his father has done, and never so revolutionary as in finding new reasons for it. Further, Christianity has no monopoly in providing new reasons for established customs. The persistence of ancient custom, unreasoningly or with new reasons, is a characteristic of human life in every phase. The differences lie for the most part in the aitiology.

We discuss, then, in this lecture, those beliefs which make the religion of the Old Testament different from other religions. In the concluding chapter we hope to indicate what these particular beliefs[1] involve for the New Testament, chiefly in the Pauline Epistles. Inasmuch as we hold that the distinctive ideas of God are at the root of the distinctive ideas of the Old Testament, we have divided our investigation in the main into a series of studies of the Nature of God as He is revealed in the Old Testament. We trust that the studies themselves will demonstrate the soundness of this method. Our conviction is that God is the Fountain and Source of this purest stream, and not that wide ocean into which all streams equally flow. He is the Foundation on which alone men may build, not the topmost Pinnacle which may mark the height of man's utmost achievement. It is He that gives meaning to all else, and not all things, nor any one thing that can explain Him, though many created things may illustrate the manner of His working.

[1] The reader is asked particularly to note these limitations, which are largely imposed by wartime time and space. See Introduction, p. 10.

Chapter II

THE HOLINESS OF GOD

THE chief and proper Hebrew word for 'holiness' is *qodesh.* This is the most intimately divine word of all. It has to do, as we shall see, with the very Nature of Deity; no word more so, nor indeed any other as much.

The word *qodesh* has a long and involved history, all the more difficult to detail because already at its earliest known stage it has come to be used exclusively in a religious context. Further, like most words in any language which deal with experiences and ideas of vital and fundamental importance in human life, its content has changed considerably with the passing centuries. Our intention in this present chapter is to deal with the history of the word and the idea in a threefold manner. Firstly, we will seek to recover the original significance of the word. This will involve a discussion largely etymological, though not exclusively so. Secondly, we hope to indicate those respects in which primitive ideas of holiness survived among the Hebrews of Old Testament times. Here we will be dealing with those elements in Hebrew religion which were held in common with other peoples. Thirdly, we propose to emphasize the first stages of that unique development in the idea of Holiness which took place among the Hebrews.

1. THE ORIGINAL SIGNIFICANCE OF THE WORD *QODESH* (HOLINESS)

Actually the etymological origin of the word is uncertain. Further, whilst it is possible to give a considered opinion as to the original significance, yet the nature of the evidence is such that there must remain a measure of uncertainty. This is inevitable in the case of a word which goes back to a very early stage in the history both of a language and of a people. Happily, the correct etymological explanation of a word is by no means the conclusive factor as to its meaning at any particular stage of its history. Whilst this approach may serve as a general guide to the meaning, and occasionally may act as a wholesome corrective, the ultimate decision must always depend upon a thorough examination of the actual use of the word itself at all stages of its development. No one word ever stands invariably for one clearly-defined, specific idea, a pin-point in expression. The analogy is more accurately a broad wedge, of which the apex may vary considerably from writer to writer, and may vary, even for the same writer, within often fairly wide limits.[1]

Something of the primary significance of the word *qodesh* may be gleaned from a comparison of the three Hebrew words which have to do with those things and affairs in which God and man are involved together, that borderland where the human and the supra-human may be said to overlap. These three words are *qodesh* (holiness), *cherem* (ban, devoted thing, destruction), and *chol* (profaneness, common). We have added an English translation in each case, not because we regard that translation as being necessarily adequate in any particular case, but because some general indication of the scope of the word is desirable, even before we attempt to be precise in respect of it.

It is convenient, as well as accurate, to use the noun in each case. The reason is that, apart from any other considerations, certainly for the first two words and for the third word also so far as its strictly religious use is concerned, the extant verb is derived from the extant noun, and not the noun through the verb, as is generally the case in these Semitic languages. The extant verb *qadash*, for instance, means 'to be *qodesh*', and the two forms of the verb *qiddesh* and *hiqdish* (the piel and the hiphil) mean 'to make *qodesh*'. The meaning of the verb, that is, depends entirely upon the meaning of the noun, and throughout the years varies with it. The fact that the extant verb is secondary to the extant noun is in itself a sufficient guarantee of the extreme antiquity of the root from which the noun itself originally sprang. It is also at the same time a warning that the original significance of any one of the three roots may prove impossible of recovery with any measure of real certainty. We are dealing here with the primary, elemental reactions of man to that mystery with which in the first days he felt himself to be surrounded. Such primitive reactions may, to some extent, be seen in comparatively recent times amongst the now largely extinct Central Australian aborigines, before they were affected to any marked extent by their contact with the

[1] Compare the varied use of the Greek *pistis* (faith) in the New Testament, even within the writings of the Apostle Paul. See Sanday and Headlam, *Romans* (I.C.C.), pp. 31–4.

whites. In particular, we refer to such a tribe as the Arunta.[1] Among the Semites, however, and certainly among the Hebrews, such days had passed away long before the time when we have any knowledge of them. The use of the Hebrew noun *qodesh* goes back into these far-off prehistoric days. The original root goes back even farther than the noun, and doubtless the beginning of the notion goes back still farther yet. Presumably the noun *qodesh* was derived in the first place from a Semitic root which contained the three consonants *q-d-sh*. This root may or may not have been known in Hebrew.[2] By this we mean that when Hebrew became a distinct language, separate from that proto-Semitic speech which was its predominant ancestor, it may have brought the noun *qodesh* with it, but left an earlier verbal form behind. Possibly the word originally was not Semitic at all, but this we regard as being a very remote possibility indeed.

Apart from the use of the word *quds* as the name of two mountains in Arabia,[3] the root does not appear to be Western Semitic, so far as the extant evidence is concerned. The Arabic equivalents, nouns, verbs, adjectives and so forth, are found in the Quran. The Arab name for Jerusalem is *Al-quds*. An Ethiopic equivalent of the root is also found, but in all cases, both Arabic and Ethiopic, the use is dominated and determined by the use of the noun *qodesh* in the Hebrew of the Old Testament. Similarly the use of *quds* and kindred words in Urdu is determined completely by Moslem usage based on the Quran. The root may have existed once as a Western Semitic root, but if so, all trace of it as such has long since been lost.

On the other hand, the other two words with which we are concerned, *cherem* and *chol*, seem to be predominantly Western Semitic words, that is, they are common in Arabic and rare in Akkadian.[4] The word *charimtu* is indeed found in Babylonian with the meaning 'prostitute', but instances of the use of the root are rare. All three roots are common in the central area, where

[1] B. Spencer and Gillen, *Native Tribes of Central Australia* (1899); *Across Australia* (1912); *The Arunta* (1927). Also Strehlow, *Die Aranda-und Loritja-stämme in Zentral-Australien* (1907).

[2] Otto Procksch thinks that the Hebrews never met the word until they came into the land of Canaan. See p. 26, below.

[3] Nöldeke, *Litt. Centralblatt* (1879), No. 12.

[4] We use the term 'Akkadian' to signify the Semitic languages of Mesopotamia, without specifying whether Assyrian or Babylonian, or whether early or late.

Mesopotamian and Arabian influences overlap. Especially for our present concern, all three roots are common in Palestine, the languages and dialects of which are essentially hybrid tongues, having affinities in grammar, syntax, and vocabulary with both Western and Eastern groups, apart from other elements which they contain.[1]

The Etymological Origin of 'Qodesh', and Its Earliest Meaning

There are two possibilities, though the choice between them has largely depended, so far as we are able to judge, upon *a priori* considerations as to the development of religion in general. One possibility is to be found in the explanation of the Babylonian *quddushu*, which the syllabaries say is equivalent to *ellu* (bright, clear). This explanation is found in Gesenius,[2] and is followed by Zimmern,[3] Dillmann,[4] Cheyne,[5] K. Kohler,[6] and others. The other possibility is the explanation offered by von Baudissin, when he said that 'a comparison with *ch-d-sh* makes it natural to conjecture that *q-d-sh* meant from the first "to be separated" '.[7] This is the explanation usually followed in modern times, though sometimes doubtfully, and depending, it is alleged, more upon an examination of the actual use of the root in the Old Testament. So, at least, Skinner[8] and Whitehouse.[9] Davidson, having originally deemed the problem insoluble,[10] later thought that the primitive meaning was ' "to be separated" or "to be lofty", or something of the kind',[11] a statement which is indefinite, not only in its conclusion, but also because it combines the two rival theories. W. Robertson Smith inclined to the idea of 'separation', men-

[1] W. Wright, *A Comparative Grammar of the Semitic Languages* (1890). G. R. Driver, *Problems of the Hebrew Verbal System*, Old Testament Studies, No. 2 (1936).

[2] *Thesaurus* (1829, etc.), but rejected by Brown, Driver and Briggs, Oxford Lexicon (1907), who prefer the other.

[3] *Babylonische Busspsalmen* (1885), S. 37, n. 2.

[4] *Alttest. Theologie* (1895), S. 254.

[5] *The Origin of the Psalter* (1891), p. 331, where he states that Jehovah's Holiness and His Glory are correlative ideas.

[6] *Jewish Encycl.*, vol. 6 (1904), p. 439.

[7] '*Der Begriff der Heiligkeit im Alten Testament*', *Studien zur semitischen Religionsgeschichte* (1878), ii. 20. This monograph, extending over some 120 pages, is a most comprehensive and searching analysis of the subject. See also Eichrodt, *Theologie des Alten Testaments*, i (1939), SS. 139–46.

[8] *H.D.B.*, ii, p. 394.

[9] *E.R.E.*, 6, p. 751.

[10] *Ezekiel* (Camb. Bible, 1892), p. xxxix.

[11] *The Theology of the Old Testament* (1904), p. 150.

tioning the Arabic commentators on the Quran at Sura ii, 28, where they say that the meaning has to do with distance, separation. Cheyne, in his additional notes, discounts the value of this comment, and so also does Nöldeke. Robertson Smith himself continued with an explanation of the difficulty of ascertaining the original significance of the root, because it was so early appropriated to religious use, and is never found in any other connection.[1]

With respect to the comparative merits of the two suggestions, the balance, in our view, is definitely in favour of Baudissin's theory, but with certain qualifications, which we shall state at the end of the present discussion.[2] Here we content ourselves with saying that the reason for the modern swing-over to Baudissin's suggestion, away from the earlier one of 'bright, clear' or the similar idea of 'freedom from defect',[3] seems to us to be due largely to the modern view that the development of religion must be traced from below and not from above. That is, the conclusion of the modern scholars is ultimately dependent on the view that religion is a movement from man to God rather than a revelation of God to man. This is the leading *motif* in the modern study of the history of religion, being a product of the application to the study of religion of the New Scientific Method with its rigid evolutionary hypothesis.

Baudissin suggested, as we have seen, that the root *q-d-sh* had to do with the idea of separation. He cited the root *ch-d-sh*, and pointed out that roots beginning with *ch-d* have something to do with cutting, piercing. Delitzsch held that the connection with *ch-d-sh* (renew) involved the meaning 'free from defect' and so 'bright'. Dillmann's argument was that the root *ch-d-sh* achieved its meaning 'renew' through the idea of a sword being renewed by being sharpened and polished, whence the third and fourth forms of the Arabic verb do actually refer to a *polished* sword. Such a suggestion is not as wild as might at first appear, since words do take the most extraordinary twists and turns in their development.[4]

[1] *The Prophets of Israel* (2nd ed., 1897), p. 224; also Cheyne's note, p. 424.

[2] See pp. 30 *ff.*, below.

[3] Delitzsch, *Real-Encycl. für protest. Theologie und Kirche* (2nd ed.), art. '*Heiligkeit Gottes*'.

[4] Cf. the English word 'restive'; see p. 98, below.

There are two difficulties. The first is that the idea of 'polished' is connected with the Arabic *ch-d-sh* and not with the root *q-d-sh* at all. The second is that the root *q-d-sh* does not appear to be an Arabic root until post-Old Testament times.

In addition to these two difficulties, we would raise the question as to whether the Akkadian *quddushu* ever really meant 'bright'.

We turn therefore to the neo-Babylonian *quddushu*. Here is to be found the crux of the whole problem, and, we believe, its solution. This is, in our view, perhaps paradoxically in the face of its equation with *ellu* (bright), that the root meant originally 'separation' and not 'bright'.

The word *quddushu* occurs sporadically in Akkadian, certainly from the time of Hammurabi (*c.* 1,750 B.C.) onwards. When it appears in neo-Babylonian (*c.* 600 B.C.)[1] in the time of Nebuchadrezzar, its association with *ellu* is certain and repeated. How does it happen that when the word occurs thus frequently in neo-Babylonian, it is regularly interpreted to mean 'bright'?

Otto Procksch holds that the Hebrews never met the word till they came into the land of Canaan, that it is probably not a primitive Hebrew word at all, and that it is Canaanite in its origin.[2] In the first place, what does Otto Procksch mean by the entrance of the Hebrews into Canaan? If he means the invasion under Joshua, then the statement must be varied to include the temporary sojourn at Qadesh-barnea (Kadesh). This site is but fifty miles south of Beersheba, so that it might be held, though precariously, to be within the sphere of Canaan. The Hebrews never deemed it such, and in any case such a variation is insufficient, for the root occurs in the form Qadesh and in kindred forms as a place name from early times. It is found as far south as Qadesh-barnea and as far north as Qadesh on the Orontes, a capital city of the Hittites and the scene of fierce fighting in the time of Rameses II, when the Pharaoh himself is said to have rivalled even Thotmes III in courage and valour. It has been the name, at one time and another, of more than one site in the

[1] For the larger part of the Akkadian evidence I am indebted to the Rev. T. Fish of the Semitics Department of the University of Manchester. He is not, of course, responsible to any degree for the conclusions which I have drawn from that evidence.

[2] *Theologisches Wörterbuch zum Neuen Testament.* (ed. G. Kittel, 1936—unfinished), S. 88

Holy Land. There was a Qadesh (Kedesh) in Naphtali, Judges iv. 6, which is possibly the same as the Kedesh in Galilee of Joshua xx. 7, and may also be the same as that in Judges iv. 11. There was a city of refuge in Issachar, 1 Chronicles vi. 72 (Heb. 57). This may have been known as Qishyon in early times, Joshua xxi. 28, but it certainly was a sacred site. Sir Charles Wilson found an inscribed altar there in 1865. The inscription is probably third century A.D., but sacred sites are not invented. They always have been. The gods vary, but the sacredness of the site persists. The inscription presupposes a Semitic deity, and underneath the site there are traces of an old pagan temple orientated to the east.[1] Further, there was certainly a place of this name in Palestine before the Ephraimite invasion under Joshua since the name appears in the Tell-el-Amarna letters in the form *Qidshi*. The root also appears in the Ras Shamra tablets as an epithet of the hero *Dan'el*.[2] He is called *b-n q-d-sh*, which may mean 'holy son', since in the myth the high-god El is represented as being his father. But it may mean that he is the son of the goddess Qadesh.

The mention of the goddess Qadesh introduces us to another weakness in Procksch's statement, for the goddess is known in cults which already had become syncretistic in the nineteenth dynasty (Sety I, Rameses II, etc., fourteenth, thirteenth centuries B.C.). On the Qadesh-stele in the British Museum she is styled 'mistress of all the gods, the eye of Re, without a second'. She is pictured nude according to Mesopotamian custom, but has Asiatic, Aegean, and Anatolian traits. On the steles at Cairo and in the Louvre, she has Egyptian accessories, but it is clear that she was known and worshipped in Syria in the middle of the second millennium B.C., and she probably had Mesopotamian associations prior to that. The name may be merely an epithet,[3] but it still is early, and the Hebrews had ample opportunity of meeting it before the Joshua invasion. Actually, if Abraham's migration from Ur of the Chaldees is to be fixed as about the time of Hammurabi (*c.* 1,750 B.C.), they knew the root even then, for it is found in the Code of Hammurabi in the form *qadishtu* (temple prostitute). The Hebrew equivalent is *qedeshah*, found in what

[1] S. A. Cook, *The Religion of Ancient Palestine in the Light of Archaeology* (Schweich Lectures, 1925), pp. 196 *f.*

[2] Dussaud, *Les Découvertes de Ras Shamra et l'ancien Testament* (1937), p. 86.

[3] S. A. Cook, *ibid.*, pp. 106 *f.* and Plate XXIV.

appears to be a very early story of the fortunes of Judah among the Canaanites, Genesis xxxviii. 21.[1] All this, whilst establishing an early Hebrew knowledge of the root as a cult term, brings us no nearer to the original meaning. If *quddushu* as equalling *ellu* really meant 'bright', how can it have anything to do with *qadishtu* (temple prostitute)?

It is assumed that *quddushu* actually means 'bright' because it is equated to *ellu* in the neo-Babylonian syllabaries. This may be correct, but the signs which represent *ellu* also form the ideogram for 'god' (*ilu*/AN). Going back beyond Akkadian to Sumerian, the ideogram for the root *q-d-sh* is that used for 'sun', 'day', etc. The equation with *ellu* (bright) and this Sumerian use of the ideogram for *q-d-sh* for such things as the sun, seem at first to settle beyond dispute that the root *q-d-sh* did actually mean 'bright' originally. But there are two considerations involved here. In the first place, whilst the evidence certainly involves an equation with the word *ellu*, yet this equation is late, and there is an earlier equation with the ideogram for 'god'. This would be a natural equation if the root *q-d-sh* already referred to that which has to do with deity.

More importantly, and in the second place, we have to remind ourselves that when we discuss the civilization of the Mesopotamian plain, we are dealing with an advanced urbanized society. There were cities in this area at a very early date, and the remarkable statement of Genesis iv. 17 has been amply confirmed by the excavations. The effect of the very early urbanization of Mesopotamia on the cultus of that area has received some attention from Svend Aage Pallis,[2] but there is room for further and more detailed investigation. The proper historical and scientific study of the Mesopotamian religious material with proper regard for the various developments and reforms is still in its infancy. There is still far too great a tendency to treat all

[1] Akkadian has three words for 'prostitute', *qadishtu*, *ishtaritu*, and *charimtu*. The distinctions are not always observed, but strictly the first two belong to the temple and the third to the street. The *charimtu* differed from the others in that she was both unveiled and unmarried, and could not adopt children. The fact that in the Judah-Tamar story the Canaanite *qedeshah* was to be found in the street may be due to some looseness of expression on the part of the narrator, since *zonah*, the ordinary Hebrew word for 'harlot', is used elsewhere in the chapter. On the other hand, she was veiled (verse 15), so perhaps Judah's messenger knew what he was doing when he used the word *qedeshah*. Both the Akkadian *qadishtu* and the Hebrew-Canaanite *qedeshah* were cult prostitutes from early times.

[2] *The Babylonian Akitu Festival* (Kobenhavn, 1926).

the Mesopotamian material as being of one stratum, and to forget that there were developments in religious thought and in ritual equally in Mesopotamia as in Palestine. Coupled with all this, and more importantly for our present purpose, is the fact that all the Mesopotamian deities, without exception so far as the later period is concerned and probably for the earlier period also, were associated with the heavenly bodies. If there ever were any deities there, apart from sky-gods and chthonic deities, or if any of these Mesopotamian deities were ever earth-gods before they were sky-gods (e.g. Tammuz), then this was before the first millennium B.C., since by that time the Assyrians had a system of gods each with a well-defined place in the pantheon, and all either sky- or chthonic-gods. Whether or not in Mesopotamia they trod the one supposedly common path beginning with pre-animism and animism or with ghost worship, and thence through all the various orthodox stages of the Tylor-Spencer-Frazer school of primitive religion, is beyond our present concern. In the period with which we are concerned all the Mesopotamian deities had their associations with the heavenly bodies. This means that for the period when *quddushu* was equated with *ellu*, the root *q-d-sh* was necessarily a cult-root associated with sky-gods. It is therefore only to be expected that it would be equated with *ellu* (bright). Compare, in this connection, Max Müller's studies of the origin of the Greek *Zeus pater* and the Latin *Jupiter* in the Sanskrit *Dyaus pitar* and the various meanings of *dyu*, namely 'sky, day, light'.[1] Our conclusion is therefore that the ascription of the meaning 'bright' to the neo-Babylonian *quddushu* is due to a misunderstanding, either on the part of those who made the syllabaries, or on the part of modern scholars. There are many cases where the meaning 'bright' is difficult, e.g. *binu quddushu* (a sacred tamarisk), and the instances where *ellu* and *quddushu* are used together of a *niqu* (sacrificial lamb), *puchadu* (lamb, kid), or a *shadu* (mountain). The Babylonian material tends to confirm our view that the root *q-d-sh* had first to do with the gods, and only secondarily came to mean 'bright' because all the gods of this later period were associated with the heavenly bodies.

We are therefore driven back to Baudissin's suggestion that the root originally meant 'separation', inasmuch as it is clear that it deals with the things that belong to the gods as distinct from

[1] *Lectures on the Science of Languages* (2nd series, 1868), pp. 426–54.

men. His statement, however, that the root *q-d-sh* signifies 'separation from, withdrawal' needs considerable qualification, especially when it is maintained that this is supported by Old Testament usage. It is true that the root stands for the difference between God and man, but it refers positively, and not negatively, to that 'Wholly Other' of whom Rudolf Otto writes.[1] It refers positively to what is God's and not negatively to what is not man's. God is separate and distinct because He is God. He is not separated *from* this, that, or the other because of any of His attributes or qualities or the like. A person or a thing may be separate, or may come to be separated, because he or it has come to belong to God. When we use the word 'separated' as a rendering of any form of the root *q-d-sh*, we should think of 'separated *to*' rather than of 'separated *from*'. The reference is not primarily to the act of separation, but rather to the fact that the object has now come into the category of the Separate. The verb in its causative form *hiqdish* means 'make separate' rather than 'be separate', but this is a derived form of the verb. We therefore insist, as of prime importance, that the root is positive rather than negative, that the emphasis is on the destination of the object and not on its initial character—all of which goes back to the fact that, in respect of the root *q-d-sh*, we must think of God first and of man and things second, and not vice versa. This is not to deny that the Hebrew *hiqdish* can never mean 'to separate, withdraw from common (i.e. human) use', but it is to say that such meanings belong to the periphery of the word and not to its central core. When Baudissin gave 'separation' as the probable original significance of the root, he may well have been correct, but only in so far as he may have been thinking in terms of a positive Other. As soon as he began to think of 'separation from' he was moving away from the central core. When he used the word 'withdrawal', he was at the outmost limits of the root.

It is natural to the modern man of our scientific age to assume that primitive man thought first of himself and of the 'human' world, and thought of it positively, and that afterwards he thought of the supra-human world and thought of it negatively as being not-human. We have forced the world into a material framework. By a strange irony we have scoffed at the geocentric

[1] *The Idea of the Holy* (Eng. tr. by J. W. Harvey, from the ninth German edition of *Das Heilige*, first published in 1917), pp. 6, 25, etc.

astronomers, only to make the whole universe and everything that is in it homocentric. The evidence of the attitude of the primitive man, in so far as there is any evidence at all, is that the one world was as real to him as the other. Further, when he reached the speculative stage, however tentatively, it is probable that he thought first of the supra-human world and secondly of the 'human' world as being distinct from it. Presumably his first speculations were not concerning the ordinary everyday world with which he was immediately surrounded, since that was ordinary and everyday. It is much more likely that when he first began to be puzzled, and to seek the explanations of what he did not understand, it was concerning the mysterious, extraordinary world. There is plenty of evidence in any book on primitive religion to show that what was mysterious was necessarily supra-human. The root *q-d-sh* has to do precisely with this supra-human world. We find no difficulty, but on the contrary every encouragement, in assuming an early positive content rather than an early negative content to the word *qodesh*. The embryo self-consciousness of man was not in consciousness of self. *Cogito, ergo sum* was preceded in the history of philosophy by *cogito, ergo id est.*[1]

There is a further qualification which we would make in connection with Baudissin's monograph. This concerns his emphatic claim that the word had originally no moral content whatever. Nöldeke[2] in his review of the monograph, noted this statement particularly and with strong approval, as being the most important conclusion which Baudissin reached. The same statement has been made with the starkest emphasis by Otto in more recent times.[3] But the terms of the statement need careful definition. All three writers, Baudissin, Nöldeke, and Otto, are thinking of morality and ethics in the developed modern senses of the words. In the way in which they used the words, the statement is, of course, undoubtedly correct, but they have forgotten that there has been a long history in the development of ethics also. It is true that in primitive religion 'the idea of sin, in any proper sense of the word, did not exist at all'.[4] But it is also true that there was no proper sense of Deity either. Further, as soon as there was any

[1] Or more accurately *operatur, ergo est.*

[2] *Litt. Centralblatt.*, No. 12, cols. 361 *f.*

[3] *ibid.* p. 6, etc.

[4] W. Robertson Smith, *The Religion of the Semites* (3rd ed., 1927), p. 410.

idea of an Other, however well or ill conceived, there was also a recognition of the danger and 'wrongness' (in a broad, almost pre-ethical sort of sense) of breaking a *taboo*, or infringing some tribal sanction. It may be said that this is a non-ethical wrongness. We would say pre-ethical, for everything is embryo here. We are dealing with embryo notions of *qodesh*, and equally with embryo notions of ethics. We maintain that the embryo *qodesh* (holiness) involves an embryo ethical content and embryo ideas of sin. If sin did not exist in the proper sense of the word, then neither did *qodesh*, and we have as little right, or as much right, to talk about the one as about the other. We therefore deny Baudissin's actual statement, though we fully accept the implications he meant to convey. The word *qodesh* originally had no moral content in our developed sense of the word 'moral', but it did involve pre-ethical restrictions, as undeveloped in content as itself.

The Etymological Origin of 'Cherem' and Its Meaning

The root *ch-r-m* is certainly Western Semitic. Procksch holds[1] that it is the primitive Hebrew root for 'holiness', and that the Hebrews brought it with them when they entered Canaan. *Al-charam* is the name of the Sacred Territory at Mecca, just as *Haq-qodesh* came to mean the Sacred Territory at Jerusalem, the modern Moslem name being *Charam esh-Sherif*. Similarly *M-ch-r-m* are the consonants of the Sabean word for Temple, corresponding to the Hebrew *M-q-d-sh*. The original meaning of the root was probably 'refuse, forbid', without any religious significance in the developed sense of the word 'religious'. Here again we are in those embryo stages, this time more specifically of *taboo*, where already we have learned to walk circumspectly. Nothing is more dangerous than the attempt to distinguish with our modern degrees of preciseness between religious and non-religious in all matters of primitive custom. Half the difficulties of the definitions of religions are due to the attempt to force modern categories on a primitive context where no such categories existed.

The meaning of the root *ch-r-m* developed along what we to-day would call secular lines in the word *chareem*, used of the women of a household, or of the part of the house (tent) where the women are wont to live. We have thus allowed to the root *ch-r-m*

[1] *Theologisches Wörterbuch zum Neuen Testament*, S. 88.

primitive negative significance which we have denied to the root *q-d-sh*. Our justification is that the idea of 'forbidden' is essential to the meaning of *cherem* in a way which is not the case with *qodesh*. Indeed, in Hebrew usage and also in such Moabite inscriptions as survive, *cherem* means nothing if it does not mean 'forbidden'.

In Hebrew the word *cherem* came to refer, with the few exceptions which are detailed below, to that which has been *qodesh* to a god other than Jehovah, and which therefore, whenever possible, was 'devoted' to Jehovah by being utterly, completely, and ruthlessly destroyed. This same use is found on the Moabite Stone in line 17, where Mesha of Moab (ninth century B.C. contemporary of Ahab; cf. 2 Kings i. 1, iii. 4 *f.*) states that the altar-hearth (?) of Jehovah was dragged before the Moabite god Chemosh and was devoted (*h-ch-r-m-th-h*). This happened at the time when 7,000 captive Israelites were massacred. All of them, like the altar-hearth, were devoted to Chemosh, because until their capture they had belonged to Jehovah. What was *qodesh* to Jehovah was *cherem* to Chemosh. Contrariwise, what was *qodesh* to Chemosh was *cherem* to Jehovah. One god's *qodesh* was another god's *cherem*. The devotees of one god therefore destroyed all they could capture of the other god's property, whether it was animate or inanimate.

Because of the implied necessity of complete annihilation which is involved in the Hebrew and Moabite use of the word, *cherem* can be used, in Palestine and its environs, in the sense of complete destruction, even when there is no connection between the object and a god, and no necessary reference to apostasy. These semi-exceptions to the normal use are 2 Kings xix. 11 with its parallels in Isaiah xxxvii. 11 and 2 Chronicles xxxii. 14; also 2 Chronicles xx. 23; Daniel xi. 44. The use is not common in Hebrew, and we have no means of telling how common it was in Moabite and kindred tongues.

A further derived use of the root *ch-r-m* is found in Leviticus xxvii. 21, 28 (P); Numbers xviii. 14 (P) and Ezekiel xliv. 29. These cases are all either in the Priestly Code or in those last chapters of the Book of the Prophet Ezekiel which are a preliminary draft for the organization of post-exilic Israel, the Atlantic Charter of the New Order. In these four cases, the word is used of things dedicated to Jehovah under specially stringent conditions. Some dedicated things could be redeemed, and so could be restored to human use, Leviticus xxvii. 13, 15, 19 (P), but not in these four instances. These refer to things which are for ever, finally, and completely separated from human use, under all circumstances unredeemable and inalienable from Jehovah. They are *qodesh qodashim*—that is, doubly *qodesh*—belonging irrevocably to Jehovah. Some of the conditions of such vows are given in Leviticus xxvii. 20 *f.* (P). We judge that the word *cherem* is used in order to make it plain that these things are completely withdrawn from man. Not even the double use of the word *qodesh* could carry the idea of complete and final withdrawal, so that the ancient word *cherem* was pressed into service.

The Etymological Origin of 'Chol' and Its Meaning

We have seen that *cherem* is non-*qodesh* to one god because of its association with another god. *Chol* is non-*qodesh* because of its association with man. It can be translated either by 'profane' or by 'common'. It means 'profane' in so far as it is regarded as being the opposite of *qodesh.* It means 'common' in that it may be free to man, being untied by any *taboo*, whether *taboo* to man because it is *qodesh* to God and free to Him alone, or *taboo* to both God and man because it is unclean. *Qodesh* is always the opposite of *chol*, but that which is *chol* may or may not be free for man. It depends upon whether it is clean or unclean. The statement in Acts x. 14, 28 is confusing, for that which is common is not necessarily unclean. There was never any objection to a Jew eating that which is common, provided that it is not also unclean.

The distinction between *qodesh* (holy) and *chol* (common) is clear in 1 Samuel xxi. 4. The priest answers David, 'There is no common bread here, but there is holy bread.' He asks if David's men have observed the sex-*taboo* of those who go forth to (sacred) war. David replies that although their journey was a common one (i.e. they are not going to war, but are on a peaceful errand; their mission is *chol* and not *qodesh*), yet actually the men have observed the sex-*taboo*, and have had no intercourse with women for the prescribed period. And their vessels will soon be holy when the holy food touches them. So the priest hands over the holy bread, actually having had no alternative before these hungry, desperate men, but having satisfied his own conscience that some sort of distinction had been made between the holy and the common.

The distinction between *qodesh* and *chol* (profane, desecrate) is clear in Ezekiel xxii. 26, where Ezekiel's charge against the priests is that they 'have profaned (*chillel*) my holy things', and 'have put no difference between the holy and the common.' Compare also Ezekiel xlii. 20, xliv. 23.

The root *ch-l-l* has cult associations from a very early date, in that wider sense of cult which would include *taboo*. It means 'untie', 'undo', and thence, as in Arabic, 'become free, lawful' and in its derived forms 'make lawful, esteem lawful', whether rightly or wrongly. Hence it can mean both 'make legitimate' and 'profane'. The verb is used of the illegitimate untying or breaking of a *taboo* in Leviticus xxi. 4, 9, xix. 29, xxi. 9 (all H); Genesis xlix. 4 (J) and its dependent 1 Chronicles v. 1. Another case is Leviticus xxi. 15 (H), but since this concerns the High Priest, who belongs to Jehovah and is therefore *qodesh*, the meaning here may be that of making un-*qodesh*.

There is also a legitimate loosening of a *taboo* whereby *chol* means 'common' and not 'unclean', as in the previous paragraph. There are four such instances—namely, Deuteronomy xx. 6 (*bis*), xxviii. 30; Jeremiah xxxi. 5. All four deal with 'making *chol*' a vineyard when men begin to 'use' (so R.V. in the first three cases), 'enjoy' (R.V. at Jeremiah xxxi. 5), 'eat' (A.V. at Deuteronomy xx. 6 and Jeremiah xxxi. 5), or 'gather' (A.V. at Deuteronomy xxviii. 30) its fruit. The theory is that all the fruit belongs to Jehovah. It is therefore *qodesh*, and no man may eat any of it. This is acknowledged in the declaration made at the presentation of first-fruits, Deuteronomy xxvi. 5–11. When Jehovah has received these as a token acknowledgement, He allows the Hebrew to retain the rest of the vintage for his own use. The first-fruits never cease to be *qodesh*, since when they are picked they are handed over to Jehovah. The rest of the vintage ceases to be *qodesh*, and therefore becomes *chol*. It is that which has ceased to be *qodesh*, and in this case is free to man. The position is made quite clear in Deuteronomy xx. 6 (Douai Version), 'made it common, whereof men may eat'.

All this is so *a fortiori* in the case of the first vintage, and indeed of any fruit from that which is newly planted. Leviticus xix. 23–5 (P) says that for the first three years after planting, the fruit must not be touched at all. 'Three years shall they be uncircumcised[1] to you', 'but in the fourth year all the fruit thereof shall be *qodesh* (i.e. it is all handed over to Jehovah), for giving praise unto the Lord (i.e. as a thank-offering). And in the fifth year ye shall eat the fruit thereof (i.e. after the first-fruits, it becomes common)'.

Conclusion

We have now given a general indication of the relative scope of the three roots which have to do with the borderland of the natural and the supernatural. From the general Semitic point of view *qodesh* and *cherem* are synonymous, both signifying that which is of the gods, the former in the centre and east, the latter in the west. But among the Hebrews and nearby peoples, *qodesh* stands for that which pertains to the native god, whilst *cherem* is its antithesis in that it pertains to any other god. On the other hand, *qodesh* and *cherem* are everywhere the antithesis of *chol*. This latter refers to that which definitely does not pertain to the gods. If it is 'clean', it is free to man. If it is 'unclean', it is prohibited to both gods and men.

2. PRIMITIVE IDEAS OF HOLINESS AMONG THE HEBREWS

When we proceed to an examination of the Old Testament use of the word *qodesh* and its derivatives, we find ourselves confronted with two aspects, clearly distinguishable each from other. Both have to do with that Otherness of things which we call holy. The difference lies in the fact that in one aspect the holy is considered as being personal, whilst in the other it is conceived as being at least semi-personal and perhaps in a wholly impersonal way.

We shall see in the next section that the word *qodesh* in its personal aspect, taken as it was among the Hebrews to refer to Jehovah exclusively, is that element which gave rise to those distinctive ideas of holiness which the Hebrews came to possess. In its semi-material or wholly material aspect, the word provides that element which the Hebrews retained in conjunction with other peoples. Frazer and his followers deal almost exclusively with this aspect. They are bound indeed to be so limited, since their whole method involves the compilation of similarities, with an accompanying tendency to neglect distinctions. We deal with

[1] Rashi explains this as meaning 'completely closed' (*wa'aṭamtem 'aṭimatho*), i.e. *taboo* to both God and man.

the semi-material aspect of *qodesh* in this section. This will enable us to be more clear as to what is similar and what is distinct, and it will leave us free in the next section, and in the following chapters, to discuss those distinctive elements which are our chief concern.

These material or semi-material ideas of holiness are those which lie at the root of the restrictive rules of ordinary life, and are also the basis of much of the Temple ritual, not only in the pre-exilic Temple, but in the post-exilic Temple also. They go back to those primitive ideas which regard holiness as being something definite and objective, quantitative rather than qualitative, neutral in morality, and such that contact with it is as undesirable as it is desirable. In this respect there is a close similarity between early ideas of holiness and early ideas of sin. Both are regarded as a mysterious something which can be transmitted by touch, or almost as a material substance which can be washed away like dirt. There are instances in the Old Testament, equally as in the surviving evidence from the early religious ideas of other peoples, where holiness, equally with sin, has to be got rid of, and similar washing rites apply to both.

We are here in the realm of *mana* and *taboo*. These two native words have come to be used as technical terms for the double reaction of primitive man to that mysterious other-than-human power whose effects he knew to be beyond his own power of accomplishment, whether they were abnormal because of their unusualness or impressive because of their regularity. Archbishop Söderblom defined *mana* as 'the general term of positive holiness as power, as distinguished from negative holiness involving the conception of danger, interdict, prohibition, which in current terminology is designated by the Polynesian word *tabu*'.[1] This does not mean, however, that *mana* and *taboo* are in all respects antithetical. There are occasions when the partition between the two is very thin, and often what is *mana* in one is *taboo* to another.

In all the confused medley of primitive notions which envelop ideas of *mana* and *taboo*, there are two features which are of importance for our present concern. Firstly, *mana* is double-edged. It can hurt and destroy as well as make blessed. Like a sharp-edged tool, it is very powerful, and must therefore be

[1] *E.R.E.*, art. 'Holiness', vol. 6, p. 731, note.

handled with great care, lest it break out and destroy innocent and guilty alike. Secondly, there is a general indefiniteness as to whether *mana* is personal or impersonal.

With respect to the first consideration—namely, the belief that *mana* is double-edged and at most barely controllable by man—it can be literally true that what is one man's meat is another man's poison. This can actually happen in the case of the chief of a tribe, who has *mana* in a special degree. This very fact renders him dangerous to others, and food, for instance, which is life to him is death to another. An example of the very great care with which an object containing *mana* must be handled is to be seen in the initiation rites of Australian aborigines. The Larakia tribe, whose home is near Port Darwin, have certain sacred wooden instruments which they call *bidu-bidu*. These belong to a class of sacred instruments known as *churinga*. They have also been called 'bull-roarers' because of the strange, eerie noises which can be made with some of them. When these *bidu-bidu* are first shown to the boys, the old men first rub them through their own armpits and across their own stomachs, before they give them to the boys for them to handle. A somewhat similar custom is observed with the sacred sticks of the Iwaidja tribe of Port Essington in the Coburg Peninsula in the Northern Territory. The rubbing of the bodies of the adult males, whether through their armpits or across their stomachs and so forth, is to reduce the magic (*mana*), so that the boys will not swell up and die.[1] Here the double-edged nature of this mysterious power is clearly in evidence.

Our second consideration concerns the discussions as to whether *mana* is personal or impersonal. Professor T. H. Robinson goes so far as to say that 'it is in no sense personal'.[2] R. H. Codrington, who was responsible for the introduction of this Melanesian word into the study of primitive religion, was much less definite. Speaking of the original Melanesian use of the word, he says that 'it attaches itself to persons and things', but 'though itself impersonal', it 'is always connected with some person who directs it'.[3] This latter reference to a person would include, possibly in Melanesia, but certainly in the generally accepted use of the word *mana*, ghosts and spirits, between which incidentally Codrington

[1] Sir B. Spencer, *Native Tribes of the Northern Territories of Australia* (1914), p. 119*f.*

[2] *Introduction to the History of Religions* (1926), p. 33.

[3] *The Melanesians* (1891), pp. 118, 120.

is rightly most careful to distinguish. Other writers think that *mana* is in some sense personal. S. A. Cook says that 'if impersonal, it tends to become personal when venerated'.[1] We would say that it tends to become personal in any case, whether venerated or not. Paul Radin's explanation of the confusion is that there are two groups of writers who depend upon two types of information. He says this by way of illustration of his belief that there are two different types of people, and in criticism of Lévy-Bruhl's theory of a pre-logical mentality common to all primitives *en masse*. 'It may be said that all people are spontaneously religious at crises, that the markedly religious people are spontaneously religious on numerous other occasions as well, and that the intermittently and indifferently religious people are secondarily religious on occasions not connected with crises at all.'[2] The markedly religious people will experience *mana* as a personal power, and the indifferently religious people more as an impersonal power. Radin's judgement is sound in so far as it allows for differences in the attitude of individual men. There has been far too much talk of man in the abstract in the study of primitive religion, as though mankind was one solid group which always and without variation thought and acted as an individual. We do not think, however, that the whole difference concerning *mana*, whether personal or impersonal, depends on the psychology of individuals. We hold that *mana* cannot be said to be either personal or impersonal, since these are modern categories, and the idea of *mana* is much more diffuse than our modern categories cater for. The idea existed in the mind of primitive man long before he had learned to be precise to any noticeable degree in any kind of thought. It is a term for a set of notions so diffuse that they are wholly indefinable, whether personal or impersonal. If we attempt to force our modern categories on to all this medley, we are immediately in difficulties, and unless we walk circumspectly we soon raise all manner of unnecessary complications. The diffuseness of the term is well illustrated by a statement of J. O. Dorsey, quoted by Söderblom, that 'no English sentence of reasonable length can do justice to the aboriginal idea expressed by the term *wakanda*',[3]

[1] In W. Robertson Smith, *The Religion of the Semites* (3rd ed.), p. 550.

[2] *Primitive Religion: its Nature and Origin* (1938), p. 11. His discussion of *mana* is on pp. 12–14.

[3] Art. 'Holiness', *E.R.E.*, vol. 6, p. 732.

the Sioux Indian equivalent of *mana*. We take it that Lévy-Bruhl used the term 'prelogical' of this diffuseness. It was an unfortunate term, since the difference between the primitives and us is not in the application of reason, but in their lack of categories.

The Hebrew *qodesh* is primitively like *mana* in both respects. It is dangerous and deadly as well as beneficent and life-giving. It is in the borderland of the personal and the impersonal.

A typical example of the destructive effect of *qodesh-mana* is the story of the fate of Uzzah, 2 Samuel vi. 6 *f.* There is nothing moral about the story, and our sympathies are with Uzzah. He acted from the best of motives, and his action was unpremeditated. He tried to steady the Ark and to save it from coming to harm when the oxen began to bolt.[1] The story still survived in the post-exilic 1 Chronicles xiii. 9, 10. The same attitude is maintained equally in the Priestly Code in connection with the story of the exclusion of the Kohathites from 'the holy things' (so R.V. margin; the Hebrew is *qodesh*), Numbers iv. 15. Or again, in the Priestly Code, we find the story of the fate of Nadab and Abihu, whose crime was that they 'offered strange fires', and whose fate was that 'there came forth a fire from Jehovah and devoured them', Leviticus x. 2. Apparently their orders were irregular, for they were not recognized in post-exilic times as being sacrificing priests according to the Aaronic rules, though there is plenty of evidence that their orders were both regular and valid in pre-exilic times. Compare also Numbers i. 51 (P), and the Chronicler's story of the fate of King Uzziah, 2 Chronicles xxvi. 19. These cases are a survival of the same set of ideas as those which appear in the slaying of Uzzah, and in the blasting of the men of Beth-shemesh who looked into the Ark, 1 Samuel vi. 19. It would appear that the post-exilic priests and the Chronicler could see that 2 Samuel xxiv. 1, 10, 15 left something to be desired from the point of view of the moral character of Jehovah (compare 1 Chronicles xxi. 1: 'Satan stood up against Israel, and moved

[1] It is difficult to determine what exactly happened. The verb used is that which is used of Jezebel being thrown from her window, 2 Kings ix. 33. The primary meaning of the word is expressed by the Septuagint, which says 'for the oxen had drawn it away' (i.e. they had gone too quickly), to which the translators added that Uzzah put out his hand to check it. This is understandable considering the extraordinary noises which they must have been making. Vulgate (and with it, Douai) says that the oxen kicked (cf. Acts ix. 5, xxvi. 14; *calcitrare*) and tilted the Ark. This latter phrase is an addition from the Old Latin and is not in the best Vulgate MSS. The strongest tradition is that the oxen let the Ark fall, or that they tilted it, but Septuagint almost certainly gives the true picture.

David'), but that when it came to a question of the maintenance of their own privileges as a priestly caste, they clung to the most primitive notions of the destructive jealousy of Jehovah, with the old-time inevitable penalty attached to illegitimate contact with holy things, whether the act was intentional, involuntary, or even accidental. We certainly get the same kind of thing among the prophets, though not later than such an early pre-eighth-century prophet as Elisha, whose conduct in the matter of the rude small boys and the two she bears does not exactly fit in with our ideas of the proper conduct of a man of God, 2 Kings ii. 23–5. Whatever the post-exilic Jerusalem priests learned from the eighth-century prophets and their successors, they evidently learned nothing which would interfere with their own sacerdotal privileges, 2 Kings xxiii. 9.

Turning to the personal-impersonal nature of *qodesh-mana*, there are instances where this power is apparently wholly material. It is regarded as being contagious, just as uncleanness is. The contagion of uncleanness is shown in Leviticus xxii. 4–6 (P), of the sons of Aaron, and again in Leviticus xv. 13 (P), in both of which cases uncleanness can be removed in running water. Similarly, the contagion of holiness is seen in Leviticus vi. 27 (Heb. 20), 'whosoever (R.V. text, 'whatsoever') shall touch the flesh thereof shall be holy (*yiqdash*): and when there is sprinkled thereof upon any garment, thou shalt wash that whereon it was sprinkled in a holy (*qodesh*) place'. Still further, it is stated in the next verse that if the blood soaks into an earthen vessel, then that vessel must be destroyed. The reason presumably is that the holiness of the blood soaks right through into the porous material and cannot be got out of it, as is not the case with brazen vessels which can be thoroughly scoured. All this is concerned with the blood of that sin-offering which is slain 'where the burnt-offering is slain' (at the north of the altar of burnt-offering). A clear distinction is made between this sin-offering, which is 'most holy' (*qodesh qodashim*), and the other type of sin-offering, of which the blood only is brought into the Tent of Meeting, Leviticus vi. 30 (23) and iv. Apparently the blood which belongs to the 'doubly holy' sin-offering is the more dangerous.

This non-moral and non-personal view of holiness is seen also in Isaiah lxv. 5 and Ezekiel xliv. 19. Here too holiness seems to be indistinguishable in its nature from uncleanness; cf. Leviticus xi.

31–8 (P), etc. Another example is Haggai ii. 12 *f*, where a new element appears. Here the question is asked of the priests by Haggai the prophet as to whether holiness is contagious. The priests answer in the negative. Dr. L. E. Browne has pointed out that the decision of the priests that uncleanness was contagious whilst holiness was not contagious, is 'in direct contradiction to the law of the sin-offering', and he suggests that the priests deliberately gave a wrong answer in order to exclude the Samaritans from the restored Temple.[1] Other examples of the contagion of holiness are to be found in the story of Elijah and his mantle, 2 Kings ii. 13 *f*.; the ritual of the High Priest on the Day of Atonement, Leviticus xvi. 4, 23 *f*; and in Ezekiel xlvi. 20. It is noticeable that these instances are all either pre-eighth-century northern Israel, or post-exilic priestly traditions.

3. THE BEGINNING OF THE DISTINCTIVE HEBREW DEVELOPMENT

First of all, we have four instances, all in Daniel iv. 8, 9, 18, v. 11 (Aram., iv. 5, 6, 15, v. 11), where the root *q-d-sh* (actually the adjective *qaddish*) is used in its personal aspect of the gods of the heathen or of gods generally. This use is similar to that in the oft-quoted Phoenician inscription on the sarcophagus of Eshmunazar (*c.* 400 B.C.).[2] All four cases are late, being second century B.C. They are unusual for the Old Testament, and are comparable to the use we have already noted in neo-Babylonian, whereby the root is applied to deities generally, as distinct from men.

The distinctive Hebrew development begins with the use of the root in its personal sense with reference to Jehovah alone. We find this in 1 Samuel vi. 20, 'Jehovah, this holy God', and in Isaiah v. 16, where the title Jehovah of Hosts is paralleled with 'El, the Holy One'. To such an extent is the root reserved for Jehovah alone that the adjective *qadosh* is actually used as a synonym for the Divine Name, e.g. Isaiah xl. 25, where the English versions are right in inserting the definite article and translating 'saith the Holy One'. See also Hosea xi. 9; Habakkuk iii. 3; Job vi. 10; Leviticus xviii. 21, where the Septuagint has 'the Holy Name' for the Hebrew 'the Name of thy God'; and

[1] *Early Judaism* (1920), p. 111. Cf. the references which he gives there; also Mark i. 41 and W. Robertson Smith, *The Religion of the Semites*, pp. 450 *ff*.

[2] *Corpus Inscriptionum Semiticarum* (Paris), No. 3. The phrase 'holy gods' occurs in lines 9 and 22.

the frequent use of the phrase 'the Holy One of Israel' in First and Second Isaiah. The plural *qedoshim* (presumably for emphasis, translated as a singular in R.V.) is found in Proverbs ix. 10, xxx. 3. When the prophet says in Amos iv. 2 that Jehovah 'hath sworn by his holiness', he means that Jehovah has sworn by His Deity, by Himself as God, and the meaning is therefore exactly the same as in Amos vi. 8, where Amos says that 'the Lord God hath sworn by Himself'. As A. B. Davidson says, 'the word "holy", when combined with the word "God", is a mere otiose epithet', and whilst the word may be used by the heathen exclusively of gods in general, 'in Israel the epithet is transferred to Jehovah'.[1]

We find such phrases as 'His holy arm' (lit. 'the arm of His holiness' *qodsho*, and similarly for the other cases), Isaiah lii. 10; Psalm xcviii. 1; 'His holy word', Psalm cv. 42, with the plural in Jeremiah xxiii. 9; and 'His holy spirit', Isaiah lxiii. 10; Psalm li. 11 (Heb. 13); and the Septuagint of Psalm cxliii. 10 (cf. R.V. margin). All these are holy because they are Jehovah's. No one else's arm, word, spirit can be holy. In the same way the Sabbath is *qodesh*, because it belongs to Jehovah, Exodus xvi. 23 (P). It is *taboo* because it is *qodesh*, and not, as perhaps might be thought, *qodesh* because it is *taboo*. Similarly, the first-born is *qodesh*, because he belongs to Jehovah, Exodus xiii. 2 (P), and has therefore to be redeemed before he can be reckoned to belong to his father or owner.[2]

The use of *qodesh* and its derivatives is extended to places, things, and persons, in so far as they belong, or have come to belong to Jehovah. Examples include 'holy hill', Isaiah xi. 9, etc.; 'holy nation, people', Exodus xix. 6 (JE); Isaiah lxii. 12; the Temple, Palestine, and even the ground near the Bush, Exodus

[1] *Ezekiel* (Camb. Bible, 1892), p. xxxix. See also his full examination of the idea of holiness in *The Theology of the Old Testament* (1904), pp. 144–60.

[2] It is true that Hebrew tradition associated Jehovah's right to the first-born son with the deliverance from Egypt. This is an aitiological association, and is a common feature of Hebrew history. Most things are traced back to the Exodus or to the forty years in the Wilderness. The same explanation is given in connection with the first-fruits, which also are holy because they belong to Jehovah. Here, although Genesis iv. 3*f.* (J) shows that the presentation of first-fruits of both field and fold was regarded as belonging to the earliest days, yet, according to Deuteronomy xxvi. 5–11, they were associated with the Exodus. We have also two reasons given why Israel is holy to Jehovah. One is because Jehovah delivered Israel from Egypt and chose him to be a peculiar people to Himself, Deuteronomy xiv. 2. The other is, in the words of Jeremiah ii. 3, 'Israel was *qodesh* unto Jehovah, the first-fruits of his increase', though even here a reference to the Wanderings is found in the previous verse.

iii. 5 (J). The word is applied to 'the holy way' through the wilderness and the solitary place of Isaiah xxxv. 8, in which the redeemed of the Lord will walk when they return with singing to Zion; for they are His, since He rescued them, and the road is His, since He made it. The heavens are holy, since they are His, Psalm cxv. 16, and He answers from there, Psalm xx. 6 (Heb. 7); cf. Wisdom ix. 10. Especially is the Temple *qodesh*, and even more so the Inner Sanctuary. In fact this latter is *qodesh qodashim*, 'the holy of holies', doubly holy, the holiest of all. Generally, everything that has a place in the Sanctuary, or is used in worship is *qodesh*, shewbread, oil, clothes, everything. Even the profits of the renewed prosperity of the harlot Tyre, after her seventy years of trade depression, will be *qodesh* to Jehovah, because, instead of Tyre hoarding her own gains, they will come 'to those who dwell before the Lord', i.e. to the Jehovah-priests or to the Jehovah-community in Jerusalem, Isaiah xxiii. 18. Or, again, the priest is *qodesh*, not because, as the Oxford Lexicon suggests,[1] he is a person connected with a holy place, but because he belongs to Jehovah. It is true that a priest is always connected with a shrine, but he himself has to become *qodesh* before he can be connected with a place that is *qodesh*. This is clear from such a passage as Judges xvii. 5 and 12; and again Exodus xxix. 44 (P). They all belonged to Jehovah, whatever their functions; priest, Leviticus xxi. 6, 7 (P); Levites, 2 Chronicles xxxv. 3; prophet, 2 Kings iv. 9; and even the Temple prostitutes, *qadesh* being the male, and *qedeshah* the female. The fact is that for far longer periods than we care willingly to admit, these Temple prostitutes are regarded as holy persons during the period whilst Solomon's Temple was standing. Probably the closing years of Solomon's Temple were the worst years of all, when the dreadful reaction set in after the untimely death of King Josiah. The destruction of that Temple was probably one of the best things that ever happened to the People of God. It gave the post-exilic reformers something like a clean start. These holy prostitutes had their place in the official cultus side by side with the priests and the cult prophets. There were times when all men, worshippers and priests alike, recognized the validity and even the desirability of their functions. Those who protested, to whom the ultimate exclusions of such untoward ministers was for the most part due, were the canonical prophets,

[1] Brown, Driver and Briggs, *Hebrew and English Lexicon* (1907), p. 872 *a*.

whose teaching was finally embodied in the post-exilic reforms. Whilst it is true that two great reforming movements started with the High Priest (Jehoiada, 2 Kings xii. 2 and Hilkiah, 2 Kings xxii. 8), yet far too often the cult prophets and the priests tolerated these things, except during the reigns of reforming kings, when they followed the lead of the kings, as indeed they had followed, meekly or enthusiastically, the lead of the other kings in the contrary direction.[1]

The verb *hiqdish* (hallow, sanctify) is used of ceremonial dedications and purifications by way of signifying to all concerned that such and such was actually Jehovah's, or to make it clear that it (he) had now come to be Jehovah's. It may be that many, or at certain stages all, thought that the actual ceremony itself was the means of hallowing; but in either case the ceremonial significance of the *hiphil* form is clear, Exodus xxviii. 38 (P); Deuteronomy xv. 19 (D); 1 Kings ix. 3; Jeremiah i. 5, etc. Other forms of the verb are also so used, e.g. the *piel*, Exodus xix. 23 (J); Deuteronomy xxxii. 51 (D); the *pual*, Isaiah xiii. 3; and the *hithpael*, Exodus xix. 22 (J). All such cases are developments from the original meaning, just as is the 'cleanse' of the Syriac, and the 'bright' of the Akkadian.

The Greek equivalent of 'qodesh'.

In view of the fact that *qodesh* refers primarily and indeed exclusively to the gods alone, and thence comes in Hebrew to be used of persons and things in so far as they have come to belong to Jehovah alone, it is curious that Otto gives[2] *hagios* as the Greek equivalent of *qodesh*, and does not mention *hieros* at all. In so far as *qadosh* equals 'numinous', which is Otto's 'special term for "the holy" minus its moral factor', then the Greek equivalent is *hieros*. This latter word originally meant 'filled with divine (supernatural) power'—that is, with *mana*. It never at any time gathered to itself any ethical meaning. For instance, *hiera* could mean 'dead-heat', because when it was impossible to decide in the Games which of two was the victor, the prize was assigned to the god. On the other hand, *hagios*, perhaps under the influence of the Greek *hagnos* (pure, chaste), came to include moral ideas, and thus came nearly to be equivalent to *katharos* (clean). Since the Hebrew *qadosh* suffered a similar development, though not to the same extent, except for the isolated 2 Samuel xi. 4, the true Septuagint equivalent of *qadosh* is *hagios*, as Otto said. But this is Septuagint Greek, and

[1] For the difference between the canonical and the cult prophets, and the sharp distinction which must be made between them, see Dr. A. R. Johnson, 'The Prophet in Israelite Worship', *Exp. Times*, xlvii. 7 (April, 1936), pp. 312–9.

[2] *The Idea of the Holy*, p. 6.

not Classical Greek. We doubt whether it is the general equivalent even in Hellenistic Greek. It is true, as Procksch states,[1] that the use of *hagios* as an epithet of the gods begins with Hellenistic times, but this is largely due to Septuagint influence, and does not seem to be characteristic of Hellenistic Greek as such. Josephus and Philo, for instance, use *hagios* under Septuagint influence, but *hieros* in speculative contexts. The word *hagios* is never found in Homer, Hesiod, or the tragedians, and is rare in Attic Greek. There are cases of its use in some of the Syrian and Egyptian mystery cults. Certain books of the Apocrypha and certain Pseudepigrapha (1, 2, 3 Esdras and 1, 2, 4 Maccabees) use *hieros* as well as *hagios*. These books, however, so far as language and style are concerned, depend upon both Hellenistic and Septuagint influence.[2] The use of *hieros* in these books is remarkable when it is compared with the rare use in other parts of the Septuagint where there is an equivalent in the Hebrew. The proportion is 109 to 12, and of these 12, there are 5 cases where the Greek *hieros* does not represent any particular Hebrew word. Only once[3] does it stand for the root *q-d-sh*, 1 Chronicles xxix. 3. Most of the 109 cases are due to the use of *to hieron* for the Temple. The word is not found in any surviving part of Aquila, and once only in Theodotion and Sexta, though in neither case for the root *q-d-sh*. Procksch is right when he says that '*q-d-sh* is related to *ṭ-h-r* (clean) as *hagios* to *hagnos*', but *hieros* is much nearer to the original non-moral use of *qadosh*. Otto is at fault when he equates *qodesh* as 'numinous' to *hagios*. He ought to have equated it to *hieros* in the first stage, and to *hagios* only when it has gathered to itself a moral significance.

The word *qodesh*, then, comes in the first place among the Hebrews to refer to Jehovah alone. From this the step is easy to use it to refer to those manifested characteristics which belong to Jehovah uniquely. Here we find it necessary to emphasize the word 'manifested', especially because of the theory that the word 'holiness' describes a relation. We strongly dissent from the statement made by W. Robertson Smith that 'holiness is not so much a thing that characterizes the gods and divine things in themselves, as the most general notion that governs their relations with humanity'.[4] We are at least equally at variance with Skinner's statement that 'Holiness in short expresses a *relation*, which consists negatively in separation from common use, and positively in dedication to the service of Jehovah'.[5] The word

[1] *Theol. Wört. z. N.T.*, S. 88.

[2] G. Schrenk (*Theol. Wört. z. N.T.*, S. 226) says that these books depend upon Hellenistic influence 'without reserve'. This is an overstatement. It might be true of the Wisdom of Solomon, but it is certainly not true of 1 Maccabees.

[3] In addition, the Septuagint Daniel i. 2 inserts 'holy' before 'vessels'.

[4] *The Religion of the Semites* (3rd ed., 1927), p. 142.

[5] Art. 'Holiness', *H.D.B.*, vol. ii, p. 395.

'relation' is correct in so far that it is the relation of a person or a thing to Jehovah which decides whether or not it is holy, but 'relation' is a dangerous word, for it hides the marked antithesis which is here. Holiness is of God, and not of man. A thing is holy only when it has passed over from one category to the other.

We have therefore used the word 'manifested' deliberately and of set intent. The God of the Hebrews was essentially active in the world which He had made. We regard it to be of the utmost importance that this fact should be recognized throughout the whole of Old Testament theology. He was no static God in the sense of the philosophers. He was never thought of by the Hebrews as apart from the world, away in splendid isolation. Any such idea among the Hebrews was a development of very much later times, and belongs to the period when the Jews had been influenced by the speculations of the Greeks. Even when such ideas of separation between God and man grew up in Jewry, there were other ideas springing up beside them in order to compensate for developing ideas of remoteness—angelology, the Law, and so forth, but all of this quite distinct from the mediatory Logos of the Greeks. God was from the beginning transcendent in that He was different from man, but He was by no means transcendent in that He was remote from man. 'I am God, and not man: the Holy One in the midst of thee', Hosea xi. 9; or, more literally, 'I am El, and not man: *qadosh* (the adjective) in thy midst.' That is, Jehovah is El, which is the general Semitic name for the High God, the great Deity who is supreme over all and distinct from all lower gods and lesser spirits. He is the High God, *qadosh*, and therefore essentially not man. But this does not prevent Him from being in the midst of His people, though He refuses to enter the city because of its sin. Transcendence does not mean remoteness. It means otherness. It can involve remoteness only when religion is treated as being primarily speculative or ethical instead of being primarily a matter of relationship, with these other elements none the less important, but definitely secondary.

Still less among the Hebrews does transcendence imply *static* remoteness, or any type of passivity. Jehovah is wholly unlike those Epicurean gods in the passage which Dr. H. Wheeler Robinson quotes from Tennyson's *Lucretius*:[1]

[1] *The Christian Doctrine of the Holy Spirit* (1928), p. 76; and again (in part) in *The Religious Ideas of the Old Testament* (1923), p. 51.

who haunt
The lucid interspace of world and world,
Where never creeps a cloud, or moves a wind,
Nor ever falls the least white star of snow,
Nor ever lowest roll of thunder moans,
Nor sound of human sorrow ever mounts to mar
Their sacred everlasting calm.

On the contrary, Jehovah is always active, always dynamically here, in this world. The Hebrew does not say that Jehovah *is*, or that Jehovah *exists*, but that He *does*. Properly speaking, the Hebrew verb *hayah* does not mean 'to be', so much as 'to come to be'. Hebrew has no real verb of 'being', but one of 'becoming'. The verb is active and not static. This attitude is most strongly marked in the Hebrew idea of God. Jehovah is known by what He does in the world. The whole of the religion is therefore concerned with the relationship of God and man. It is not, however, the relationship which is Holiness, but the God who is known only in the relationship.

To such an extent is *qodesh* an essential characteristic of Jehovah that there are many instances, particularly in the Priestly Code, where it is synonymous with *kabod*, in the sense of the burning Splendour of the Presence of the Lord. These are the cases which are cited to support the derivation of the root *q-d-sh* from the Akkadian *quddushu* (? bright, clear).[1] The connection is established in Leviticus x. 3 (P); and Exodus xxix. 43 (P), where it is stated that Jehovah will meet with the children of Israel at the door of the Tent of Meeting, and it 'shall be sanctified (*niqdash*) by My glory (*kabod*).' Such a positive use is not confined to the theophanies of the Priestly Code, though it is sufficiently common there as to be a characteristic feature. We find the association of *qodesh* and *kabod* in Isaiah vi. 3, part of a paragraph which is important in the study of the idea of holiness from more than one point of view. The verse reads 'Holy, holy, holy is Jehovah of Hosts; the whole earth is full of His glory (*kabod*).' The word *kabod* is used as an indication of the Presence of the Lord some seventeen times in the Book of the Prophet Ezekiel (i. 28, iii. 23, etc.). See also Psalm xxvi. 8, cxiii. 4, viii. 1 (Heb. 2); and as early as 1 Samuel iv. 21 *f*., where the loss of the Ark of Shiloh to the Philistines is described in the terms 'the Glory is departed from

[1] Cheyne, *The Origin of the Psalter* (1891), p. 331. See p. 24, above.

Israel'. Another outstanding example is Exodus xv. 11, 'Who is like unto Thee, glorious in holiness?' where the verb translated 'glorious' is *'adar*, originally meaning 'to swell out'; cf. the Arabic *'adira*, 'to have a hernia'. From 'swelling out' the root came to mean 'grand, magnificent'. Compare Psalm xciii. 4, where the same root is translated 'mighty', being used of the mighty swelling of the seas.

In all such cases as these the positive content of the word *qodesh* is clear. It is therefore not enough to say that the word stands for a relation, nor even to say that it stands for the separation between God and man. It comes to stand for the positive activity of that Personal Other, whom the Hebrews recognized as Jehovah. He shines forth positively, radiantly, Deuteronomy xxxiii. 2; Psalm l. 2, lxxx. 1 (Heb. 2), xciv. 1; Job x. 3; just as the light shines forth, Job iii. 4; or again 'and the Light of Israel shall be for a fire, and His Holy One for a flame', Isaiah x. 17. In such a way as this, at the dedication of Solomon's Temple 'the cloud filled the house of the Lord, so that the priests could not stand to minister by reason of the cloud: for the glory of the Lord filled the house of the Lord', 1 Kings viii. 10 *f.*; 2 Chronicles v. 13 *f.* The development of this experience, and of this figure of speech in describing it, is seen in the Shekinah of later Jewish tradition, and in the cloud of the Transfiguration, Mark ix. 2–8.

We are here once more merging into the realm of the 'numinous' as described by Otto,[1] with its Awefulness, Overpoweringness, Urgency, Wholly Other, and Fascination. We have previously seen that *qodesh* strictly has to do with the Wholly Other. These last cases deal with the first Hebrew developments of the ideas of Overpoweringness, Urgency, and Fascination in the human experience of the Holy One. In them we get that element which is fundamental to true religion, that creature-feeling in the Presence of Deity.

The actual connection between Holiness and Awefulness in the Old Testament is seen in the association of 'holy' and 'reverend', e.g. Psalms cxi. 9: 'Holy and dreaded (R.V., "reverend", but the word is the ordinary Hebrew verb for "fear") is Thy Name.' See also Psalm xcix. 3, where it is probable that the original psalm read, 'Dreaded and holy is thy Name', but that it was altered to make 'dreaded' (R.V., 'terrible') go with the first part of the line,

[1] *The Idea of the Holy*, pp. 8–41.

in order that there might be a triple refrain, 'Holy is He.' The New Testament refers to the Awefulness of the Presence of God, when, in describing the experiences of Moses in Exodus xix, the writer of the Epistle to the Hebrews says, 'And so fearful was the appearance that Moses said, I exceedingly fear and quake.' This is Hebrews xii. 21, a passage which is derived from the Septuagint of Deuteronomy ix. 19 with the addition of a reminiscence of 1 Maccabees xiii. 2. Similarly Jacob, awaking at Bethel after having seen visions of God, says, 'How dreadful is this place. This is none other than the house of God, and this is the gate of heaven', Genesis xxviii. 17. It is probable that the original reading of Deuteronomy xxxii. 17 was 'new gods before whom your fathers did not shudder'. In Isaiah vi. 3 *f.* even the very door-posts quiver and shake before Jehovah in His overpowering Holiness. Compare also Eliphaz's description of the effects upon him of that supra-human Presence which came to him in visions of the night, Job iv. 12–15. Other passages are Genesis xxxi. 53 (E), where God is called 'the Fear of Isaac', and the use of the Aramaic *dachala* (fear) in the Targums, e.g. Jonah i. 5, 'they prayed each to his fear'. These last three passages belong perhaps to notions of the awful holiness ascribed to deities in general, but, as we have seen, the distinctive Hebrew development is in the use of *qodesh* to refer to Jehovah alone. This narrowing of the application of the root paves the way for the great step forward which was initiated by the eighth-century prophets. This we discuss in the next chapter.

Chapter III

THE RIGHTEOUSNESS OF GOD

WE proceed to discuss the effect on the idea of holiness of the teaching of the eighth-century prophets. With them we have the first truly distinctive development among the Hebrews. The effect is seen in the association of Holiness and Righteousness, but it is Righteousness with a special emphasis. If we were to choose a passage of Scripture as indicative of the new content of *qodesh*, it would be Isaiah v. 16: 'the holy God (*ha-'el haqqadosh*) is sanctified (*niqdash*) in righteousness', though the verse does not indicate that special emphasis involved in the word 'righteousness' which began in these prophets.

We have described that preliminary stage by which *qodesh* came to refer to that which pertains to Jehovah alone. This forms the necessary basis for the distinctive Hebrew development. Already before the time of the eighth-century prophets, the word 'holiness' had come to be conditioned by man's understanding of the Nature of God. It is the glory of Israel that to them first there was revealed a deeper understanding of that Nature. This distinctive element, due mainly to the eighth-century prophets, is generally said to be a 'moral' development. As we shall see, this statement needs considerable qualification.

Writing of this so-called moral development, Sellin said that in this way Holiness came to mean the Inner Nature of Deity, and that this was without parallel. We find this statement to be wide of the mark, since Holiness plainly had this significance from the beginning. The root *q-d-sh* has always been descriptive of the supra-human Otherness, both among the Hebrews, and also in Canaan and Mesopotamia. With the establishment of a true monotheism among the Hebrews, it came to stand pre-eminently for the Nature of Jehovah. To say that it 'came to mean' this, is accurate only because of the distinctive development of ideas of God among the Hebrews. Whatever that Other was realized to be, that was Holiness. *Qodesh* never meant anything else among the Hebrews. It meant precisely that which at any period was recognized to be the inner Nature of Deity. What is without parallel, is the new content which the eighth-century prophets gave to the word. This they did because they had a conception of Deity which was without parallel.

There are two other observations which must be made prior to a proper examination of the teaching of the eighth-century prophets in respect of Holiness and Righteousness.

Firstly, when we say that they gave a new content to the idea of Holiness by their association of it with the idea of Righteousness, we do definitely mean that it was a new content. We go so far as to say that it was a distinctive content. Particularly, we mean that it was distinctive in origin, in emphasis, and, finally, in content, from those moral ideas which we have received from the Greeks. We say this because of the common tendency to equate the moral teaching of the Hebrew prophets with the ethical speculations of the Greeks. This we hold to be definitely an error, and to show a complete misunderstanding of the function and message of these prophets. It should also be pointed out that, even if the ethical teaching were identical, Amos preceded Socrates by some three centuries or so, and Aristotle by rather more than four.

Secondly, if it should be argued that the prophets were aware of the true Nature of Deity as against primitive and immature notions, or as against the erroneous ideas of the heathen, then we agree, though tentatively. For the understanding of the Nature of God on the part of the eighth-century prophets is true only relatively to these other and immature ideas. Their work was by no means final, even so far as the Old Testament is concerned. The step which they took was but the first stage in a long process. Apart from the different emphasis of the Prophet Jeremiah, there was certainly one other prophet—namely Second-Isaiah—who came still nearer to the truth, and this in connection with that very word Righteousness which is one of the characteristic words of these eighth-century prophets. Further, the Christian knows that there is One who rightly claimed Himself to be the Truth.

I. THE USE OF THE ROOT *Q-D-SH* BY THE EIGHTH-CENTURY PROPHETS

The actual words *qodesh* (holiness), *qadosh* (holy), etc., are rare in the eighth-century prophets apart from Isaiah of Jerusalem. Amos and Hosea use the root only in its earlier sense of that which belongs to God alone as God, whilst Micah does not use the word at all. The two cases in Amos are 'my holy Name', ii, 7, and 'hath sworn by His holiness', iv, 2. The one case in Hosea is xi. 9: 'for I am God and not man; the Holy One in the midst of thee'.

All four prophets combine into a solid unanimity in repeatedly reiterating the fact that Jehovah by His very Nature demands right conduct from His worshippers and will be content with nothing less. The specific and clearly-expressed connection between *qodesh* (holiness) and *tsedaqah* (righteousness) is found twice, both instances being in the Book of Isaiah the Prophet, v. 16 and vi. 1–5. We quoted Isaiah v. 16 at the beginning of this chapter. The parallelism of Hebrew poetry shows that 'exalted high' is an equivalent of *niqdash* (be sanctified). This is in accordance with those ideas of *qodesh* which we have previously considered. But still further, and here we have the new contribution, this sanctifying or hallowing is to be done in *tsedaqah* (righteousness); that is, men see the holiness of Jehovah by the exaltation of righteousness in their midst.

The second passage, Isaiah vi. 1–5, also forms a bridge from the pre-eighth-century ideas of holiness to the new content given by the eighth-century prophets. Isaiah says that when he was in the Temple on one occasion in the year of King Uzziah's death, he saw Jehovah of Hosts seated on a highly exalted throne, attended by His heavenly court of seraphs. We have already[1] noted the awful effect of the Presence of the Lord in the shaking of the very door-posts before Him, whilst the Temple is full of smoke and the heavenly choir antiphonally chant His glorious praise, declaring with a triune refrain His transcendent holiness. But the prophet goes further than this. He does not describe the effect upon himself as a shuddering sense of awe, though doubtless this was an element in his experience, but as a sincere conviction of his own sinfulness. 'Woe is me', he cries, 'for I am undone; because I am a man of unclean lips.' He is convinced of his own and of his people's sin, and all this because he has seen a vision of the King Jehovah, the Holy One. The connection between holiness and righteousness is unmistakable.

Other instances of the use of the holiness-words by Isaiah fall into two groups. The first comprises those cases where the word

[1] See p. 50, above.

is used in the old style to denote that which is holy because it belongs to Jehovah, xi. 9, xxvii. 13; of the Temple Mount as belonging to Jehovah. The third case is iv. 3, where the remnant that is left in Zion-Jerusalem 'shall be called holy'. This chiefly is because they will be consecrated to Jehovah, though the basis of their consecration is that they have been left as survivors when all the filth and shed blood shall have been washed away.[1]

The second group of instances contains the eleven (twelve, if we include xxxvii. 23) cases where the phrase 'the Holy One of Israel' is found as a title of Jehovah. They are i. 4, v. 19, 24, x. 20, xii. 6, xvii. 7, xxix. 19, xxx. 11, 12, 15, xxxi. 1. In addition we find the phrases 'the Holy One of Jacob', xxix. 23, and 'his (Israel's) Holy One', x. 17. The phrase is found with equal frequency in Second-Isaiah, but elsewhere seven times only, one of which is 2 Kings xix. 22, a parallel to Isaiah xxxvii. 23. The other six cases are Jeremiah l. 29, li. 5; Ezekiel xxxix. 7; Psalm lxxi, 22, lxxviii. 41, lxxxix, 18 (19). See also Jeremiah ii. 2 (Septuagint). In these eleven cases in First-Isaiah, we have very much more than a plain ascription of Deity to Jehovah as the God of Israel. The prophet gives to the word that new content which is to be found in the new appreciation by all four eighth-century prophets of the Nature of God and of the demands which He makes upon the people Israel because of His Nature. These demands can be seen in the charges which are made against the people because of their conduct.

Amos's Charges against the People

Amos makes general charges of injustice, v. 7, and of the persecution and victimization of honest and upright men who are prepared to speak out against such misdoings and perversions of justice, v. 10. He knows that the command of God to all Israel is 'to hate the evil and to love the good', v. 15; and his fervent impassioned prayer is that 'judgement roll down like waters, and righteousness like a mighty stream', v. 24. He makes one other general charge, that of a man and his father having sexual intercourse with the same woman, ii. 7, thereby profaning God's Holy Name. It is difficult to say what exactly this offence is. In view

[1] We do not regard 'the holy seed', vi. 13, as being from Isaiah of Jerusalem. The last clause is almost certainly a gloss. It is not in Septuagint. Also, we regard xxiii. 18 as being in an exilic (or post-exilic) supplement to what may very well be a genuine Isaianic prophecy concerning Tyre.

of Hosea iv. 2 and Ezekiel xxii. 11, it may be adultery and incest, though the actual word used for 'woman' is strange in that case. On the other hand, it may be Temple prostitution, but whatever exactly the charge which is involved, it is one which is made against all and sundry, and that is the point with which we are concerned here.

Apart from these general charges, Amos's condemnation of the House of Israel is a condemnation of the rich for their oppression of the poor. It may be that in the foregoing cases he is thinking of the rich rather than of the poor, but he does not say so. In such passages as ii. 6–8, iii. 9, 10, v. 11, 12, viii. 4–6, however, he is certainly accusing the wealthy and the powerful. His complaint is that they do not seem to realize that such bribery and corruption with its perversion of ordinary justice between man and man has anything to do with religion. They seem to think that worshipping God is one thing and that 'business' or 'politics' is another, and that there is no connection between the two worlds. They even go so far as to make use in their religious feasts, more feast than religious, of that which they have unjustly wrung from the poor and needy. They use clothes which they have taken in pledge in order to make themselves comfortable as they recline to eat and drink their sacred meals before the altar.[1] They drink that which they have obtained by extortion, that is, by making full and privileged use of the law to extort fines from the poor and ignorant, ii. 8. They reprove those who speak uprightly, v. 10; they even go so far as to urge Nazarites to break their vows of abstinence and to seek to prevent the prophets from speaking, ii. 11 *f.* Perhaps in this last instance Amos is thinking of his own fate at Bethel, when the priest Amaziah hounded him out of the place, vii. 10–17.

So indignant is Amos at the incongruity between the fulsome worship of his day and the glaring injustices of the rich, that he roundly condemns the whole ritual, and declares Jehovah's abhorrence of the whole affair, v. 22 *f.* It may be that, as many argue, Amos's objection is not to the actual worship itself, but that the worshippers are those who oppress the poor and are generally lacking in what we would call the humanitarian virtues. But he does not say this. He asks if there were sacrifices and

[1] Septuagint understands the passage to mean that they bind the clothes with cords to make curtains near the altar.

tribute offerings during the forty years in the Wilderness, v. 25. The sense of Scripture is that the question expects the answer, No. Amos may have been right or he may have been wrong, both in his knowledge of the past and in his judgement of the value of ritual worship. These things have to be decided on other grounds. For our part, it is quite clear that unless his words are 'looking-glass' words, he did definitely believe that there was no cultus in the desert days comparable to the cultus of his own day. In this he was supported by Jeremiah, vii. 22.

Hosea's Charges against the People

Hosea's charges are quite general. He does not single out any particular section of the community. His complaint is that there is no trustworthiness anywhere: 'there is no truth (*'emeth*), nor troth (*chesed*),[1] nor knowledge of God in the land', iv. 1. In Hosea iv. 2, Hosea follows his general statement of Jehovah's 'controversy' with the inhabitants of Israel by proceeding to define it as a charge of 'swearing (to keep covenants) and breaking faith'. This issues in 'killing and stealing, and committing adultery, and breaking out' (i.e. widespread lawlessness in contrast to isolated incidents) to such an extent that 'blood toucheth blood', i.e. the pools of shed blood lie so thick upon the ground that they run together into one gory mass. The same charge of failing to keep faith with God is found in x. 4.

In respect of worship, we find a double charge. Firstly, we get the same contrast between ritual worship and social conduct; 'for I desire keeping troth and not sacrifice; and the knowledge of God more than burnt-offerings', vi. 6. 'Ephraim (the Northern Kingdom, Israel) has multiplied altars . . . to sin', viii. 11. But Hosea, whatever be the case with Amos, is not against the cultus as such, iii. 4, viii. 13, ix. 5. This is especially clear in iii. 4, where Hosea regards it to be a great calamity that 'the children of Israel shall be many days without king, without prince, without sacrifice, and without pillar, and without ephod or teraphim'. Here there is enough sacred furniture, most of it even pre-Deuteronomic, to satisfy the most ardent ritualist. Hosea's second charge is that of turning away from Jehovah to worship other

[1] For the meaning of *chesed*, often translated 'mercy, loving-kindness', see pp. 99*f*., below. Here it is sufficient to say that, with few exceptions, the word has to do with covenants and keeping faith in respect of them.

gods. This, in view of ii. 8 (Heb. 10), probably refers to the contamination of the worship of Jehovah with the fertility cults of Canaan. It is as well to realize that neither Amos nor Hosea knew any cultus apart from one which was everywhere more or less saturated with these elements. In any case, Hosea insists that ritual worship is secondary to sound ethical conduct.

Micah's Charges against the People

Micah follows the Amos tradition in making his charges particularly against the rich. It is part of Micah's general tirade against the city-dweller. This peasant of Moresheth-gath has little use for the capital city and everything in it, the Temple among the rest. He speaks against those who lie awake at night to think out new schemes whereby they can rob the poor man of what little he has, ii. 1, 2. Amos told men to love the good and hate the evil, Amos v. 15, but Micah finds that they persist in hating good and loving evil, iii. 2. They 'skin' the people, iii. 2, 3. The courts are full of bribery and corruption, whilst both priests and prophets are out for all that they can get, thinking of nothing except making money, iii. 11. Again and again close parallels can be seen between eighth-century B.C. Micah and Langland's fourteenth-century A.D. Piers Plowman. To such a state are things come in Micah's time, that any windy gas-bag who raves from wine and strong drink is greeted as a true prophet, ii. 11. This we take to refer to the excited garrulousness of the talkative drunkard and to his general incoherence, which is taken to be the equivalent of the exalted ecstasy of the true prophet.

If the first three chapters alone are indeed all that can genuinely be ascribed to Micah of Moresheth-gath, then we find nothing specific in his preaching concerning the shrines and the cultus. There is a general denunciation of Zion, and a complete certainty of its utter destruction, iii. 11, 12; but this is part of his deliberate contradiction of such optimistic preaching of Isaiah as is found in Isaiah xxxi. 4–6, xii. 6; and reflected in Psalms xlvi-xlviii. See also Jeremiah xxvi. 18. Later in the Book of Micah, we have the famous passage, vi. 6–8, which, if not actually from the hand of Micah himself, is a good summary of the preaching of the eighth century prophets: 'Wherewith shall I come before Jehovah, and bow myself before the high God? Shall I come before Him with burnt offerings. . . . He hath showed thee, O man, what is good;

and what doth Jehovah require of thee, but to do justly, and to love *chesed* (E.VV., "mercy", but "keeping troth" is better), and to walk humbly with thy God.'[1] Here again is the old contrast not so violently expressed as by Amos, but comparable with Hosea vi. 6.

Isaiah's Charges against the People

Isaiah of Jerusalem joins the chorus of protest against the general wickedness of the times, and once more particularly in respect of the behaviour of the rich and powerful. He is also at one with the others in his condemnation of the cultus he knew. In both respects, in his attitude both towards the wealthy and towards the cultus, he is the most remarkable of the four. He himself was an associate of the well-to-do. From his youth he was a companion of the counsellors of kings, and in his manhood he himself was counsellor to Ahaz and to Hezekiah. Further, on his own evidence, it was in the very Temple itself, even during the offering of the sacrifices, that he himself had that vision of God which made him conscious of the central core of his message as a prophet, vi. 1–end.

Isaiah charges Judah with being 'a sinful nation, laden with iniquity', i. 4. At the close of his condemnation of festivals and religious occasions generally, i. 11–15, he breaks out into one of the most impassioned pleas for repentance ever uttered, 'Wash you, make you clean . . .' i. 16, 17. God is weary of all these new months and sabbaths and the like, these innumerable sacrifices. He will not listen to prayers from those whose outstretched hands are dripping with blood, i. 11–16. They are a people of unclean lips, vi. 5. They honour God with their lips, but not in their hearts, xxix. 13. They call evil good, and good evil, v. 20. Where the prophet looked for judgement (*mishpaṭ*), he found oppression (*mispach*), and instead of righteousness (*tsedaqah*), he heard a cry (*tse'aqah*), v. 7. Everywhere men are profane evil-doers, ix. 17. The land is full of drunkenness, v. 11, 12, 22, xxviii. 7 (Ephraim); and of oppression, bribery, and corruption, i. 23, iii. 14, 15, v. 7, 23, x. 2, xxx. 12. The leaders of the people publish unrighteous decrees, x. 1; the prophets teach lies, ix. 15; the leaders lead the people astray, ix. 16, so that they are destroyed through ignorance,

[1] Moffatt's translation of this passage is inadequate, unfortunate, and indeed wholly at variance with the whole conception of God which these prophets held.

v. 13 (cf. Hosea iv. 6). The wealthy landowners are continually enlarging their estates to the detriment and even extinction and ruin of the small peasant, whom to-day we would call the crofter or the smallholder, v. 8–10. Meanwhile the painted ladies of Jerusalem walk with the mincing steps of harlots, decked out in extravagant finery, iii. 16–24, whilst the poor are robbed of their little all, iii. 14*f.*, and the widow and the fatherless are oppressed, i. 23.

From these summaries of the messages of the four eighth-century prophets, it is clear that we have a new and distinctive conception of the demands of God for Judah-Israel. Jehovah, say these prophets, one and all, demands right conduct from His worshippers. This means justice, honesty, and fair dealing between man and man. Because of this emphasis these prophets have been called 'the ethical prophets of the eighth century'. Their message is recognized by all as marking a considerable advance on all previous ideas. We find it worth while to consider carefully just exactly in what their new emphasis consists. This distinctive element in their message is not always adequately, or even, in our view, correctly understood, particularly in respect of the relation of their ethical teaching to that of the Greeks. There are two aspects in which their message is unique, differing in each case from the ethical ideas of the Greeks. We proceed to deal with these two aspects in turn, and at some length.

2. RIGHTEOUSNESS AS PRIMARILY A RELIGIOUS TERM

Righteousness is Theocentric

Firstly,[1] if the phrase 'ethical prophets' is understood to mean that their new emphasis was made in the realm of ethics, then the phrase may well stand. But it is essential to realize that ethics was not their primary concern. They were ethical prophets almost incidentally. Primarily, they were religious prophets; only secondarily were they ethical teachers. By this we do not mean to detract even to the slightest degree from the importance of their ethical teaching. We insist, however, that their insistence upon right conduct was religious in its origin, and at root was never anything else than religious. We regard this fact as being of the utmost importance, all the more since it does not appear to be

[1] The second aspect is discussed on pp. 68*ff.*, below.

generally recognized. Their whole attitude was dependent directly upon their new-found knowledge of God. This knowledge was religious, rather than speculative. By this we mean that their knowledge was not based upon any notion of the best human conduct, nor upon any theories of 'the good for man'. Their insistence upon the necessity of the humanitarian virtues did not rest upon any theory of the equality of man, nor upon any conviction as to the brotherhood or solidarity of mankind, even though that might include in practice, as often still it does, only men of their own race or colour or class. They made no idealization of human conduct. The idea of the Supreme God as the god of virtue, in whatever sense, may have arisen among other peoples as an idealization of human conduct on the part of the philosophers, but this was not the case in respect of these prophets. The standard by which they judged was not an ethical code. Their standard was what they themselves knew of the very Nature of God Himself. It was because they were so passionately religious that they were so insistently ethical. Knowledge of God came first, and the understanding of right action second. This, firstly, is what is unique in the message of these eighth-century prophets. God first, ethics second, was the order of their preaching.

Sin is 'Theofugal'

The fact that the prophets based their conception of righteousness upon their knowledge of God, and not upon an ethical code is further to be seen in their attitude to sin. How, then, did the eighth-century prophets think of sin?

The answer to this question is of great importance, not only for the proper understanding of the message of these prophets, but also in the study of all subsequent theology, both Jewish and Christian. Actually there are two strands running through the whole of Christendom, and they are quite distinct. The world 'sin' can be used either in an ethical sense of transgressing a moral code, or as a religious term in the sense of rebellion against God, and so being alien to Him. From this latter point of view, sin is 'theofugal'; it leads away from God. The eighth-century prophets thought of sin in this way. Primarily, it was rebellion against God. If the prophets had been in the first place teachers of ethics, they would have spoken of sin as a transgression against a code. A man need not be religious in order to speak in this way. On the other hand, no man can talk about sin as being rebellion against God unless he is religious. Such a man realizes that religion primarily is a matter of relationship with God, and secondarily is a matter of ethics. The religious man is also ethical, if and when his conception of God is ethical. These religious prophets of the eighth century were ethical prophets because their knowledge of God demanded it. The order religious-ethical is vital. Herein is the reason why Christian ethics are different from Jewish ethics. The Christian conception of God is different from the Jewish conception of God. The two conceptions of ethics march parallel with the two conceptions of God. There are certain things which a Christian must do, because He is a Christian. There are other things which the Christian may do, and indeed must do, in common with others. The Ten Commandments, for instance, are incumbent upon Jew and Christian alike. But there are other standards of conduct which arise directly out of the Person and Teaching of the Lord Jesus, and they are incumbent upon the Christian, because he is a Christian. There are certain things which others may do according to their codes, but the Christian may not do them. The prohibition does not lie in any code of ethics, however splendid that code may be. It lies in the Nature of the God in whom the Christian believes, the God who is revealed in the Lord Jesus. The Nature of God is the deciding factor. This is why 'the other cheek' and 'the second mile' are not merely desirable for the Christian, but his plain minimum duty. This is why Christian ethics involve more than decent, honourable living. The God of the Christians is more than right action, honour and truth.

Sin is Rebellion. (*a*) *Amos*

In the first two chapters of the Book of Amos, all the nations within the purview of the ordinary Palestinian, who as yet knew nothing of the still-distant threat of Assyria, are in turn arraigned and condemned for their 'rebellions' against God: i. 3, Syria-Damascus; verse 6, Philistine Gaza; 9, Phoenician Tyre; 11, Edom; 13, Ammon; ii. 1, Moab; and lastly Judah and Israel. The English Versions translate 'transgressions', but the Hebrew word means 'rebellions'. The Douai Version has 'crimes', but this version does not pretend to be a translation of the Hebrew except through the Vulgate, and 'crimes' is sound for the Latin *scelera*.

The charges are of brutal atrocities upon captives and helpless women. The charge against Moab is obscure, but it seems to have involved the double crime of desecration of the dead, and of the desecration of the sacred body of a king. It is noteworthy that the crime was not against Judah or Israel, as were the rest, but against Edom, a people who were rarely anything other than deadly enemies of Israel-Judah. Apart from the Moab charge, all the charges are with reference to the normal customs of Semitic warfare, crimes which also have been perpetrated by invading armies with ignoble persistency throughout the centuries. They involve the infringement of those humanitarian principles which are the foundation of any ordered society. Such infringements are called 'rebellions'. According to ii. 4 (perhaps not from Amos himself), the rebellions of Judah are against the Law of Jehovah. Such an indefinite charge is scarcely in accordance with Amos's direct and specific style. This style shows clearly in ii. 6, where the rebellion of Israel is described as 'selling the righteous for silver, and the needy for a pair of sandals'. The prophet follows with charges of drunkenness, oppression of the poor, and (possibly) adultery and incest. Rebellion, therefore, is Amos's word for the non-observance of those ethical demands which it was his chief duty as a prophet to declare. The going of the people to Bethel and Gilgal is rebellion, iv. 4. Whatever his exact reason for such a statement, it is clear that he regards such conduct as the opposite of seeking Jehovah.[1] The idea of rebellion is further shown in his complaint that they have not ceased from their evil ways and have not 'returned' (*shub*) to God, iv. 6, 9, 10, 11. In v. 12, we get the equation clearly set forth: 'For I know how manifold are your rebellions (R.V., "transgressions") and how mighty are your sins.'

Sin is Rebellion. (*b*) *Hosea*

Hosea has the same attitude in respect of God and sin. He says that the people have 'sinned against'[2] God, iv. 7, that 'they have left off to take heed to Jehovah', iv. 10, and that 'Israel hath behaved himself stubbornly, like a stubborn heifer', iv. 16. He speaks of 'revolters', v. 2, ix. 15, who have dealt treacherously against God, vi. 7. This latter is the phrase he uses when he speaks

[1] And so also in respect of going to Beer-sheba, if the text is sound.

[2] The Hebrew has 'in respect of', equivalent to the classical 'dative of reference'.

of transgressing the covenant. The equation is not surprising when we remember that before the Exile the covenant was thought of entirely as a personal relationship towards Jehovah, the idea of a written law being a later and mostly post-exilic idea. Israel's attitude was one of wandering away from God, and of rebelling against Him, vii. 13.

Sin is Rebellion. (*c*) *Micah*

Micah speaks of the 'rebellion of Jacob' and of the sins of Israel, i. 5, iii. 8; and, further, that he is empowered 'by the spirit of Jehovah and of judgement and of might' to declare unto Judah this rebellion, iii. 8. The meaning of ii. 8 is obscure, but it seems to mean that God's people have risen up to be an enemy to Him in that they have oppressed and robbed passing travellers (caravans?).

Sin is Rebellion. (*d*) *Isaiah*

The same attitude is pronounced in Isaiah. His opening verse is: 'I have nourished and brought up children and they have rebelled against me', i. 2. The theme is continued in verses 4–5. In his plea for true repentance which begins 'Come now, and let us reason together . . .', i. 18, the alternative which Isaiah places before the people is, 'If ye be willing and obedient . . . but if ye refuse and rebel . . .', i. 20. The 'converts' of verse 27 of the English Versions are 'those that return (*shub*) of her', as the margin rightly explains. The rebels and the sinners are those who forsake God, i. 28. Men have rejected the teaching (*torah*) of Jehovah of Hosts, and have despised His word, v. 24. The people (or leaders) of Judah are rebellious children in that they go for counsel elsewhere than to Jehovah, xxx. 1, or in that they will not listen to His teaching, xxx. 9. In connection with Isaiah's attack on the pro-Egyptian policy, he urges Judah to turn back (*shub*) to Him from whom they have deeply turned aside (E.VV., 'revolted'), xxxi. 6. The remedy is that men should return, turn back, even though there be but a remnant, ix. 13, x. 20, 21. This message is embodied in the name of Isaiah's son, Shear-yashub, meaning 'a remnant shall return to God'.

Sin is Rebellion rather than Transgression

All these four prophets, then, are unanimous in thinking of sin as fundamentally a rebellion against God. Their most characteristic word is *pesha'*, the word which is translated 'transgression' by the English Versions (Amos i. 3, etc.), but actually means 'rebellion'. Dr. H. Wheeler Robinson says that the noun is 'inadequately rendered "trespass" or "transgression" '.[1] The fact of the matter is that such renderings are quite misleading, because they give the impression to those who read only the English Bibles that the prophets are thinking of sin as a transgression against a law. This translation 'transgression' is an illustration of the way in which the predominant Jewish *motif* of Law-*nomos* has been interwoven with the characteristic Christian *motif* of Love-*agape*. It began very early, as early in fact as the *Didache*,[2] towards the end of the first century A.D. The idea that the prophets thought of sin as a transgression against a law is further strengthened by the fact that the Bible of all Western Christendom from the fifth century to the Reformation was the Latin Bible, which, as we have seen, here reads *scelus* (crime). This rendering is sound in so far as it refers to the heinousness of sin, but definitely wrong in its complete neglect of the meaning 'rebellion'.[3] It is not the case that the Hebrew *pesha'* means 'transgression', 'trespass', or 'crime'. The word means 'rebellion', and should always be translated this way. The corresponding verb is often used of a revolt in the historical books, notably 2 Kings i. 1 of the revolt of Mesha of Moab against the domination of Israel. Hosea viii. 1 should read, 'because they transgressed my covenant, and rebelled against my law', and the book should end with the stumbling of 'rebels', xiv. 9. Similarly the word translated 'backsliding', Hosea xi. 7; xiv. 4; means 'turning away', 'apostasy', and the remedy is therefore 'return' (*shub*) to God, Hosea vi. 1, vii. 10, xii. 6, xiv. 1, 2. Later Jewish tradition was well aware of the significance of the word *pesha'*, when it is used of sins, for it is said in the Talmud, *b. Yoma* 37 *b*, '*pesha'im*: they are rebellious acts (*meradim*)'.[4] Additional confirmation is to be found in the Septuagint. These translators varied considerably throughout the Greek Bible in their rendering of this word *pesha'*,

[1] *The Christian Doctrine of Man*, (2nd ed., 1920), p. 44.

[2] See A. Nygren, *Agape and Eros*, Part II, Vol. I (Eng. tr. by P. S. Watson, 1938). The majority of scholars hold that the *Didache* dates from A.D. 80–100.

[3] Compare also the way in which the Hebrew *tsedaqah* and the Septuagint *dikaiosune* have been influenced by the Latin *justitia*.

[4] Cf. *Tosef.*, *Yom.* II, 1, where the contrast is between *meradim* as deliberate acts against God and *zedonoth* as unpremeditated acts of passion.

but they made no mistake when they dealt with the eighth-century prophets. With one[1] exception only (Isaiah i. 28), they have translated by *asebeia* (noun) and *asebeo* (verb), of which the meaning is 'contrary to God'. The Greek *adikia*, as commonly used, is an act against man, but *asebeia* is an act against the gods.[2] Luther explains the phrase 'for three transgressions . . . yea, for four' as 'for ungodliness in its worst form'. The word 'ungodliness' is a good rendering of *asebeia*.

The Prophets' Serious View of Sin

We find it necessary to emphasize the most serious view of sin which the prophets took, especially in that they thought of it as rebellion rather than as transgression. Particularly is this emphasis necessary in view of deprecatory references which are sometimes made to the attitude of the prophets concerning sin. The late Canon Quick, for instance, regards their attitude as seriously inadequate.[3] His complaint is that they are 'distinctly libertian and Pelagian, in insisting that the chosen people, and the individuals which compose it, can always obey God and be righteous, if they will'. 'They assume without question that he can (change his way of life), if only he will make the effort.' This attitude of minimizing the prophetic teaching in order to exalt the priestly elements of the Pentateuch is common amongst those who to-day hold to a sacerdotal view of religion, and wish to emphasize the efficacy of the Sacraments. Micah vi. 8, for instance, is quoted, with the comment that 'Micah almost speaks as if it were an easy task'. Such a statement as this depends upon interpreting the 'but' of the English Versions to mean 'only'. The Hebrew makes it clear that this is not so. The original is *ki-'im*, the usual construction to indicate the contrary after a negative or after a question which involves the denial of what has previously been said. In this particular case, the *'im* is a strengthening of the adversative *ki* (but).[4] The prophet means that God does not require sacrifices and substitutions, but, on the contrary, he certainly requires . . . Again, it is true that the prophets assume

[1] There is also Amos iv. 4 in Codex Alexandrinus, but not in Codex Vaticanus. But even here the Greek is *anomeo*.

[2] Cf. Xenophon, *Cyropaedia*, 8, 8, 7.

[3] *Doctrines of the Creed* (1938), pp. 216–20.

[4] See the large number of instances of this type in the Oxford Lexicon, p. 475*a*. It is rare for *ki-'im* to mean 'only'.

that a man can change his way of life if he will. But they realize that man does not so will. They never anticipated that more than a very small remnant would ever turn back to God. This is clear in Isaiah i. 9, vii. 3, and especially Ezekiel v. 1–4, where the prophet expects the salvation of only a few of a third part.[1] The prophets knew very well that man's will is corrupt. Men are fast bound by their deeds, so that they cannot turn, Hosea xi. 7.[2] If there is ever to be any turning, then God Himself must turn them, Jeremiah xxxi. 18. Why is it, asks Jeremiah in viii. 4–7, a context where he is dealing with the problem of man's persistent apostasy, that the migratory birds know the proper time to come back, but God's people do not know? Hosea's explanation is that 'a spirit of whoredom' has caused the people to go astray, iv. 12. By this he means that they are possessed by a *ruach* (spirit), which dominates their will, so that they are no longer able themselves to control their actions.[3]

It is said that Isaiah i. 18*f.* is 'all the gospel which Isaiah knows'. The passage in question is a call to repentance, and a promise of happiness and prosperity following that repentance. But in Isaiah xxii. 14 the prophet says 'this iniquity shall not be purged away from you till you die'. The prophet uses the word *kipper*, that great atonement word which is always being emphasized as belonging to the priestly circles. It is therefore ridiculous to say that the prophets have nothing more to say than simply to call to repentance, and to threaten punishment. Isaiah, at any rate, talks of atonement. Jeremiah and Ezekiel say that God will give men new hearts and will put His spirit in them, not 'in a dim and distant future', but in the days of the return from exile and of the rebuilding of Jerusalem. This immediacy is quite clear from the contexts. If the suggestion of a far-distant future be made because it is thought that the references are apocalyptic, then we have a most extraordinary misapprehension of apocalyptic thought, of which the whole point is that the crisis is near at hand, and that the New Age is imminent. To suggest otherwise is a most amazing error.

For our part, we find 'the priestly religion, which produced the sacrificial code in the Pentateuch' to be singularly inadequate.

[1] If Canon Quick includes the Priestly Code in his discussion, we are perfectly entitled to include such earlier prophets as Ezekiel and Second-Isaiah.

[2] Surely this is the very antithesis of Pelagianism. It equals anything in Augustine. The thought is as far removed from Pelagianism as white is from black.

[3] See our study of the use of the word *ruach*, pp. 143*f.*

This system has little to say about deliberate sins except death and excommunication. It deals only[1] with sins 'by error', i.e. by inadvertence (*bishegagah*), mistakes in which there is no intention of doing what is not right. When therefore it is said that 'in Leviticus there is a note of pastoral care and tenderness for erring souls', we do not think that it is the prophets who have an inadequate idea of sin. When it is said that there is nothing like this tenderness for erring souls in the prophets, we wonder what is the meaning of such a passage as Isaiah xl. 10*f.* or Isaiah xliii. 2, and many other passages in Second-Isaiah, Hosea, and Jeremiah, especially Jeremiah xxxi. 20. All this is apart from those psalms which are in the prophetic tradition, e.g. Psalm xl, which incidentally also includes verse 6 (Heb. 7).

In view of the comparative inability of the Priestly Code and its sacrificial system to deal with premeditated and deliberate sin,[2] except by the death of the sinner, we fail to see how, for one moment, it can seriously be maintained that this priestly religion had deeper sense of sin than the prophetic tradition.[3] We find that the idea of the taint of sin in the Priestly Code is a survival of the early *qodesh-mana* ideas, whereby 'holiness' is equally to be got rid of as 'uncleanness'.[4] On the other hand, the prophets knew very well man's inability to turn. What is lacking in the earlier prophets is filled up by Jeremiah and Ezekiel. Jeremiah ix. 6 (Heb. 5) says that the reason why the people refuse to know God is 'through *mirmah*'. The word is translated 'deceit', but the root means 'to become putrid, corrupt'.

And, lastly, we wish that writers who seek to extol any sacrificial priestly system, would, when they use the word 'sacrifice', cease to interpret the word to mean 'gain through loss', and then assume this notion everywhere. All such interpretations make strange reading beside any book on the history of religion, and they bear no relation to G. B. Gray's scholarly and factual study of these matters in his *Sacrifice in the Old Testament* (1925).

It is difficult to say when deliberate personal sins came to be

[1] The one exception is Leviticus vi. 1-7 (Heb. v. 20-6).

[2] Is there really any other kind of sin than this? There are many who would deny that unpremeditated sin is really sin at all.

[3] We are speaking here of the priestly tradition of the Priestly Code, and wish to make it quite clear that we do not refer to moderns of sacerdotal tendencies, concerning whose serious views of sin no one who knows them and their work can have the slightest shadow of doubt.

[4] See pp. 41*f.*

associated with the Day of Atonement, that highest pinnacle of Jewish forgiveness and sacerdotal efficacy. That Leviticus xvi. 30 did ultimately come to be interpreted to refer to every sin, deliberate as well as unintentional,[1] is clear from modern Jewish prayers.[2] The earliest reference of which we are aware, wherein Leviticus xvi. 30 is taken to include deliberate sin, is in the classification of Rabbi Ishmael[3] at the beginning of the second century A.D. He says that there are four ways of atonement. Firstly, if a man transgresses a commandment by not fulfilling it (i.e. omits it by error), and immediately repents, then God forgives, and the Scriptural reference is Jeremiah iii. 22. Secondly, if he deliberately breaks it and repents at once, then God suspends punishment, and the Day of Atonement atones, and the Scriptural reference is Leviticus xvi. 30. Thirdly, if he deliberately breaks a commandment where the penalty is death or excommunication, and then repents, then repentance and the Day of Atonement suspend punishment, and visitations cleanse the sin away. Fourthly, if he profane the Name, then there is no power in repentance to suspend punishment, nor in the Day of Atonement to atone, nor in visitations to cleanse away, but all three together suspend punishment, and death cleanses, Isaiah xxii. 14. From this classification several facts emerge. First, repentance is essential, and apart from this nothing at all can be done. Second, even in Rabbi Ishmael's time, the Day of Atonement can atone only for sins where the penalty is not death or excommunication. Third, in all cases of deliberate sin, the Day of Atonement at most combines with repentance to suspend punishment, but is never itself efficacious even for that, still less for atonement. Rabbi Ishmael, for all his zeal, evidently has a lower estimation of the value of the sacrificial system *per se* than some of its modern admirers.

3. RIGHTEOUSNESS IS MORE THAN ETHICAL

The Bias of Righteousness in Favour of the Helpless

We turn now to the second truly distinctive element in the teaching of these eighth-century prophets. Even the statement that their teaching was ethical in a secondary sense needs considerable qualification. There is a deep-seated and fundamental bias at the root of their ethical teaching. This element is a special

[1] Again, if there really is such a thing as unintentional sin.

[2] Singer, *Authorised Jewish Prayer Book*, pp. 259–61.

[3] *Mechilta*, 20, 6.

consideration for the poor and down-trodden. It crops up again and again. As we saw in our résumé of the messages of the eighth-century prophets, whilst they made general charges, and proclaimed a general standard of true humanitarianism, they nevertheless made particular charges against the wealthy on behalf of the poor. It is true that they spoke against the particular evils which were rampant in their day, and that they said such things because such things needed particularly to be said. The fact remains that, whatever the reason, these things were said.

When they emphasized *tsedeq* (righteousness) in relation to the needs of the widow and the orphan, the poor and the needy, this does not mean that the depressed classes ought to receive any treatment different from the rest of the community. It does not mean that they were to receive better things. Still less does it mean that wrong actions which are condemned in the rich are to be condoned in the poor. Theoretically, there is no doubt, the prophets held that there should be one law for all, rich and poor alike. But their message arose out of the frank recognition that here most in human affairs there was room for improvement. In practice these unfortunates did not receive the same treatment. That is why the prophets singled them out so markedly. Their need was greater. Further, it was evident that unless God Himself did something for them, then nothing would be done at all. The wealthy and the noble, the aristocrats and the business men would continue on their self-appointed way, selling up the poor, building up their own estates, and all within the law as administered in the courts. The poor had no redress there, for where the oppressors themselves were not the judges, they controlled the judges by influence and bribes. The poor and helpless had no helper but God. 'The helpless committeth himself to Thee; Thou hast been the helper of the fatherless', Psalm x. 14; 'He shall deliver the needy when he crieth; and the poor that hath no helper', Psalm lxxii. 12.

Inasmuch, therefore, as it is God's concern to establish *tsedeq* (righteousness) in the land, He must perforce pay particular attention to the case of the poor and outcast, the widow and the orphan. The result is that, even as early as the eighth century, *tsedeq* is more than a barely ethical word. Already it is invading the salvation vocabulary. *Tsedeq* certainly stands for the establishment of justice in the land. We would not detract to any degree from the importance of that, but, important as it is, it is but half the truth. It is incidental that *tsedeq* stands for justice. It is incidental because *tsedeq* actually stands for the establishment of God's will in the land, and secondarily for justice, because that in part is God's will. It is 'in part', because God's will is wider than justice. He has a particular regard for the helpless ones of earth to rescue them from the clutches of those that are stronger than they.

The Post-Biblical Use of 'Tsedaqah' (Righteousness)

The word *tsedeq* (with *tsedaqah* as the feminine form) has from the first a bias towards the poor and needy. It means not only the establishment of righteousness on equal terms for all, but also the vindication by God of those who cannot themselves secure their own rights. We find this idea in Hannah's prayer, 'He raiseth up the poor out of the dust . . .', 1 Samuel ii. 8, and from thence it is carried on into the Magnificat and elsewhere into the New Testament. See also Psalm cvii. 40 *f.*, etc.. Already in the Old Testament there is evident, to use Dalman's phrase, 'a righteousness which is better than that of the scribes'.[1] The Hebrew *tsedaqah* is specially connected with giving to the poor, Psalm cxii. 9, and in Daniel iv. 27 (Aram. 24) the Aramaic *tsidqah* is equated with 'shewing mercy to the poor'. In post-Biblical Hebrew and in the Targums and Talmud, the Hebrew *tsedaqah* and the Aramaic *tsidqah* most frequently mean 'almsgiving' and 'benevolence'. Dalman gives[2] illustrations of this, of which the most striking example is *Tos. Sanh.* i, 3: 'wherever there is justice (*din*), there is no *tsedaqah*, and wherever there is *tsedaqah*, there is no *din*'. The normal Aramaic word for ethical uprightness is *zaku* (*zakutha*). The only instance where the Aramaic *tsidqah* is used in the Targum of Onkelos for the Hebrew *tsedaqah* in anything like its ethical sense is Genesis xviii. 19. Here the ancient commentary on Genesis, *Bereshith Rabba* 49, makes full use of this apparent waywardness of the Targum, and contrasts *tsedaqah* (as meaning charity, benevolence, indiscriminate hospitality) with *mishpaṭ* (strict justice), thus understanding the word in its later sense. Further evidence of the later tendency of *tsedaqah* may be found in Strack-Billerbeck.[3]

[1] *Jesus-Jeshua* (Eng. tr., 1929), p. 67.
[2] *Jesus-Jeshua*, pp. 67–9; see also his earlier *Die richterliche Gerechtigkeit im AT* (1897).
[3] *Kommentar zum neuen Testament aus Talmud und Midrasch* (1925), iv, 537–610.

The Greek translators of the Old Testament were fully aware that the word *tsedaqah* could mean 'a benevolence going beyond strict justice', as is clear from Ezekiel xviii. 19, 21 and Psalm xxxiii. (LXX, xxxii) 5, where *eleos* (pity, mercy) is found. See also Daniel iv. 27 (Aram. 24), where both Septuagint and Theodotion have *eleemosune* (pity). This provides evidence that such views were not confined to Palestinian circles.[1] Another notable instance is Matthew vi. 1, where the better text is: 'Take heed that ye do not your righteousness (*dikaiosune*) before men'. The Textus Receptus has *eleemosune* (pity, almsgiving, charity). It is difficult to resist the inference that this latter assimilation to the next verse shows a true understanding of Matthew vi. 1. Strack-Billerbeck[2] are against the meaning 'almsgiving' and insist on 'righteousness', as in Matthew v. 20, but Dalman shows[3] clearly that even in Matthew v. 20 the word means more than ethical righteousness, and he also gives good ground for supposing that Jesus never used the word *zaku*, but always *tsidqah*. Dr. Dodd agrees[4] with the equation of verses 1 and 2 in Matthew vi. In Urdu the development has gone even farther. *Tsadqah*, from meaning 'alms' has come to mean not only 'gift' but even 'sacrifice'. For instance *tsadqah karna* means 'to make a sacrifice on behalf of another'.

We do not claim that the later use of the word *tsedaqah*, and its Aramaic and Urdu equivalents, in itself proves anything with regard to the Old Testament use of the word. Nevertheless, where there is smoke, there is fire. We hold that it may be taken as a legitimate development of an element which was contained in the root from the beginning, especially since we have seen that such a meaning is found already in the Old Testament. The meaning 'benevolence' could not have been fathered on to just any word. There is every reason for this being the word. Also 'of thorns men do not gather figs, nor of a bramble bush gather they grapes'.

We hold strongly therefore, that, in spite of all that is said about the ethical teaching of these prophets, justice between man and man is not the fundamental basis. Even their ethical teaching is more than ethical. Here is no Justice, blindfoldedly holding the

[1] See C. H. Dodd, *The Bible and the Greeks* (1936), pp. 45*f.*

[2] *loc. cit.* i. 386.

[3] *Jesus-Jeshua*, p. 68.

[4] *The Bible and the Greeks*, p. 46.

scales in just equality. She watches for the rich, and, Brennus-like, throws in her sword against them.

The Origin and Meaning of the Word 'Tsedaqah' (Righteousness)

The Hebrew words for 'righteousness' are *tsedeq* (masculine form) and *tsedaqah* (feminine). There is no difference in meaning. The choice is independent of date, and is a matter of style or caprice. The masculine form occurs 117 times and always in the singular; the feminine 155 times, of which fifteen are in the plural. When we say that they mean 'righteousness', we mean that this is the usual rendering, and that on the whole it is probably as near the true meaning as any one English word can be. The weakness is that this rendering by no means contains the whole significance. Sometimes *tsedaqah* means 'salvation'; it can even be paralleled with 'wealth', Proverbs viii. 18; it can mean 'prosperity', Joel ii. 23, where R.V. has 'in just measure'. The deliverance from Egypt was a *tsedaqah*, 1 Samuel xii. 7 *f.*; Micah vi. 5. Yet again, the word is so frequently found in close connection with *mishpaṭ*,[1] that there must be a close similarity between the meanings of the two words.

The original meaning of the root *ts-d-q* is most easily found by contrast with its antithesis. The opposite of *tsedeq-tsedaqah* is *resha'-rish'ah* (wickedness), again with two forms, masculine and feminine, but this time with a decided preference for the masculine, the proportion being two to one, the actual numbers being thirty against fifteen. The contrast between the two sets of words is plain in Psalm xlv. 7 (Heb. 8): 'Thou hast loved righteousness, and hated wickedness.' Compare also Exodus xxiii. 7 (E); Deuteronomy xxv. 1. The primary distinction between the roots *ts-d-q* and *r-sh-'* is to be seen in Arabic, though there is some difference of opinion as to what precisely this distinction is. Nöldeke and Delitzsch take the original meaning of the Arabic *tsadaqa* to have been 'to be straight, firm', but Skinner holds to the idea of 'hardness'. The discussion has centred round the meaning in two particular instances. Does the phrase *ruch tsadq* mean 'a straight spear' or 'a trusty spear'? Again, when the word is applied to a knotted reed, does it refer to the straightness of the sections or the hardness of the knot? It seems better to take the original meaning to have been 'straightness', for this, contrary to

[1] See below, pp. 74 *f.*

the opinion of Skinner, seems to account better for the later developments of the root in Semitic languages.[1] The root *r-s-*ʿ in Arabic meant 'to be loose, slack' in the sense of not being straight. Both roots in all Semitic languages found a place in the vocabulary of ethics, the two ideas being apt metaphors the whole world over for the description of the two main contrasting categories of human conduct. The cognate languages also give warning that even in Hebrew another application may have taken place other than that in the realm of ethics, and that the use of neither root is confined to this sphere. For instance, there is an inscription in which the verb *tsadaq* is used to mean 'favour, endow',[2] whilst in Ethiopic *rasa*ʿ*a* means 'to forget' more often than it means 'to err, be wicked'. We have already noted the post-Biblical Hebrew, the Aramaic and the Urdu meanings of the root *ts-d-q*.

We take therefore the original significance of the root *ts-d-q* to have been 'to be straight'. The word thus very easily comes to be used as a figure for that which is, or ought to be, firmly established, successful and enduring in human affairs. It stands for that norm in the affairs of the world to which men and things should conform, and by which they can be measured. We are of the opinion that Skinner is quite mistaken in denying this, and in saying that 'nothing of the kind can be inferred from the cases where the word is used of material objects'. On the contrary, just balances and just measures are those which conform to the proper standards, Deuteronomy xxv. 15; Leviticus xix. 36 (H); Ezekiel xlv. 10; Job xxxi. 6. An original idea of 'hardness' is far removed from this application of the root, and this applies to the following cases also. The sacrifices of Deuteronomy xxxiii. 19; Psalm iv. 5 (6), li. 19 (21) are the correct and proper sacrifices, those that conform to the regulations. The same idea applies to the Arabic use in the real as against sham bravery in battle, and also to such Hebrew cases as Genesis xxxviii. 26 (J); Job ix. 15, 20; all three referring to conduct which conforms to the established standards of the time. This is particularly clear in the story of Judah and Tamar, where Judah admits that Tamar, in spite of having played the harlot and thereby coming to be with child, has conformed more closely to the accepted standards than Judah himself in that he

[1] Skinner, Art. 'Righteousness' in *H.D.B.*, iv, p. 274; and the references there. Also Delitzsch, *Commentary on the Psalms* (Eng. tr., 1892), i, p. 84.

[2] *Corpus Inscript. Semit.*, iv, p. 198.

had not given her in marriage to his third son. We would explain in this way the only case where the niphal form of the verb is used: 'the holy place shall be put right' (i.e. into proper order, after it has been desolate and trodden under foot), Daniel viii. 14. This is much to be preferred to the 'cleanness' of the English Versions, following the Greek and Latin, to the 'sanctified' (*wieder geweihet werden*) of Luther, or to the 'justified' of the margins of the English Versions.

The Origin and Meaning of 'Mishpaṭ' (Judgement, Justice)

We said at an earlier[1] stage of this discussion that the message and teaching of these eighth-century prophets was rooted in their knowledge of the Nature of God. This position is confirmed not only by the origin and meaning of *tsedeq* (righteousness), but also by the origin and meaning of the word *mishpaṭ* (judgement), a word which is frequently found in close conjunction with *tsedeq-tsedaqah*.

The root *sh-ph-ṭ*, from which the noun *mishpaṭ* is derived, is found in Eastern and Central Semitic languages, i.e. in Akkadian, Phoenician, and Hebrew. From these it is found in Biblical Aramaic, and in Punic, for the official name of the judges in Carthage was *supheṭ*. The root has to do with the verdict given by a judge (cf. the Latin *judicium*), and it is used of every phase of a judge's work, discriminating the truth, Zechariah vii. 9; deciding controversies, vindicating or condemning, and even, in the niphal form, of entering into a controversy to see who is in the right, Isaiah xliii, 26. The noun *mishpaṭ* means the judgement which is given by the *shopeṭ* (judge), whence the word can mean justice, ordinance, legal right, and so forth.

So much for the basis of the word, and for its use as a legal term in the courts, comparable to our own use of such words. In Israel, however, the word has a history which makes it mean very much more than this, of which the effect has been largely lost because the Old Testament came to us first in a language other than the original Hebrew. Neither this word, nor its early companion *torah* (later 'The Law') can ever wholly be separated from God. For us, 'justice' means either the demands of some moral law, or, more often, the king's justice. To the Hebrew it meant the demands of God's law, and God's justice. It is a

[1] See p. 60, above.

common characteristic of religions and peoples in the early stages of their development that justice should have a close contact with, and should be closely intertwined with, religion. This is the stage before that codification of custom and law which usually leads men to follow the code itself rather than the god whom they have believed to be the author of it. It is true that post-exilic Jewry did tend to exalt the Law, and that the Jews were apt to make the law itself the be-all and end-all of religion. Nevertheless, there was a saving factor even in this legalism, though this is generally forgotten by anti-legalists. They were prevented from following the normal line of development because of their continued insistence on the personal activity of God in the common affairs of this world. They never lost the connection between God and the Law. This was due to that theocentric emphasis on the part of the eighth-century prophets on which we are taking such pains to insist. Doubtless there were legalists of the most pernicious type, but it was God's Law which they were at such pains to exalt. All this shows itself in the history of the word *mishpaṭ*.

Both *mishpaṭ* (judgement) and *torah* (instruction, law) were regarded in Old Israel as being the definite word of Jehovah. When a cult-official, priest or cult-prophet, was asked for a ruling on a matter of faith or conduct, the answer he gave was regarded as being the command of God with regard to the particular point which had been raised. If the question had never been asked before, then the official consulted the divine oracle, by sacrifice or sacred lot if he were a priest, by dream or in ecstasy or vision, if he were a cult-prophet. The word which came to him, and which he thereupon communicated to the questioner, was a definite instruction from God. It was called a *torah* (that which was taught, an instruction). When the same question was next asked, there was no need for the consultation of the oracle, for there was now a precedent. The official gave exactly the same answer as had been given on the previous occasion, but because he was now following a precedent, his answer was no longer a *torah*, but a *mishpaṭ*. The two words are synonymous to the extent that both are the declared word of God. They are different in that *torah*, at this early stage, meant an original pronouncement, whilst *mishpaṭ* meant a decision according to precedent. But both equally are the word of God. Because of this idea of precedent, the word *mishpaṭ* can mean 'manner, custom', 1 Samuel ii. 13,

xxvii. 11; 2 Kings xvii. 33; or 'what manner of boy, man . . .' Judges xiii. 12; 2 Kings i. 7. When the word means 'right, privilege, due', Deuteronomy x. 18, xviii. 3; Jeremiah xxxii. 7; etc., it signifies a right as established by custom.

The primary idea according to usage is judgement by custom, for the function of a judge is to give decisions according to custom or precedent. But no judge, whether priest or prophet, could give any other judgements than those which are regarded as being the veritable word of God. It is necessary therefore to think of 'doing *mishpaṭ*' (Micah vi. 8) as meaning 'doing God's will as it has been made clear in past experience'. In Amos v. 24 it means the declaration of God. According to one line of development, then, *mishpaṭ* is of God, being His declared will, whilst the 'secular' meaning is 'habit, custom'.

For the proper setting of these righteousness-judgement words, it is necessary to emphasize those considerations which we have already noted in connection with *qodesh* (holiness). The first consideration is that God was regarded as being essentially active in this world. He was to be known by what He had done, firstly, at the Creation, and afterwards by what He kept on doing all the time in His created world, particularly with reference to His chosen people. This means that *tsedeq-tsedaqah* must be understood as that which God has established, or will establish in this world. All other ideas are secondary to this, important as some of them are. *Tsedeq* is that which God Himself established as the proper norm, and which, on that account, is firm and straight, steady and immovable. It is the norm which God set up in the beginning, by which also He will judge the world, Psalm xcviii. 9. He made the world in 'righteousness', and He will judge the world in 'righteousness'. *Mishpaṭ* is *tsedeq* in that men can learn what is God's norm through common experience or by the repeated declarations of those through whom He speaks and declares His sovereign will. *Mishpaṭ*, however, tends always to be more closely connected with the law-courts than *tsedeq*, though not to the extent which the Septuagint equivalent *dikaioma* or the Vulgate *judicium* would suggest.

The second consideration which must be re-emphasized is that, just as God is always active in this world and is not an Idea abstracted from it, so *tsedeq* is nothing that is abstracted from this world of affairs. In this it is quite distinct from the Greek *dikaiosune* of the philosophers. *Tsedeq* is something that happens here, and can be seen, and recognized, and known. It follows, therefore, that when the Hebrew thought of *tsedeq* (righteousness), he did not think of Righteousness in general, or of Righteousness as an Idea. On the contrary, he thought of a particular righteous act, an action, concrete, capable of exact description, fixed in time and space. He could take note of *tsedeq* actually happening. If the word had anything like a general meaning for him, then it was as it was represented by a whole series of events, the sum-total of a number of particular happenings. When the feminine plural form is used (fifteen times), it means 'righteous acts', and it is a natural and ordinary plural. It is not to be explained as a 'plural of majesty, intensity', as, for instance, the *behemoth* of Psalm lxxiii. 22, which S. R. Driver so admirably translated 'very beast was I before thee.'

Conclusion

Tsedeq, with its kindred words, signifies that standard which God maintains in this world. It is the norm by which all must be judged. What this norm is, depends entirely upon the Nature of God. This is why *tsedeq-tsedaqah* meant sound ethical conduct to the eighth-century prophets. It is also why it meant more than sound ethical conduct, and shows a persistent tendency to topple over into benevolence, and easily to have a special reference to those who stand in dire need of a Helper. There is to the Hebrew no *Ananke* (Necessity) and no *Dike* (Justice) to which both gods and men must conform. God is His own necessity. Justice is what God wills because such is His Nature. If His thoughts were as our thoughts, then He would insist upon justice first, which usually means retribution, as *dike* tended to do among the Greeks. If His ways were as our ways, then He would seek first to establish a Kingdom of Justice. But His thoughts are not as our thoughts, and His ways are not as our ways. God knows that justice is not enough. Rashi[1] knew this. In his commentary on Genesis, he notices that Genesis i. 1 has *Elohim* for 'God', and not the Sacred Name. He says this is 'because at first God intended to create it [i.e. the world] to be placed under the strict measure of justice, but He realized that the world could not thus endure, so He gave

[1] Rabbi Solomon ben Isaac of Troyes (1040–1105), the most popular of all Jewish commentators, even to this day.

precedence to the rule of Mercy, and joined it with the rule of Justice'. And so, says Rashi, when the Creation is referred to a second time in Genesis ii. 4, we get both the Sacred Name and *Elohim*, with the Sacred Name coming first. This means Mercy first and Justice[1] afterwards. Let all men, Christians and Jews alike, who have forgotten that we must all pray to be judged by the Mercy of God rather than according to the strict measure of Justice, learn from this eleventh-century Jew.

[1] The idea that *Elohim* is the Name of God as Judge comes from such passages as Psalm l. 6 and Psalm lxxv. 7 (8).

Chapter IV

THE SALVATION OF GOD

We have seen that Holiness signifies the essential Nature of Jehovah. It means 'Jehovah-ness'. 'Thy way, O God, is in holiness', Psalm lxxvii. 13 (Heb. 14), R.V. margin. When the eighth-century prophets realized that Righteousness is of the very Nature of Jehovah, Holiness came to include Righteousness as the main element of its content. Our argument in the last chapter was that this is perfectly sound, provided it is remembered that, even in the eighth-century prophets themselves, there is a marked tendency for Righteousness to have special reference to the need of the poor, the widow, and the orphan.

Because of this, we deplore that development which has made Holiness to include almost exclusively such ideas as purity, morality, and ethical rectitude. That it has come to involve these ideas is, of course, one of the glories of that tradition in which Jew and Christian together can rejoice. But it is not its greatest glory, for Holiness has thus stopped short of expressing that wider activity of God on behalf of the helpless ones, which to the Hebrew was implicit even in the eighth century. Whatever Judaism may have become when it was legalized[1] on a predominantly ethical basis, and however our modern Christianity has come to be equated with 'the good life', the religion of the prophets was certainly far more than a matter of ethics. If their tradition is anything to go by, then, just as religion is more than ethics, so holiness should be regarded as being more than awefulness plus moral perfection. It should be regarded as involving Salvation to at least an equal extent as Righteousness. God is Saviour at least as surely as He is Judge.

We have also seen that, whilst Holiness stands for the difference between God and man, yet it never involved an 'away-ness' from man. Whatever 'away-ness' there was, is

[1] Even in the most legalistic period, there was far more than 'the strict measure of justice' than is generally allowed. See Rashi on Genesis i. 1 (p. 77, above). See also *Jer. Sanh.*, x. 2, and the story of the hole in the firmament of Heaven, which God Himself caused to be bored beneath the very Throne of His Glory, in the first place for repentant Manasseh's prayer, but also for the encouragement of all penitents for all time to come.

enshrined in 'the priestly religion which gave rise to the sacrificial code in the Pentateuch', with its zeal for separation between the clean and the unclean, and that whole system of *Habdalah* (Separation) which was the watchword for the last centuries of the pre-Christian Era. God truly is a different category from man. He is different, separate, but He is assuredly always near. Righteousness is the visible effect of this nearness of God in the affairs of this world. The reason why Skinner and Robertson Smith spoke of Holiness[1] as involving a relation is, we ourselves are satisfied, because this Righteousness, this visible nearness of God, is more than ethical, and is in fact a personal relationship at root. It is because Righteousness involves Salvation. This nearness and personal activity of the unique Holy God is of the utmost importance both in Hebrew and in Christian religion. Without it there could never be any connection between Holiness, Righteousness, and Salvation. Because of this connection, it is a travesty of both faiths to think of any one without the other two. Unless the three were inextricably involved, the Holy God could never be the Saviour.

All this is superlatively clear in Second-Isaiah. There is no prophet who insists more completely and harps more insistently on the uniqueness of Jehovah. Again and again, in varied forms, the question rings out, 'To whom then will ye liken Me, that I should be equal to him? saith the Holy One', Isaiah xl. 25. And yet it is this very prophet who proclaims those mighty words which have been the strength and consolation of the faithful Jew for two and a half thousand years: 'When thou passest through the waters, I will be with thee; and through the rivers, they shall not overflow thee: when thou walkest through the fire, thou shalt not be burned; neither shall the flame kindle upon thee. For I am Jehovah thy God, the Holy One of Israel, thy Saviour', Isaiah xliii. 2 *f.* There were never words more intimate than these, except for the Christian when the Word of God Himself was made flesh and dwelt alongst us.

No prophet, we say, has insisted more completely upon the uniqueness of God. No prophet has insisted more certainly upon the nearness of God to His people Israel, and to His saving activity on their behalf. The prophet who most clearly teaches the transcendence of God is the prophet who most clearly teaches His

[1] See p. 46, above.

immanence. If First-Isaiah brought the word Holiness into the vocabulary of ethics, then Second-Isaiah brought it right into the vocabulary of Salvation.

1. THE UNIQUENESS (TRANSCENDENCE) OF GOD IN SECOND-ISAIAH

Second-Isaiah shares with First-Isaiah his marked preference for the phrase, 'the Holy One of Israel' as a title for Jehovah.[1] Second-Isaiah also uses the phrase eleven times, xli. 14, 16, 20, xliii. 3, 14, xlvii. 4, xlviii. 17, xlix. 7, liv. 5, lv. 5, and, in addition, 'His Holy One', xlix. 7, 'your Holy One', xliii. 15, and '(the) Holy One', xl. 25. The phrase is also used twice in the dependent Isaiah lx. 9, 14. In all cases, both in First- and in Second-Isaiah, the phrase is used to signify the Separateness and the Uniqueness of Jehovah.

The Holy God: His Incomparable Power as Creator

Second-Isaiah is continually emphasizing the uniqueness of God in respect of His incomparable power. Jehovah is the Creator of the heavens and the earth, and of all that is in them both. But majestic as are these works of Creation, they are as nothing before Him. God the Creator is vastly more wonderful and magnificent than they. So great is He that He used but the cup of His hand to measure out the waters of the seas. He used but the span of His hand to measure out the heavens. He used a small tierce measure for all earth's dust, and with that He weighed out mountains and hills. Alternatively, as the Vulgate puts it, He poised the whole mass of earth on three fingers. The Gentiles and the isles of the sea which they inhabit are as the small dust of the balances. This means that they are like the fine dust in the scales which can be neglected in the weighing, or, if we follow the Greek and Latin Bibles, they are like the last smallest particle which tips the beam, xl. 12–15. Though men burn all the cedars of Lebanon and every wild beast in its forests, all that were far too poor an offering for Him. These things Israel ought to have known from the beginning. The facts of Creation ought to have been enough to convince them of God's tremendous power, xl. 21 (R.V. margin). Jehovah is the El, the High God, 'He that created the heavens and stretched them forth; He that spread abroad the earth and that which cometh out of it', xlii. 5. He sits

[1] See p. 54, above.

on high, and the horizon is a circle far below, xl. 22. He is the Former of light and the Maker of darkness, xlv. 7. He made the stars, and He makes them rise night after night in their proper order, none ever rising out of turn or failing to answer His muster-call, xl. 26, xlv. 12. Equally on earth does He accomplish His sovereign will. He makes the rivers spring forth in barren lands, and every kind of tree to flourish in the wilderness, xli. 18 *f.* So with cedar, acacia, myrtle, oleaster, fir, elm, and box, He rivals the splendid gardens or 'paradises' of the Persian kings, wherein every kind of tree was cultivated. Actually He outrivals them, because He makes His paradises in the sultry, waterless wilderness. See also xlix. 9, xliii. 19, and so on, again and again.

The Holy God: Arbiter of Nations and Men

Not only is Jehovah the Master of all the natural world of earth and sea and sky, but He is also supreme Arbiter of the fate of nations and men. Egypt, Ethiopia, and Seba are but pawns in His hands, xliii. 3, xlv. 14. Even mighty Babylon, 'the lady of kingdoms', and the all-powerful Chaldaeans are subject to His will, xliii. 14, xlvii, and especially xlviii. 14: 'He shall perform His pleasure on the Chaldaeans.' At the bidding of Jehovah, the heathen will bring back to Palestine scattered Israel, however far they be scattered. They 'shall bring thy sons in their bosoms, and thy daughters shall be carried on their shoulders. And kings shall be thy nursing fathers, and their queens thy nursing mothers' xlix. 22 *f.* God will vindicate His servant, and 'will divide him a portion with the great', liii. 12. It is God and none other, Jehovah the Holy One of Israel, who has raised up the new conqueror in the north and east. It is of Jehovah that nations and kings are like dust and wind-driven chaff before this conqueror's sword and bow. He will trample the rulers of the heathen as the potter stamps his clay in the mortar. No doors nor bars of gates can keep him out. All this is of God, who raised up Cyrus for His purpose, and uses Cyrus for His purpose, though Cyrus never knew Him, xli. 2–5, xlv. 1–5. But most of all God has the power and the will to redeem His people Israel. He always had the power, but now is the time which He has chosen to show it forth. By His incomparable power, which none can gainsay, Jehovah will redeem Israel. His word is strong and sure.

The Holy God: No other God; no Other Saviour

The prophet never tires of this theme. There is none like God, xl. 18, 25, xlvi. 5, xliv. 24. He is unique in glory and in praise, xlii. 8, xlviii. 11. There is none other but He, xliii. 10, 11, xliv. 6, 8; and again He is the first and the last, xli. 4, xliv. 6. He is all powerful, xliii. 13. He alone can declare the end from the beginning, xli. 4, 26, xlii. 9, xliv. 7, xlvi. 10, xlviii. 3. He needed no counsellor, neither in His work of Creation, xl. 14, nor when He determined to redeem captive Israel, xli. 28. There was never such a God before Him, and there can never be any such after Him, xliii. 10, 11. There is no other God, no other Saviour.

The prophet particularly pours scorn on the idols of Babylon. With blistering sarcasm, he condemns the folly of those who first make these idols and then bow down to what they have made. What can be more ridiculous than that a man should take a tree, use part of it to make a fire, at which to warm himself and on which to cook his food, and then use another part of the selfsame tree for a god, to whom he prays and at whose hand he asks deliverance? Jehovah is different from these things of wood, which have to be piled upon beasts of burden if they are to have any chance of surviving in the day of disaster. Even then they cannot escape. They have no power to save themselves, xl. 18–20, xli. 6, 7, xli. 29, xliv. 9–20, xlviii. 5, xlvi. 6, 7, xlvi. 1.

Jehovah equally is different from men. Man's steadfastness is but for a moment, here to-day and gone to-morrow, fading as quickly as the wild flowers fade. But the word of Jehovah by contrast endures for ever, xl. 6–8.[1] God needed no man (the Hebrew is *'ish*) to instruct Him or to give Him counsel at the time of Creation, xl. 13. When strong and vigorous youths faint and are weary, then God gives new and wondrous strength. The prophet does not mean that God revives the strength they have, but that He gives them new strength, strength of a different kind. He gives them new pinions as of eagles, those mighty, high- and far-soaring vultures of the desert, xl. 30 *f.*

2. THE NEARNESS (IMMANENCE) OF GOD IN SECOND-ISAIAH

Much as Second-Isaiah emphasizes the uniqueness of Jehovah, He emphasizes His nearness with equal insistence. Whatever

[1] See p. 105, below.

holiness with its ideas of separateness may have come to mean in the priestly tradition with its survivals of primitive ideas of *taboo*, it never created in the prophets any gap between God and man. This is nowhere so clear and patent as in Second-Isaiah. When the policy of *Habdalah* (Separation) became the dominant theory of post-exilic Jewry, with its rigid separation and exclusion of all who did not, or could not fulfil the ritual laws, it was not of the prophets that this came to pass. When Montefiore objected to the Christians saying that Jewry had removed God far away, he was thinking of such a prophet as Second-Isaiah, and such a passage of Scripture as Isaiah xliii. 2. He was right. Without the firm conviction of the nearness of God, Jewry could never have survived all the hatreds and jealousies of the heathen. The strict observance of the Law has been in point of fact the rallying point of Jewry, but not all her legalizers, nor all the Deist-isolationists could have saved her, if it had not been for this other also. Her persistence, alone among the nations of antiquity, has been the fruit of the sure knowledge that the Incomparable God has been intimately concerned for her.

The whole prophecy of Second-Isaiah is directed to convincing captive Israel of the nearness of the God who is about to rescue him. God has always been active on Israel's behalf. He still is active and He is near. There have been good reasons why He has not delivered him hitherto. It was not in the least because He was far away, or inactive, or incapable. In fact, the very Exile itself was His doing, xlii. 24. It was because of their sin against Him, and their refusal to walk in His way, or to be obedient to His instruction, xlii. 24. So also xlvii. 6, xlviii. 3, 4, l. 1, li. 17, 20, liv. 7. But the time of condemnation is now past, and the day of consolation is near. The hiding of His face was but for a moment, liv. 8.

This insistence upon the redeeming activity of God and the consequent alteration in the fortunes of Israel can be seen by the way in which, whenever the prophet mentions the sins of the past, he immediately speaks of forgiveness and redemption. In xl. 2 he mentions the iniquity of Jerusalem only to say that it is pardoned. Similarly xlii. 24, 25 is followed by xliii. 1; again, xliii. 22–4 by xliii. 25; again, xliii. 27 by xliv. 1 *f.*; again l. 1 by l. 2; then li. 17–20 by li. 21–3; and lastly liv. 7*a* by liv. 7*b* and 8. In addition the last of the four so-called Servant poems deals with the whole matter of the cancellation of sin in the expiatory suffering of the Servant, lii. 13–liii. 10. Yet again, even xlviii. 1–10, which deals with the still unrepentant inhabitants of Palestine, says that, in spite of continued stubbornness, God will yet defer His anger, and will not cut them off for His own Name's sake, if not for their sakes, xlviii. 9, 11.

The evidence of God's redeeming activity can be multiplied. The prophecy opens with the Divine Command that words of effective comfort are to be spoken to toiling, weary Jerusalem, xl. 2. The command 'Comfort ye' does not mean that consoling words are to be spoken to one in the midst of sorrow, in order that the sorrowful one may continue bravely in tribulation. It means that words are to be spoken which will make an end of sorrow, and so will comfort *out of* sorrow, not *in* sorrow. God is Israel's Shepherd, now Himself about to lead His flock with all due care on from one oasis to another, xl. 11. Exhausted Israel will find new strength, that strength which is the strength of God. A mother may forget the babe she has suckled, but God will never forget Zion, xlix. 14 *f.* Abraham was God's friend, xli. 8. They are His people, xl. 1, xliii. 20, 21, etc. He is their husband, liv. 5. In such intimate terms as these the prophet describes the redeeming activity of God.

God is Redeemer

This is one of the two characteristic epithets which Second-Isaiah uses of Jehovah. The other is Saviour.

The word for Redeemer is *Go'el.* The word is used of the next of kin whose duty it is to see that the deceased gets his full rights. Some commentators have therefore explained the prophet's use of the word as emphasizing the kinship between God and Israel. This may possibly be the case, since the relationship is certainly a personal one. It is unlikely, however, that this is why the word is used, since the relations between God and Israel, close as they are, are by no means those of equal and equal. Even the idea of husband (liv. 5) implies nothing of equality, since the name means 'lord'. Israel is His bond-slave, not only in the so-called Servant[1] Songs, but even more outside them (nine times). It is therefore more likely that Second-Isaiah's use of the word *Go'el* is connected

[1] The translation 'servant' is far too mild for the Hebrew *'ebed,* as also it is too mild for the Greek *doulos.* Cf. Romans i. 1 (R.V. margin).

with the idea of causing a slave as property to revert to the original owner, as could be done by payment of an assessment, Leviticus xxvii. 9–25 (P). Israel belonged to God before the Exile, but God sold him, Isaiah l. 1, though without receiving any money for him, lii. 5. He therefore will not pay any money to redeem him, lii. 3. We take this last passage to be decisive as regards the meaning of the word *Go'el*. Again and again we find the word used of God bringing Israel out of Exile and back again to Himself. Again and again we find the statement that He is Israel's Redeemer, xli. 14, xliii. 14, xliv. 6, 24, xlvii. 4, xlviii. 17, xlix. 7, 26, liv. 5, 8. He will certainly redeem His people, xliii. 1, xliv. 22, 23, xlviii. 20, lii. 9, also li. 10, lii. 3. In addition there are six instances in those parts of Third-Isaiah which are dependent on Second-Isaiah, lix. 20, lx. 16, lxii. 12, lxiii. 4, 9, 16, and one more in the very similar Isaiah xxxv. 9. Apart from these cases, there are twenty instances only in other parts of the Old Testament where the word is used of Jehovah. Not all of these by any means are used in the strict sense of 'redeem, buy back', or in a true salvation sense.[1] Out of the twenty, there are five which refer to the Egyptian bondage, all late except Exodus xv. 13; and perhaps four to the Babylonian Exile. The use, therefore, of the root *g-'-l*, in connection with the relations of God and Israel, is predominantly, though not exclusively, Second-Isaiah, and usually when it is found elsewhere, it owes this use to his frequent usage.

God is Saviour

This appellation is by no means confined to Second-Isaiah, for it is the theme of many psalms and of most of the prophets. The name Saviour is, however, so frequent in Second-Isaiah as to be a marked feature of his vocabulary, e.g. xliii. 3, 11, xlv. 15, 21, xlix. 26. The prophet insists that there is no saviour apart from Jehovah, xliii. 11, xlv. 21, xlvi. 7, xlvii. 13. He speaks often of God's salvation, li. 5, 6, 8, lii. 7, 10, xlix. 6, xlv. 8, also xlix. 8, xlvi. 13; and especially 'but Israel shall be saved of the Lord with an everlasting salvation', xlv. 17.

In so far, therefore, as Holiness signifies the essential Nature of Jehovah, Second-Isaiah has brought the word into the centre of

[1] E.g. Job xix. 25, where the word means 'vindicator', and indeed probably does not refer to God at all, but to one who will vindicate Job against God.

the salvation vocabulary, just as certainly as the eighth-century prophets brought it into the vocabulary of ethics. We see this from his general teaching about God, and it is emphasized by the way in which he makes the word *qadosh* (holy) a characteristic Name for God.

'Tsedeq' as meaning Vindication, Salvation, Victory

We have seen that the eighth-century prophets use the word *tsedeq-tsedaqah* (righteousness) in an ethical sense, but with a tendency to shade off into a salvation sense. In Second-Isaiah we find a further stage of this development, for here the word means 'vindication' and even 'salvation' to a far greater extent than 'ethical rightness'. The meaning now is chiefly soteriological, and only to a slight extent ethical. The word forms part of Second-Isaiah's salvation vocabulary.

This increased emphasis arises chiefly out of the thought of God's active participation in the affairs of his world, but viewed from a somewhat different point of view. The eighth-century prophets tended to give *tsedeq* this wider meaning because they thought of it as that which God is seeking to establish in this world. It thus gained its significance from what they knew of this active, immanent God. Second-Isaiah thought of *tsedeq* more from the point of view of that which actually is established in this world. It is that which triumphs and prospers, the assumption being that such is the will of God. Something of this is indeed implicit in First-Isaiah, but the emphasis is unmistakable in Second-Isaiah. The use of the root *ts-d-q* in the sense of triumph is seen in Isaiah v. 23: 'which justify (i.e. put in the right, cause to triumph: the word is the niphal participle of the verb *tsadaq*) the wicked for the sake of a bribe, and the right (*tsedaqah*) of the righteous (*tsaddiqim*) they turn aside from him'. That is, they make the wicked triumph, and take away from the righteous the triumph which properly is theirs. The verb is used without any moral significance, meaning solely 'cause to prosper'.

There are a number of instances of the use of the root *ts-d-q* in this sense throughout the Old Testament. Pharaoh says, 'Jehovah is the righteous one (*tsaddiq*), and I and my people are the wicked ones (*resha'im*)', Exodus ix. 27 (J). There is no ethical meaning here. The writer means that Pharaoh and his people have been beaten, and have lost. Jehovah has won the victory, because He discomfited the Egyptians, and yet preserved the Israelites in Goshen. Another example is Jeremiah xxiii. 6, where the reason given for the new Name 'Jehovah-our-righteousness (*tsedeq*)' is that in the days of the deliverer of David's line, 'Judah shall be saved and Israel shall dwell securely'. Here the word for 'righteousness' has been brought into the same context as the salvation root *y-sh-'*. This occurs also in Isaiah xlv. 21: 'a just (*tsaddiq*) God and a Saviour', and again in the well-known description of the Deliverer in Zechariah ix. 9: 'Behold thy king cometh unto thee, righteous (*tsaddiq*, victorious) and saved (passive participle of *yasha'*).' The next word is 'meek', so that once again we find the emphasis of the eighth-century prophets that the meek and the humble are God's peculiar care, an idea which became more and more prominent in later times when the Jews identified themselves with the meek, cf. Psalm xxxvii. 11 and Matthew v. 5. It is often said that the Hero of Zechariah ix. 9 was a Messiah of peace because He rode the ass and not the war-horse. It is quite probable that the Lord Jesus attached this meaning to the passage when He Himself fulfilled that Scripture. Actually the prophet meant that the Messianic King had already triumphed, and that having triumphed and having been made victorious, He then proclaimed His rule of peace. He had finished with chariot and horses, and with the battle bow, and now would speak peace to the heathen. *Ts-d-q* in this context means victory and triumph, and, of course, inevitably in this world. Along this line the word can even mean wealth and riches, Proverbs viii. 18; prosperity, Psalm lxxxv. 10 (Heb. 11); or the blessings of a bountiful harvest Joel ii. 23. Here the R.V. text has 'in just measure',[1] and the margin 'in (or "for") righteousness'.

The argument which leads to such a use of the root is as follows. God is going to establish His will and vindicate the right. He is going to do this with particular reference to the righteous poor, a phrase which in time comes to mean the godly humble remnant of Israel who, through all the perils of their way and in spite of every disability and oppression, have conformed to the norm (*tsedeq*) which God has established. Further, if this norm is going to be established, then where is God going to establish it?

[1] A.V. has 'moderately' in the text and 'according to righteousness' in the margin. Douai has 'He hath given you a teacher of justice', following the Vulgate *doctorem justitiae*, which reads the same vowels for the Hebrew consonants. Luther follows the Vulgate with *Lehrer zur Gerechtigkeit*.

It must be either on this earth, or not on this earth. If a people has no belief in any life beyond the grave worthy of the name, then of necessity this *tsedeq* (vindication of right) must show itself in this life, on this earth, and in the things of this life. It follows therefore that the *tsedeq* which God establishes must involve the blessings of honour from men and of general prosperity. These are the things of this life by which any good favour must be judged. Even the conclusion of the Book of Job admits this. The point as to whether the Book of Job is all from one hand or not, or all from the same period or not, is of no account in this connection. The last man to touch the book left it as it is now. Presumably he was satisfied with the ending, for certainly no considerations of prior authorship, antiquity, authority, or anything else, prevented wholesale alterations. The vindication of Job is demonstrated by his increased prosperity and his new progeny in the final outcome of the story.[1] How else was an author to demonstrate the final triumph of faithful Job, when there was no other world in which it could be demonstrated?[2]

[1] The literary criticism (Higher Criticism) of the Old Testament has often forgotten that those who pieced the Old Testament together, pieced it together as we have it now. They chose the order we have. The analysis of the sources is but the first step in literary criticism. The editors had the final say, and they used all the material from its varied sources in order to teach their particular message. This message, that of Scripture as a whole, can never be found so long as we think of the Bible only with respect to its literary sources. This is why the fundamentalists, with all their errors, are sometimes nearer to the truth than the literary critics. We need both elements in Bible study, the message of the men who under God were responsible for the various strata, and the message of those who under God were the final editors. In both the truth of the Bible is to be found. See the summary of the contents of the Pentateuch which we have given in *The Speaker's Bible*, Vol. XXXIV, No. 1, pp. 1–6, where it is shown that JEDP has its message as a whole as well as J and E and D and P. In the New Testament, the fact that there are a number of Lucan sources has never prevented us from speaking of the message of that Gospel as a whole. But in the Old Testament we have been so busy with the trees that we have sometimes neglected the wood.

[2] We find two passages only which speak of a resurrection life beyond the grave, and none at all of any immortality of the soul, which is not a Biblical idea at all. One passage is Isaiah xxvi. 19, where the Israelite dead are to rise from the dust and live. This passage is in Isaiah xxiv-xxvi, probably early third century B.C., of the time of the rivalries of the Ptolemies and the Seleucids in Palestine. The other is Daniel xii. 2 (first half of second century B.C.), where we read of a partial 'general resurrection', 'some to everlasting life, and some to shame and everlasting contempt'. The question is raised in Job xiv. 14, but the poet turns away from it, as too much to hope for. The idea is scouted as being ridiculous in Ecclesiastes iii. 18–21, ii. 16. Other passages are held, though we believe erroneously, to refer to a resurrection life after death. E.g. Psalm lxxiii. 24 *f.*, but the argument is valid only in the English Version. The Hebrew reads 'the heavens'. He is speaking geographically. Further, *kabod* (glory) means honour and prosperity in the things of this life; it means heavenly bliss only with English Evangelicals of a former generation. The 'after' means after these temporary distresses. Cf. Luther 'and at last thou dost receive me with honour',

The Use of 'Tsedeq-tsedaqah' in Second-Isaiah

The only case where *tsedaqah* can be said to approach the meaning of the eighth-century prophets is Isaiah liv. 14, where being established in *tsedaqah* (righteousness) is equivalent to being far from oppression. Even here we are well beyond any purely ethical meaning, and it is probable that the phrase refers definitely to the salvation which God is about to accomplish. The meaning therefore is probably the same as elsewhere in Second-Isaiah, i.e. soteriological.

There are four cases where the root *ts-d-q* is used in a forensic sense, xli. 26, xliii. 9, 26, l. 8. These cases refer to the reliability of witnesses, trustworthy in the sense of their statements being verified by events, or by the defendant getting the verdict. To this group we may add another four cases, xlviii. 1, xlv. 23, xlv. 13, 19.

In a number of cases the root *ts-d-q* means 'victory'. It cannot be said that the ethical element is at all in evidence, since some of these instances deal with the victories of Cyrus. Here the ethical element is absent, except that the triumph is regarded as being ultimately that of God's will, and therefore the ethical element must have some part in it, since it is of God. The translation of xli. 2 is far from easy, but it is certain that *tsedeq* means victory.[1] We would translate: 'Who hath roused one from the east? Victory meets him at his feet. (God) sets nations before him, and kings he (the conqueror) subdues, makes (them) like dust with his sword and like wind-driven chaff with his bow.' In xli. 10, God says, 'I have strengthened thee, yea, I have helped thee, yea, I have

substantially as in R.V. margin. For verse 25, Luther has *Wenn ich nur dich habe, so frage ich nichts nach Himmel und Erde*, which, in Catherine Winkworth's translation of Luther's hymn *Herzlich Lieb hab' ich dich*, becomes—

'The whole wide world delights me not,
For heaven and earth, Lord, care I not,
If I may but have Thee.'

The famous passage in Job xix. 25–7 can be made to refer to life after death only by a most liberal latitude in translation, a strong attachment to the Latin Version, and reminiscences of Handel's Messiah. The Hebrew text is difficult, but it is unlikely that the vindicator is God, and Job almost certainly means that he will be vindicated before he is dead. Yet again, Isaiah liii. 8–12 can be made to refer to life after death, if it is first assumed that the Servant is an individual, if an emended text such as that of Duhm is used (as in Oesterley and Robinson, *Heb. Rel.*, 2nd ed., p. 353), and if the reader forgets to remember that death and resurrection are figures for the Exile and the Return, Ezekiel xxxvii. Another geographical passage is Psalm cxxxix. 7–10; see the Douai Version marginal reference to Amos ix. 2.

[1] The difficulties of the Hebrew are discussed in the commentaries.

upheld thee with My victorious right hand (lit. the right hand of My *tsedeq*).'[1] Or again, Isaiah xlii. 6 reads: 'I have called thee in *tsedeq*, and have grasped hold of thy hand, and I will guard thee. . . .' The text continues (if verses 5–9 do actually belong to verses 1–4) with the mission of the Servant in reference to the opening of blind eyes and the releasing of them that are bound. Whilst therefore verse 4 may lead us to suppose that the meaning of *tsedeq* is 'victory', yet verse 7 reminds us of that emphasis which we noted in the eighth-century prophets—namely, that God has a peculiar regard for the helpless ones of earth. Again, in xlv. 24 we have '*oz* (strength) coupled together with *tsedaqoth* (righteous acts), both having their source in Jehovah. The passage continues, 'even to him shall one[2] come, and all that are incensed against him shall be ashamed. In Jehovah shall all the seed of Israel be victorious (*yitsdequ*, R.V., "shall be justified") and shall boast themselves.' The context demands that the verb *tsadaq* shall be translated 'victorious', since the word coupled with it means at the least exaltation in triumph, and may even mean exultation over beaten foes. Yet again, as the text of xlix. 24 stands, *tsaddiq*[3] means 'victor'. 'Can the prey be snatched from the warrior, or can the captive of the victor be snatched away?'

The full meaning 'salvation, redemption' is to be found in xlv. 23, xlv. 8, li. 5, xlvi. 13, li. 6 and in all other cases except four. Two of these four are li. 1, 7, where pursuing after *tsedeq* is equated with having His Torah (Law) in the heart. These sixth-century passages belong to the realm of personal relationship rather than that of ethical rules. We are left with liv. 17 and the difficult liii. 11. In the former case *tsedaqah* has a composite meaning, forensic, victory, general prosperity: 'No weapon that is formed against thee shall prosper, and every tongue which shall stand up with thee in judgement thou shalt put in the wrong (hiphil of *r-sh-'*; cf. Exodus ix. 27 and p. 72, above). This is the inheritance of the servants of the Lord and their *tsedaqah* from me, saith the Lord'. Here *tsedaqah* is that vindication and triumph which God gives to His servants in the judgement court of the whole world of mankind.

[1] The verbs are probably 'prophetic perfects', in which case they should be translated, 'I will certainly strengthen thee. . . .'

[2] R.V. has 'men', but the Hebrew has the singular.

[3] Some would change this to '*arits* (violent), and so make the verse fall exactly into line with verse 25.

The remaining passage, liii. 11, is one of those verses in Isaiah liii which almost every commentator seeks to emend. It is clear that verses 10 and 12 both provide a context where the emphasis is on victory and triumph. The presumption is that verse 11 also has to do with this. We see no need for emendation, provided that we take 'Jehovah' to be the subject of the verbs in the first part of verse 11. The end of verse 10 reads: 'and the purpose of the Lord will prosper in his hand'. We continue translating: 'He (God) will see of his (the Servant's) travail, and will be satisfied by His knowledge.' That is, when God sees the suffering of the Servant and knows it, then He will be satisfied. Compare Isaiah xl. 2, where an accurate translation gives 'her iniquity (i.e. her punishment; cf. Genesis iv. 13) is accepted *(r-ts-h)*'. Jehovah now speaks. 'The righteous one, my servant, will make many prosperous (hiphil of *tsadaq*), for it was their iniquities (i.e. punishments) he was bearing. Therefore will I give him a share with the many (i.e. with the many whom he has made to prosper)'.[1]

Conclusion

We see therefore that in Second-Isaiah the word *tsedeq-tsedaqah* (righteousness) has come to mean 'salvation'. The Righteousness of God shows itself in His saving work. Whilst the ethical content must by no means be neglected, yet the emphasis is on God's mighty work in saving the humble, those devoted ones who trust in Him though it be through flood and fire. For the barely ethical meaning of the root *ts-d-q* we must turn to Proverbs, but in the Prophets and in the Psalms the salvation *motif* steadily becomes supreme. Second-Isaiah reaches his greatest heights of inspiration in such passages as xlii. 7, xlix. 6, and in the suffering of the Servant, bruised and dying in order that the many transgressors may be brought once more to prosperity according to the good pleasure and will of God. The idea of Salvation is everywhere dominant. This mission is re-echoed in Isaiah lxi. 1 *f.* It is not without significance that when the Lord Jesus declared His

[1] This involves only a change of accents in the Massoretic Text, *zaqeph qaton* on *beda'o*, and probably *pashta* on *yir'eh*. The word *tsaddiq* can scarcely be an adjective qualifying 'my servant', for then it should follow and also have the article. But it can be translated as if it has the article, since Second-Isaiah regularly neglects the article, though only if it is treated as the subject with 'my servant' in apposition. In this way we may take 'righteous' to mean 'victorious', in that he has fulfilled God's purpose. Perhaps *tsaddiq* may be due to a reminiscence of 1 Kings viii. 32, where also the article is curiously absent. See also Deuteronomy xxv. 1.

Mission in the synagogue of Nazareth of Galilee, Luke iv. 17–21, He based His claim on Isaiah lxi. 1 *f.* And again, when John the Baptist sent from prison two of his disciples to ask if the Lord Jesus was indeed 'He that cometh', the Lord bade them return, saying, 'Go your way and tell John what things ye have seen and heard: the blind receive their sight, the lame walk, the lepers are cleansed, and the deaf hear, the dead are raised up, and the poor have the gospel preached to them,' Luke vii. 22.

Chapter V

THE COVENANT-LOVE OF GOD

THE Hebrew word is *chesed*. In the English Versions it is translated, with few exceptions, by 'mercy, loving-kindness', the latter being a rendering which we owe in the first place to Miles Coverdale. Luther used the word *Gnade*, his New Testament rendering of *charis* (Grace). We have been sorely tempted to use the word 'Grace' in the title of this chapter, but have rejected it on the grounds that the New Testament 'Grace' is at once both a wider and equally a narrower term.[1] Apart from this, the word *chesed* has a double development in the Old Testament. When it is used of God, it moves steadily on towards 'grace'; when it is used of man, it develops into 'piety' in the sense of the Latin *pietas*. The particular meaning of *pietas* to which we refer, is that of the Vulgate in (say) 2 Peter i. 6 or 2 Maccabees iii. 1, where R.V. has 'godliness'. It signifies that love and duty which is shown towards God by doing His will. The meaning is a combination of the dutiful, filial love of *pius Aeneas* for his father Anchises in the *Aeneid*, and that respect for the gods which marks the highest point of the religion of classical Rome.[2]

The usual translations 'mercy, loving-kindness' are to be found, for instance, in Hosea iv. 1; vi. 6, Micah vi. 8; Psalm xxxvi. 10 (Heb. 11); 2 Samuel x. 2; and often elsewhere, especially in the Psalms. Whilst in some cases these renderings may be regarded as not unsatisfactory, they are nowhere really adequate, and on occasion are definitely misleading. These English translations owe their origin to the traditional meaning as shown in the Septuagint *eleos* (pity) and in the Vulgate *misericordia* (pity), both being the usual equivalents in those versions.

DISTINCTION BETWEEN *CHESED* AND *'AHABAH*

It is necessary to distinguish between these two words, since both mean 'love'. The difference lies in the fact that *chesed*, in

[1] See pp. 175*f*. It includes *chesed* and in addition *chen* (good favour apart from the covenant), and at the same time involves a transformation because of the Christian setting.

[2] Cicero, *Topica*, 23, 90, *De Finibus*, 3, 22, 73, etc. See also the first chapters of Walter Pater, *Marius the Epicurean*.

all its varied shades of meaning, is conditional upon there being a covenant. Without the prior existence of a covenant, there could never be any *chesed* at all. The word represents that attitude to a covenant without which that covenant could not continue to exist. It has no meaning apart from a covenant previously instituted, and apart from such a case as Isaiah xl. 6,[1] it is always conditioned by the terms of the covenant. On the other hand *'ahabah* is unconditioned love. It is not limited by the conditions of any covenant, but only by the will or the nature of the lover. Actually God's *'ahabah* (love) for Israel is the very basis and the only cause of the existence of the Covenant between God and Israel. *'Ahabah* is the cause of the covenant; *chesed* is the means of its continuance. Thus *'ahabah* is God's Election-Love, whilst *chesed* is His Covenant-Love.

We propose to deal with God's Election-Love (*'ahabah*) in the next chapter. In this present chapter we deal with the word *chesed*. We propose first to discuss the etymological origin of the word, since this is vital to its proper meaning everywhere. Next we propose to trace the meaning of the word as it developed in Hebrew, particularly in its relation to the idea of the Covenant. Next we will seek to show the distinctive Old Testament development of *chesed* when it is used of God. Further, in order to complete the study of the word, we propose to trace its development when used of man, i.e. its development towards the meaning *pietas* (godliness) as that word is used in ecclesiastical Latin. We will conclude the chapter with a note on the difference between *chesed* and *chen* (good favour apart from any covenant association).

1. THE ETYMOLOGICAL ORIGIN OF *CHESED*

The general opinion is that there is very little to be gained from this, and nothing with certainty. We are of the opinion that there is much more to be gained than is usually maintained. Indeed, in the earlier suggestion of 'eagerness' as the original meaning of the root, we find that common link of complete devotion and utter earnestness which is the essence both of the Grace of God and of the godliness of the pious man of the type of Onias the High Priest, 2 Maccabees iii. 1. The whole problem, however, of the origin of this noun *chesed* is beset with difficulty.

This difficulty arises from the fact that in Leviticus xx. 17 (H)

[1] See p. 105, below.

and in Proverbs xiv. 34 the word *chesed* clearly means 'shame, reproach, defilement'. The corresponding verb with the same meaning is found in Proverbs xxv. 10. It is not easy to see how one word could have such contrary meanings as 'kindness' and 'defilement, shame', or a verb such contrary meanings as 'to be kind' and 'to revile'. The two words are extant in Aramaic also, and with the same two contradictory meanings. The same situation is found in Syriac, where Bar Hebraeus distinguished them by making the 'd' hard in the one case (reproach) and soft in the other (kindness). This is probably a device to make the distinction, and has no scientific value. W. Robertson Smith thought that there were probably two different roots, represented in Arabic by *chashada* ('assemble', with special reference to the hospitality due to a guest) and *chasada* (envy). The former is the derivation of the Hebrew *chesed* (kindness), which is favoured by Brown, Driver and Briggs.[1] There are difficulties in this equation of the Arabic letter *shin* with the Hebrew *samek* and the Syriac *semkath*, but such an equation, though rare, is known.[2] The satisfactory feature of this derivation is that it involves that virtue which is the bond of society, and, as we shall see, *chesed* has a very great deal to do with the bonds which bind men together. Such a derivation was particularly acceptable to Robertson Smith because of his theories of the totemistic origin of Semitic and other religions.

But the other Arabic root (*chasada*) is a perfectly sound and exact equivalent from the linguistic point of view for the Syriac and Hebrew words. Indeed, if the word *chashada* had not been known, and further, even if it had been known and there had been no difficulty of contrary meanings, then no one for a moment would have doubted that *chasada* was the Arabic equivalent, and we would have had to make the best we could of its meaning 'envy'. This Arabic meaning 'envy' is certain. It is confirmed by the Urdu *chasad* (jealousy, envy, ambition).

Gesenius, in his *Thesaurus* (p. 502), suggested 'keenness, ardent zeal (*acer studium*)' as the primary meaning of the root. We find this suggestion to be satisfactory in that both meanings, different though they are, can be derived from it. Further, the idea of 'sharpness (*acer*)' has support in roots beginning with *ch-s*, *ch-ts*

[1] Oxford Lexicon, p. 339.

[2] W. Wright, *Lectures on the Comparative Grammar of the Semitic Languages* (1890), p. 59.

and *ch-d*. The one line of development is 'ardent desire' showing itself in love and kindness for a person, whilst the other line shows itself in emulation, ending in envy or ambition. In Arabic, Aramaic, and Syriac the idea developed in a bad way, but in Hebrew it developed in a good way. The bad meanings in Hebrew are due to Aramaic influence, and the good meanings in Aramaic and Syriac are due to Hebrew influence. The three occasions in which the bad meaning is found in Hebrew, Leviticus xx. 17; Proverbs xiv. 34, xxv. 10, do not involve a greater influence upon Hebrew on the part of Aramaic than is generally recognized to have taken place. The large number of good meanings which are found in Aramaic and Syriac are amply accounted for by the association of the Hebrew noun *chesed* and the adjective *chasid* with the Law in post-exilic times.

If it should be argued that it is unlikely that two such contrary meanings could possibly have been derived from the same root, then we cite two other Semitic roots in justification. Doubtless there are others. The first is *q-n-'*. The Arabic *qana'a* means 'to become very red, black through dye'. This colour significance is found in Syriac also, but in Hebrew, Aramaic, and Ethiopic, the word can mean both 'zeal for' and 'envy against'. Compare especially Psalm cvi. 16 and Numbers xi. 29 (J). In each case we have exactly the same syntactical construction, but the first means envy against Moses, and the second zeal on his behalf. In a case like 1 Kings xix. 10, 14, where Elijah says, 'I have been very jealous (*qanno' qinne'thi*) for the Lord of Hosts', it is impossible to decide whether 'jealous' or 'zealous' is the better English rendering. A.V. and R.V. have 'jealous', but Douai has 'zealous'. The common ground of the two words is the ardour or intense emotion which shows itself in the redness of the face. A similar situation has arisen in the case of the Greek *zelos*, which can be used both as a noble passion distinct from *phthonos* (envy), and also as the equivalent of *phthonos*, the origin of *zelos* itself being supposed to be *zeo* ('boil, seethe' of water).[1]

The second case is the root *ch-ph-ts*. The original meaning is 'attention, be mindful of', and so 'keep, protect' as in the Arabic verb. This is reflected in Urdu, where *chifazat* means 'safety, protection, custody'. In Arabic the root came to mean 'excited attention', and thence 'excitement, anger' as in *chafiytsat*. But in

[1] The references are given in Liddell and Scott, and include Hesiod and Plato.

Hebrew it came to mean 'delighted attention', whence the noun *chephets* (delight); cf. the name Hephzi-bah (my delight is in her), 2 Kings xxi. i. Later this word came to mean 'will, purpose', as in Second-Isaiah, viz., Isaiah xliv. 28, xlvi. 10, xlviii. 14, and even liii. 10. From this it came to mean 'business, occupation' as in Isaiah lviii. 13, Proverbs xxxi. 13 (R.V. margin); Psalm i. 2, of the scribe whose full-time occupation is in the Law of the Lord; cf. Ecclesiasticus xxxix. 1–11. Still later the word came to mean 'matter', Ecclesiastes iii. 1, 17, etc., until in post-Biblical Hebrew it meant little more than 'thing', having lost every vestige of decisive meaning and having become almost entirely featureless. There could be no greater difference than between 'anger' and 'pleasure' with the featureless 'thing' at the zero mark between the two.

The same kind of thing has happened in the case of the English word 'restive', which means 'characterized by restlessness', the very opposite of what it ought to mean from the philological point of view. Some say that the word has always meant what it means now, but an archaic meaning 'being at rest' is given in Funk's *Standard English Dictionary* (Ward, Lock & Co.). This is what the word ought to mean. From this it came to mean 'seeking to continue at rest in the face of encouragement to move', e.g. 'our restive clay', whence comes the idea of resisting compulsion, and so being restless under the constraint of being made to rest. Thus we have turned the full circle.

2. THE HEBREW DEVELOPMENT OF *CHESED* AS A COVENANT WORD

The etymological origin of the word established 'keenness, eagerness' as the core of the meaning of the word, but in Hebrew the main factor is that it is used definitely in connection with the idea of covenant. The root means 'eagerness, steadfastness' and then 'mercy, loving-kindness', but all within the covenant. It never meant 'kindness' in general to all and sundry. Unless this close and inalienable connection with the idea of the covenant is realized, the true meaning of *chesed* can never be understood. This applies to both uses, whether of God or of man. It applies to the Old Testament *chesed* of God, His covenant-love for Israel. It applies also to the New Testament development in *charis* and in the Grace of Protestant theology. Whilst there is a general benevolence to all, and whilst there is that 'prevenient Grace' which is the New Testament equivalent of the Old Testament *'ahabah*,[1] there is also that state of grace in which we come to stand when we are 'in Christ', i.e. within the New Covenant which He Himself sealed with His own blood. It applies also to that complete devotion of the pious which is contained in the Hebrew *chasid*, usually translated 'saint' or 'holy one' in the Psalms, e.g. Psalm xxx. 4 (Heb. 5), xvi. 10.

The original use of the Hebrew *chesed* is to denote that attitude of loyalty and faithfulness which both parties to a covenant should observe towards each other. It may have come to be used thus because of the zeal which the two parties may be supposed to have shown in thus coming together to bind themselves in a blood-brotherhood. Sir George Adam Smith suggested 'leal-love' as a good rendering. This includes the two essential elements of love and loyalty. We find this suggestion to be adequate only for the first stage of the development of the word, when it was used of covenant in general. When the word came to be used predominantly of the Covenant between Jehovah and Israel, it was realized by the prophets that such a covenant could be maintained only by that persistent, determined, steadfast love of God, which transcends every other love by its nature and depth. The rendering therefore does not suffice for the later and developed stages of growth. If it were not for the special New Testament content of the word 'Grace', we would use that word for Old Testament as well as New Testament. Again, we find Dr. C. H. Dodd's suggestion[2] of 'piety' in the sense of the Latin *pietas* unsatisfactory, because, although it is an admirable rendering of man's dutiful *chesed* towards God, it neglects entirely all that is involved in the *chesed* of God. Actually, to use a former metaphor, the word represents a broad wedge of which the apex varies between 'love, mercy' at the one extreme, and 'loyalty, steadfastness, faithfulness' at the other. The word means 'faithfulness' rather than 'kindness', for we find the word to involve, in almost every case, a substratum of fixed, determined, almost stubborn steadfastness. If therefore we were compelled to choose one word in a case where the exact significance was not made clear by the context, we would choose 'faithfulness' in preference to 'kindness'.[3] The best word is

[1] See pp. 175 *f.*, below. [2] *The Bible and the Greeks*, pp. 60 *f.*

[3] So J. Lindblom, *Profetismen i Israel* (1934), pp. 394 *f.*

'covenant-love', using 'covenant' deliberately in preference to 'leal', because it is more specific and accurate. Next to this, when the word is used of God, we would use the phrase 'sure love',[1] unless it is clear that we ought to say 'covenanted mercies' as the outcome of God's sure love.

'Chesed' is, primarily, Determined Faithfulness to a Covenant

There are forty-three cases where the noun *chesed* is linked by means of the copula with another noun. Such a construction can be used only when the two nouns thus joined together are almost synonymous, or have some more than ordinary bond between them. Of these forty-three instances, twenty-three are *'emeth* and *'emunah* (fidelity, firmness, truth),[2] derived from the root *'-m-n* (confirm, support) which in derived forms means 'be trustworthy, have faith in, believe'. Compare the Hebrew *'amen* (verily, truly) of the liturgies; Isaiah lxv. 16 (twice); 2 Corinthians i. 20; and especially Revelation iii. 14. Of the remainder, seven are *berith* (covenant).[3] We are left with thirteen cases. Of these, four are the two righteousness words *tsedaqah* and *mishpaṭ*;[4] one is *ṭob* (prosperity), Psalm xxiii. 6; one is *metsudah* (stronghold), Psalm cxliv. 2; one is *chen* (general kindness where there is no special tie), Esther ii. 17; whilst six are *rachamim* (compassion).[5] To sum up, out of a total of forty-three, there are thirty associations with 'faithfulness' and 'covenant' and one 'stronghold' as against seven 'kindness', of which latter, two are connected with 'righteousness'.

If we consider the parallels to the word *chesed*, we find the

[1] Cf. John Wesley's translation of von Zinzendorf's hymn '*Du ewiger Abgrund der seligen Liebe*' (*Methodist Hymn-book*, No. 63, verse 4)':

'To thy sure love, thy tender care.'

[2] Genesis xxiv. 27, 49 (J), xlvii. 29 (J); Exodus xxxiv. 6 (E); Joshua ii. 14; 2 Samuel ii. 6, xv. 20; Psalm xxv. 10, xl. 11 (Heb. 12), lvii, 3 (4), lxi. 7 (8), lxxxv. 10 (11), lxxxvi. 15, lxxxix. 14 (15), 24 (25), xcviii. 3, cxv. 1, cxxxviii. 2, Proverbs iii. 3, xiv. 22, xvi. 6, xx. 28.

[3] Deuteronomy vii. 9, 12; 1 Kings viii. 23; Daniel ix. 4; Nehemiah i. 5, ix. 32; 2 Chronicles vi. 14.

[4] Hosea xii. 6 (7) and Proverbs xxi. 21; Psalm ci. 1 and Jeremiah ix. 24 (23), where all three words occur.

[5] Jeremiah xvi. 5; Hosea ii. 19 (21), where the pair is immediately preceded by 'in righteousness and in judgement'; Zechariah vii. 9, preceded by 'judgement'; Psalm xxv. 6 (7), ciii. 4; Daniel i. 9.

proportion to be substantially the same. By 'parallels' we mean that characteristic of some[1] Hebrew verse whereby we have couplets in each verse, wherein the same statement is made, but with different words in each line. This is the form of poetry called 'synthetic parallelism', whether the parallelism be complete or incomplete. An outstanding example of complete parallelism is 'I-will-divide-them in-Jacob, and I-will-scatter-them in-Israel', Genesis xlix. 7, which is a two-word couplet with exact parallelism. See also Isaiah xlix. 2 and especially the Prayer of Baruch, Apoc. Bar. xlviii. 2–24.

There are eighteen cases of parallelism where *chesed* is one member. All of these involve exact parallels so far as the words in which we are interested are concerned, except perhaps Psalm cix. 12, where the second line might be taken to extend the imprecatory prayer of the first line into a wider sphere. Of the eighteen cases, nine are *'emeth* and *'emunah*, the two fidelity words.[2] There are four cases where the parallel is one of the two righteousness words, *tsedaqah* and *mishpaṭ*.[3] In addition, we have Hosea vi. 6, 'knowledge of God'; Psalm lix. 17 (18), 'strength'; whilst the other three are Psalm cix. 12, *chonen*[4] (have pity); Genesis xix. 19 (*chen*) and Psalm lxxvii. 9 (10), *rachamim* (compassion). This gives a total of seventeen cases, of which ten are 'firmness, strength' against (at most) two 'kindness'. Actually, in both this and the preceding paragraph, all the cases of association with 'righteousness' have to do with the keeping of the covenant, so that the final proportions are: total, sixty; 'keeping faith, being firm, covenant', forty-eight; 'kindness', nine. This does not include the five cases in Genesis and two in Exodus where the Septuagint translates

[1] We use the word 'some' deliberately, because in the Psalter there are many cases of triplets. It is not realized that the accent *'oleh wayored* often marks a break in a verse equally as decided as *'athnach*. Sometimes indeed it marks the main dichotomy in *'athnach's* clause, just as *segholta* does in prose. This is the statement made in books on the accents, such as those by Wickes, and it is assumed in studies on Hebrew parallelism, e.g. G. B. Gray, *The Forms of Hebrew Poetry* (1915), T. H. Robinson, 'Hebrew Metre and Old Testament Exegesis', *Exp. Times*, Vol. LIV, No. 9 (June, 1943), pp. 246–8. But this is not the whole truth, for at other times *'oleh wayored* and *'athnach* equally mark main dichotomies in *silluq's* clause, the sole difference being that *'oleh wayored* comes first and *'athnach* second.

[2] Isaiah xvi. 5; Hosea iv. 1; Micah vii. 20; Psalm xxvi. 3, lxxxviii. 11 (12), lxxxix, 2 (3), xcii. 2 (3), cxvii. 2. Particularly Isaiah lv. 3, where the word *berith* (covenant) also occurs.

[3] Isaiah lvii. 1 (*tsaddiq*); Hosea x. 12; Micah vi. 8; Psalm xxxvi. 10 (11).

[4] Possibly a 'climbing' parallelism. Same root as *chen*, Esther ii. 17.

chesed by *dikaiosune*, one of its regular equivalents of *tsedaqah* (righteousness).[1]

These detailed instances involve a preponderance in favour of the meaning 'firmness, steadfastness' which is often neglected. We do not desire by any means to deny the meanings 'loving-kindness, mercy' which *chesed* often has. On the contrary our aim is to insist that these renderings are often far too weak to convey the strength, the firmness, and the persistence of God's sure love.

There are eight cases where the plenteousness (seven) or the greatness (one) of God's love is paralleled with His slowness to anger.[2] There are also twelve cases where the plenteousness (or greatness) of His *chesed* is associated with words or ideas of mercy and forgiveness.[3] Perhaps the most notable example of all is Isaiah liv. 8: 'In overflowing wrath I hid My face from thee for a moment; but with everlasting *chesed* will I have mercy upon thee.' Here undoubtedly, as in all these cases, *chesed* has to do with mercy and forgiveness, but its true significance, as the *chesed* of God, is that it is everlasting, determined, unshakable. Wonderful as is His love for His covenant-people, His steady persistence in it is more wonderful still. The most important of all the distinctive ideas of the Old Testament is God's steady and extraordinary persistence in continuing to love wayward Israel in spite of Israel's insistent waywardness.

The covenant association of *chesed* has been most clearly demonstrated by Dr. W. F. Lofthouse,[4] and the fact that it expresses a firm adhesion to the conditions of the covenant, is, we trust, clear from the examples we have instanced above. The word *chesed*, says Dr. Lofthouse,[5] 'is not used indiscriminately where any kind of favour is desired, but only where there is some

[1] Genesis xix. 19, xx. 13, xxi. 23, xxiv. 27 (with 'truth'), xxxii. 10 (11: also with 'truth'); Exodus xv. 13 (parallel to 'strength'), xxiv. 7, where *dikaiosune* is in a forgiveness context. Genesis xxiv. 27 has been included in an earlier count.

[2] Exodus xxxiv. 6 (JE); Numbers xiv. 18 (J); Joel ii. 13; Jonah iv. 2 (Heb. iii. 12); Psalms lxxxvi. 15, ciii. 8; Nehemiah ix. 17; also Psalm cxlv. 8.

[3] Exodus xxxiv. 7 (JE); Numbers xiv. 19 (J); Isaiah lxiii. 7; Jeremiah xxxii. 18; Lamentations iii. 32; Nehemiah xiii. 22; Psalms v. 7 (8), lxix. 13 (14), lxxxvi. 5, cvi. 7, 45, cxlv. 8.

[4] '*Chen* and *Chesed* in the Old Testament', in *Zeitsch. f. d. altt. Wissenschaft*, 20 Band, Heft 1 (1933), SS. 29–35. See also C. H. Dodd, *The Bible and the Greeks* (1935), pp. 60–5. Dr. Dodd is interested chiefly in the Septuagint rendering, and, in our view, has not given sufficient emphasis to Dr. Lofthouse's conclusions. This is due to the fact that he was dealing with Greek, and so was concerned with the *chesed* of man rather than with the *chesed* of God. Also N. Glueck, *Das Wort Chesed* (1921).

[5] *ibid.*, S. 33.

recognized tie'. Indiscriminate favour is *chen*, and except for the unique Esther ii. 17, the distinction between the two is everywhere observed. The idea of 'favour' belongs to the word *chesed* also, but only to that line of development which deals with the *chesed* of God, and even then only within the Covenant. The meaning '*firm* adherence' is truer to the significance of the word in all its occurrences. This is the virtue of Sir George Adam Smith's rendering 'troth'.[1]

We proceed to give three instances of the use of *chesed* in connection with a covenant. The first is 2 Samuel x. 1 *f.*, where we read that David wished to perpetuate with Hanun the relations which he had had with his father Nahash. We suspect that the two parties to the treaty were by no means equal in the matter, and that the relation of Judah to Ammon was comparable to that of Germany and her allies in the Second World War. 'And David said, I will make *chesed* (i.e. make a treaty and keep faith in it; the R.V. 'shew kindness' is misleading) with Hanun son of Nahash even as his father made *chesed* with me.' Undoubtedly David sent Hanun his condolences in his bereavement (verse 2), but there was more in the embassy than this. The relation which David desired to establish with the son was similar to that which had existed between the dead father and David. This is expressed in the text by *chesed*. We judge that this word therefore does not refer to the expressions of sympathy. The whole affair was an abortive attempt by David to retain his suzeranity over Ammon at the accession of the new king. David was seeking to renew a treaty.

Another example is 1 Samuel xx. 14–16, where we read of the making of a blood-brotherhood between David and Jonathan. By this covenant they are to show each other 'the *chesed* of Jehovah', and David is not to 'cut off his *chesed*' from Jonathan's house for ever. The similar phrase '*chesed* of God (*'elohim*)' is found uniquely in 2 Samuel ix. 3, but again of the covenant between David and Jonathan. Every covenant was regarded as being witnessed by God, from the compromise between the mutually suspicious (and each with very good reason) Jacob and Laban, Genesis xxxi. 49, to the truest and most honourable blood-brotherhood imaginable. But the phrase '*chesed* of Jehovah' means a covenant *chesed* so strong and true that it can never pass

[1] *Jeremiah* (Baird Lecture, 1922), p. 104.

away. Virtually, this covenant was a promise made by David that when he became king he would not exterminate the sons of Jonathan in following the normal custom of destroying 'all the seed royal'.[1] David did actually slay the sons of Saul, but on another plea, 2 Samuel xxi. 6. He spared Jonathan's son Mephibosheth, however, because of the *chesed* of his covenant with Jonathan, 2 Samuel xxi. 7, ix. 1–13. Mephibosheth could not have been king in any case, since 'he was lame on both his feet', 2 Samuel iv. 4, ix. 3.[2] David was fortunate more than once in being able to combine great piety with a happy issue out of personal difficulties.[3]

The third case is that of Hushai, who came to Absalom with profuse expressions of loyalty, 2 Samuel xvi. 16. Absalom knew that of all men Hushai was closely bound to David, since he was 'the friend of David'. So Absalom said, 'Is this thy *chesed* with thy friend?' That is, Is this the way you keep faith? Is this what your loyalty to your covenant with David amounts to?[4]

But especially the word *chesed* is used of faithfulness in the Covenant between Jehovah and Israel, both of the firm faithfulness of God, and of the fitful faithfulness of Israel. Micah vii. 20 reads: 'Thou wilt perform (establish, maintain) truth (*'emeth*) to Jacob, *chesed* to Abraham, which thou hast sworn to our fathers from days of old.' This is typical of a large number of cases where the word is used of His persistent, sure covenant-love for Israel all through the years. For the other side of the picture, we turn to Jeremiah ii. 2; where the Hebrew means, not 'the kindness of thy youth', as in R.V., nor even 'the piety of the youth', as the Oxford Lexicon suggests, though it would be wrong to deny that either idea was included, but 'thy youthful faithfulness to the

[1] Athaliah in 2 Kings xi. 1; Jehu and Ahab's sons, 2 Kings x. 1–11, especially verse 11; the fear expressed in 2 Samuel xiii. 30; Abimelech and the sons of Gideon, Judges ix. 5.

[2] Was Asa deprived of his kingship when 'in the time of his old age he was diseased in his feet', 1 Kings xv. 23, just as David was deposed because of his incapacity, 1 Kings i? If so, this might account for the apparent interregnum of four years between the accession of Zimri (who reigned seven days, 1 Kings xvi. 15) in the twenty-seventh year of Asa, and the accession of his successor, Omri, in Asa's thirty-first year, 1 Kings xvi. 10, 23.

[3] The Amalekite who claimed to have assisted Saul to die; the two men who murdered Ish-bosheth at a time when his death was most opportune; the death of Abner, which certainly saved complications in the High Command.

[4] Hushai's answer has been obscured by the Massoretes lest it should be said even wrongly that any king except the true Davidic king was 'the chosen of the Lord'.

covenant'. This includes the warmth of Israel's marriage love, and also her first glad obedience to God's demands in respect of conduct, but both these are secondary to the main idea of faithfulness to the marriage bond. The same idea of Israel's early loyalty is expressed in Hosea vi. 4: 'Your *chesed* has been like a morning cloud.' The force of this simile is not easily appreciated by us who live in these cloudy northern lands. The writer lived by the Mediterranean,[1] where, for the most part of the year, any lingering night clouds are soon dispersed by the warmth of the rising sun.

There is one case where *chesed* means 'firmness' without any suggestion of 'kindness'. This is Isaiah xl. 6. We hold that the Hebrew text here is perfectly sound, and that there is no need to emend the text as the commentators do. The word means 'steadfastness'.[2] All the versions except the Targum were puzzled here. Perhaps the Targum was puzzled also, but the sense of the passage enabled the translators to keep right. Septuagint has the unique rendering *doxa* (glory, splendour), and so the Vulgate *gloria*, and the Syro-Hexapla, following the Septuagint as usual. The Syriac Peshitta goes even farther with 'beauty'. The versions all think of the glory and splendour of the wild flowers. These are not the only cases where mankind has been led astray from a true understanding of God by the appreciation of the beauties of Nature. The Targum alone has realized, with its 'their strength', that the prophet was speaking about the frailty of wild flowers and not about their beauty. He means that man is like the grass and the wild flowers, here to-day and gone to-morrow, never continuing in one stay. The contrast is with the Word of the Lord, which is reliable, steadfast, trustworthy, enduring for ever. 'All man's *chesed* is like the wild flowers'; cf. Hosea vi. 4.

There are four[3] other cases where *chesed* is used unusually. These are Psalms lix. 10 (Heb. 11), 17 (18), cxliv. 2; Jonah ii. 8 (9). In all four cases God is referred to as the *chesed* of those that trust in Him. The first two cases are probably due to accidents of

[1] See Tacitus, *Agricola*, xii, for the judgement of another Mediterranean writer on our British climate.

[2] For further details and a fuller discussion see 'The Exegesis of Isaiah xl. 5, 6' in *Exp. Times*, LII, 10 (July, 1941), pp. 394–6.

[3] For further details, see 'The Meaning of *chesed*' in *Exp. Times*, LV, 4 (January, 1944), pp. 108–10.

transmission, that at the end of Psalm lix being due probably to a corrupted gloss, and that earlier in the psalm to a misguided attempt to restore what was believed to be an ancient chorus. As the last phrase now stands, Luther's translation, *mein gnädiger Gott* (my God of Grace), is fully acceptable, and is much better than such renderings as 'the God of my mercy' (R.V.) or even E. G. King's 'my merciful God'. But an examination of the Hebrew text in conjunction with the versions shows that there are complications which are not at first evident.

With respect to the other two cases we suggest 'my surety', i.e. the source of my confidence, for the one, and 'their surety' for the other. Such translations as 'my mercy' and 'my loving-kindness' are unsatisfactory, since, whilst *chesed* can certainly stand for God's sure love, yet *chasdi* must mean 'my sure love for some one else, and not 'some one else's sure love for me'. If, however, the word be understood more after the pattern of Isaiah xl. 6, then the meaning 'confidence, security', which is demanded by the contexts can be achieved without the emendations which the commentators suggest, and also without doing violence to the Hebrew.

And so there is, we hold, always some notion of 'strength, firmness, steadfastness' in this word *chesed*.[1] We hold this tendency to have been inherent in the word from the beginning, and to be a direct result of its origin from the root which in Arabic means 'eager, ardent desire'. The result of this is that in respect of both developments of the word, the idea of eagerness, ardour, intense devotion persists. It is to be found in that sure love of God which will never let Israel go, and also in that loyal devotion of the Chasidim, whose firm devotion and willing sacrifice for the Law may have been equalled, but has never been surpassed, 1 Maccabees ii. 42.

Before we trace this element of ardour and intense devotion, in respect both of God and man, it is necessary first to indicate the development among the Hebrews of the idea of the Covenant between Jehovah and Israel, since each development of the idea of *chesed* marches parallel with that.

[1] This is so even in Psalm cix. 12. The texts of the E.VV. are misleading here, 'let there be none to extend mercy to him'. R.V. margin is better, 'to continue loving-kindness'. But the meaning is to maintain *chesed* with him in spite of his unseemly conduct (verse 16). Compare the *chesed* of Jehovah towards Israel, which He persists in maintaining in spite of all Israel's waywardness; see pp. 100*f.*

The Development of the Idea of the Covenant

The idea of the Covenant is fundamental to both the Old and the New Testaments. We acknowledge this every time we speak of either, for the word 'testament' is nothing but an anglicized form of the Latin *testamentum*, itself the Vulgate rendering of the Hebrew *berith* (covenant). To such an extent is it the case that the idea of the Covenant is fundamental to Hebrew religion, that Eichrodt has built the whole structure of the first volume of his recent three-volumed *Old Testament Theology* on the idea of Jehovah as the Covenant-God.[1] Except for the introductory chapter of Vol. I, of which the general title is *Gott und Volk* (1939), there is no chapter which does not contain in its title the word *Bund* (covenant). This is a perfectly sound conception, since whatever else Jehovah is, He is first and last a *Bundesgott*. Similarly, if Israel of old had not been, and had not realized himself to be the *Bundesvolk*, there would never have been any Israel at all after the Babylonian Exile. Yet again, the Israel of God in every age is a *Bundesvolk*.

The word *berith* (covenant) is found in the earliest records. It is used of the Covenant which Jehovah made with Abraham, Genesis xv. 18 (J), and of that which He made with His people Israel at Sinai, Exodus xix. 5, xxiv. 7, 8 (E), xxxiv. 10, 27, 28 (J). In the Deuteronomic Code, and onwards from that time, the word became more frequent. Indeed it was the Deuteronomic writer(s) who invented the term 'the Ark of the Covenant', Deuteronomy x. 8. Previously it had been called 'the Ark of God' or 'the Ark of the Jehovah', though the phrase 'the Ark of the Covenant of Jehovah'[2] occurs twice in J, Numbers x. 33, xiv. 44. In J and E the idea of the relationship between Jehovah and Israel is not materially different from that which other nations of the period conceived to exist between themselves and their gods. In D the idea of Israel as a special nation, 'a peculiar people', comes into full prominence, and this accompanies the beginnings of the distinctive Hebrew-Jewish ideas of the Covenant.

The seeds of all subsequent developments of the ideas of both *chesed* and covenant are to be found in Amos and Hosea, each representing one strand in the double cord, the one dealing with the requirements of God in the Covenant, and the other more

[1] Walther Eichrodt, *Theologie des alten Testaments* (1935–9).

[2] The reference to the Covenant may well be a Deuteronomic interpolation here.

particularly with God's persistent love towards His Covenant people. Amos holds that God chose Israel in a special and unique way. 'You only have I known of all the families of the earth', iii. 2. With this choice there are certain specific ethical demands. We have already discussed these, especially in their tendency to have a wider scope than the merely ethical. More importantly for our present purpose, we notice that the choice comes first and the demand second. The prophet first speaks of the Divine Election of Israel, and, secondly, says: 'Therefore I will visit upon you all your iniquities.'

Out of these first distinctive ideas of the Covenant between Jehovah and Israel, four points of importance arise. Firstly, Jehovah existed before Israel. Secondly, if He once existed without them, He could do so again. Thirdly, if He chose them, He could also reject them. Fourthly, He was different from other gods in the demands He made upon His people as their part in the Covenant. These four points are of the utmost importance. Without them, Israel's religion could never have grown to what it actually did become. The development is wholly wrapped up with the special relations between God and His people. These relations were centred in, and summed up in the Covenant. The Covenant involved these four special and peculiar conditions.

The great barrier to religious progress was the belief that a god could not exist without a people, and that he must in the last resort rescue his people for his own credit's sake. Nay, he must save them, if he himself was to continue to exist, or to have any place in the dwelling-houses of the gods. So long as men believed that their god was bound to save them whatever they did, or to whatever extent they flouted his commands, the ethical demands of the eighth-century prophets were so much wasted breath. It was mostly because the masses of the people failed to realize the truth of these four elements, that the seed which the prophets sowed, bore so little fruit. The bitter experiences of the Exile did indeed convince some men of the truth of the words of the former prophets, but apparently only a remnant believed even then. Men persisted in thinking that they had a hold upon God. The prophets disposed of the illusion, so far as the truly religious were concerned, that there was need for God to have fellowship with men. There are moderns who have forgotten this, and speak of the 'necessity' of Creation in order that God might create beings capable of holding fellowship with Him. God is still God, though all men be liars and apostates. There is no 'must' about God, so far as any human circumstances are concerned. The only 'must' is what He Himself wills because of His own Nature. Men can know something of this 'must' in their experience of Him, but not in any speculations concerning the Good or the Right. God chose Israel because He willed to choose them, Deuteronomy vii. 6–8. It was not because of any necessity laid upon Him from outside. It was all of His own free, unfettered, and sovereign will. The realization of this is essential to the understanding of both Old and New Testaments.

The pre-eighth-century idea of the Covenant and its demands on the people are contained in the Book of the Covenant, Exodus xx. 22–xxiii. 33, the name being derived from Exodus xxiv. 7. Israel is evidently here an agricultural people. The code 'compares favourably with the English criminal law in the eighteenth century, and with the statutes of the slave states of America in the earlier half of the nineteenth century'.[1] It is comparable with the Code of Hammurabi, found in 1902, and dating from about 1,750 B.C. This represents Hammurabi, sixth king of the first dynasty of Babylon, receiving the code from the sun-god Shamash. This Mesopotamian code[2] is urban as against the Israelite agricultural. From the point of view of humaneness, there is little to choose between the two codes, each having points in which it is superior to the other. Both are examples of general traditional law and custom as known and observed in ancient times throughout the Middle Semitic East. It is probable that the Israelite Code was Palestinian in origin, and it may well have belonged to those elements which never left Palestine after Jacob returned from Padan-Aram.

With the promulgation of the Deuteronomic Code we get a transformation. This now becomes the Book of the Covenant, 2 Kings xxiii. 2 *f.* It is founded upon those ideas of Election, and on the demands consequent therefrom, which we have discussed in connection with Amos iii. 2. Previously we had a covenant consisting of the ordinary commands of an ordinary god upon an ordinary henotheistic (more or less) people. After Deuteronomy,

[1] W. H. Bennett, *Exodus* (Century Bible), p. 13.

[2] C. H. W. Johns, 'The Code of Hammurabi' in *H.D.B.*, V, p. 584–612; S. A. Cook, *The Laws of Moses and the Code of Hammurabi* (1903).

we have a Covenant consisting of the special commands of the Only God upon a people specially chosen by Him. In the Priestly Code, the whole Deuteronomic idea of the Covenant is strengthened and developed. Those elements in it which the Exile had shown to be most important for the separate preservation of this special people, received additional emphasis. Circumcision, the strict observance of the Sabbath, now came to be the outward signs of the Covenant. The Covenant was traced back with all its special terms and conditions to the patriarchs; to Noah, Genesis ix. 9–17; to Abraham, Genesis xvii. 2–21; to Jacob and Isaac, Leviticus xxvi. 42. Circumcision came to be from patriarchal times the token in the flesh of the Covenant between Jehovah and the seed of Abraham, Genesis xvii. 11, 13. From the time of Ezra onwards, Jewry clung more and more to the Covenant as it was manifested in these strict, exclusive forms. A whole corpus of tradition gradually developed, all of it to ensure the more exact observance of the Law, as enshrining Israel's obligations under the Covenant. This strict adherence in utter devotion was Israel's *chesed*, and the Israelite who kept the Law was *chasid* (pious, saint). The more the Covenant was exalted, and the more the Law was exalted as the means by which Israel on his side could maintain the Covenant, the more exalted became the ideas associated with the words *chesed* and *chasid*.

3. THE *CHESED* OF GOD

We have seen that, according to the pre-exilic prophets, Israel's *chesed* to God was characterized mostly by its fitfulness, Hosea vi. 4. They were not faithful in the Covenant. The result is that, not only in Hosea, but in the rest of the pre-exilic prophets also, we have the perennial problem of the broken Covenant, with its allied problem of what attitude God is going to adopt towards those who have broken it. Experience proved that whatever is to be done about this broken Covenant must be done by God Himself. The first move must come from Him. The position is summed up in Romans vii. 18, whilst 'to do is present with me', yet 'to do that which is good is not'. Even if men will to do the things of the Covenant, there remains a wide gap between will and performance.

The 'Chesed' of Jehovah in Hosea

Hosea was a Northerner. The identification of his father. Beeri, with the Beerah of 1 Chronicles v. 6 gave rise to the tradition that he was a Reubenite, whilst other traditions make him of Issachar and of Gilead. All these are without any genuine foundation,[1] though his frequent mention of Gilead may well be due to personal association. There does not always seem to be adequate reason in the context itself for the mention of this area. But whatever the exact district from which he came, or whatever his particular tribe, it is almost certain that he was an Israelite of the North. He is speaking of the waywardness of his own section of the Hebrew people, and not of that other section in the south, with which his own folk were nearly always at enmity. This may well account for his special tenderness as contrasted with the hardness of Amos, who preached to the North, though himself a Southerner.

Hosea's own domestic experience taught him what *chesed* could mean to Jehovah. Because of his own attitude to his wayward wife, he came to know that the *chesed* of God meant God's steadfast determination to be true to His share of the Covenant obligation whatever Israel did on her part. Hosea's love for Gomer-bath-Diblaim was so strong and sure that not all her adulteries could kill it. He realized that Jehovah's love for Israel was at least as sure and strong as his own love for his wife. Jehovah's love was both a 'sure love' and a 'love unswerving'.[2]

Hosea makes his own experience with Gomer-bath-Diblaim an allegory of the relations of Jehovah and Israel. He treats of these relations mainly[3] under the figure of a marriage. This is a bold simile for a true prophet of Jehovah, since the idea of the fertile divine marriage was one of the chief elements, perhaps the chiefest element, in the fertility cults of Canaan. Perhaps this is the very reason why he used the simile, desiring to transform into a new significance the actual central theme of the popular religion. This is the attitude of the missionary evangelist in all ages, transforming through sympathetic understanding, and not curtly refusing to have anything to do with native custom.[4] Viewed in this light, Hosea is starting from the popular idea, and is trying to transform

[1] The tradition that he was of Benjamin is due to the seventeenth-century Cabalist, Zacuto, and is falsified by the very context out of which it arose, 1 Chronicles v. 4–6.

[2] This phrase occurs most happily in Robert Bridges' translation of Johann Heermann's hymn, *Herzliebster Jesu, was hast du verbrochen*, in *Methodist Hymn-book*, No. 177, verse 5.

[3] The figure is of a vine in x. 1, and a son in xi. 1–4.

[4] C. P. Groves, *Jesus Christ and Primitive Need* (Fernley-Hartley Lecture, 1934), p. 222.

the whole religion on to a new basis. Hosea was no wholesale reformer in cult matters. He himself regarded as serious the loss of such cult objects as the pillar, the ephod, and the teraphim, all of which the reformed cultus of post-exilic days looked upon with the utmost horror. But he did earnestly desire that faithfulness in the Covenant and true knowledge of God should be realized to be of greater importance than sacrifices and burnt-offerings.

Hosea thinks of the time in the wilderness as the time of courtship, ii. 15 (17). This is a figure which Ezekiel used later, and amplified with a wealth of detail which is foreign to modern ideas of what is seemly. To Hosea, the time when Jehovah brought Israel-Ephraim out of Egypt was the time of espousals and youthful love. The trouble began in Canaan, when the new wife Israel was enticed away from her true Husband by her lovers, the Baals. She played the harlot with them. She fell into the snare of the Canaanite cults, and came to believe that she received all the goodness of the land of Canaan from the Baals and the Astartes, ii. 5 (7). This was the old-time religion of the land, Jeremiah xliv. 18 *f.* Israel did not realize that it was Jehovah who gave her all these things, and that they were the pledges of His love to her. So she prostituted them all to the service of the Baals, ii. 8 (10). And so Israel broke the marriage covenant. The proper penalty was the withdrawal of these gifts, and an end of fruitfulness. She had to learn that the Baals had not given her the fruit of vineyard and olive-tree, ii. 9 (11). Still further she was to lose all the blessings of proper government, and 'abide many days without king, and without prince', and without the cult objects of her worship, iii. 4.

But through all the troubles which beat against and broke the marriage covenant between Jehovah and Israel, there was one factor which never changed. This was God's sure love for Israel. Because of this sure, unswerving love, the Covenant can never be finally and completely broken. It takes two to make a covenant, and it also takes two to break it. Israel may have rejected God, but God has not rejected Israel. He will allure her back once more to the wilderness, back to the scene of their first love. There He will make love[1] to her again, as He did in the former time. Then once more He will lead her into the land of vineyards. The

[1] Heb., 'speak to her heart'. E.VV., 'speak comfortably to her'. For the meaning, see Genesis xxxiv. 3.

Valley of Achor, through which Israel entered Canaan at the first, Joshua vii. 26, has indeed proved to be a valley of *'achor* (troubling), but when Israel enters Canaan a second time, it will be a valley of hope. There will be a clean cut with the past. This time there will be no more *baal*. This old Semitic word for 'husband' will be cut right out of the vocabulary. It will be no longer *ba'ali* (my lord), but *'ishi* (my man). The horrid word will be excised. There will be a newer, sounder Covenant, ii. 18 (20), and all things living will be involved in it. 'And I will betroth thee to Me in righteousness (*tsedeq*) and in justice (*mishpaṭ*), and in *chesed*, and in mercies', ii. 19 (21).

All this speaks of Jehovah's determined, steadfast love for chosen Israel. It is a love which nothing can destroy, not all her waywardness, nor her apostasy. This attitude on the part of Jehovah appears not only in the first three chapters of Hosea, where the figures of betrothal and marriage are maintained, but elsewhere in the book, and in parts which cannot by any means be held to be later insertions. We deprecate the tendency to deny to Amos and Hosea all sections which speak of a restoration, and to leave only passages which contain messages of doom. Such exegesis is based on *a priori* assumptions, often with little justification except the belief that the prophets were always condemnatory. The hope for better times is clear in Hosea xi, where Israel is God's son, the child whom He called out of Egypt, the small boy whom He taught to walk, carried in His arms, and healed of childhood's knocks and bruises, xi. 3. 'I drew him with cords of a man, with bonds of love', xi. 4. But Ephraim was determined to turn away from God, xi. 7. Then comes the heart-broken cry, 'How shall I give thee up, Ephraim? How shall I surrender thee, Israel? How shall I make thee as Admah? How shall I set thee as Zeboim?[1] Mine heart is turned within Me, My compassions are kindled together. I will not execute the fierceness of My anger, I will not again (or "turn to") destroy Ephraim', xi. 8 *f.*

We see then that the idea of God's undying love and His great reluctance to let Ephraim go, are clear and pronounced in passages indubitably Hosea's. This is independent of Hosea xiv, which some allege to be of later date.

[1] Two cities of the Plain destroyed with Sodom and Gomorrah.

The 'Chesed' of God in Jeremiah

Jeremiah's heart was with the North. He was 'of the priests that were in Anathoth in the land of Benjamin', i. 1. This makes him a descendant of the House of Eli, the ancient priesthood of the Ark from Egypt, 1 Samuel ii. 27 *f*. Abiathar alone survived the massacre at Nob. His grandfather Ahitub was a grandson of Eli, 1 Samuel xiv. 3, xxii. 20. This Abiathar followed David in all his varied fortunes, and in the days of success shared the Jerusalem priesthood with Zadok.[1] In the intrigues which marked the end of David's reign, Abiathar supported the unsuccessful Adonijah, and was exiled to Anathoth. Jeremiah's descent from Abiathar shows itself also in his interest in Shiloh, vii. 12–15, xxvi. 6.

Jeremiah had therefore great symapthy with the North. Neither he nor his family could be expected to have any great love for the Zadokite priesthood at Jerusalem. The attempt on Jeremiah's life by the men of Anathoth may well be explained by his (to them) traitorous adherence to the centralizing Deuteronomic movement, Jeremiah xi. 1–8 and 18–23. This support was short-lived, Jeremiah viii. 8, perhaps because he soon found that the Jerusalem priests were determined not to admit any of the country priests to share the increased privileges under the centralization order, 2 Kings xxiii. 9. Jeremiah had no love for the Temple at Jerusalem nor for the priests there. He called it a den of robbers, vii. 11 *f*., a phrase whose point is enhanced if the priests there clung to the increased profits and refused to share them with the provincial priests whose livelihood had thus been taken away from them. Jeremiah had little but condemnation for Jerusalem, except for the few who went into exile with the young Jehoiachin in 597 B.C. But he is always looking forward to the time when the old Israel of the North shall return to a renewed prosperity, when the purged of Judah shall reunite with a restored Ephraim in worship at Jerusalem.

Jeremiah thought tenderly of the North-country, and hoped always in that same unswerving love of God which Hosea had first learned to know. If Hosea learned something of the *chesed* of Jehovah because of his rejected love for Gomer-bath-Diblaim, then Jeremiah, childless and friendless, learned something of Jehovah's deep longing for Ephraim, His dear son, His pleasant

[1] Zadok was probably the pre-Davidic Jebusite priest; see H. H. Rowley, 'Zadok and Nehushtan' in *Journal of Biblical Literature*, LVIII, No. 11 (1939), pp. 113–31.

child, now long since strayed and lost, Jeremiah xxxi. 20. He knew of that undying love which never would let Israel go, or, having been forced to let Israel go into exile to a far land, could never cease from tears and longing until one day He should see the wanderer return. All that devour Israel, 'holiness to Jehovah, the first-fruits of His increase', 'shall be held liable:[1] evil shall come upon them', ii. 3. See also iii. 12 *ff.*, xvi. 14 *ff.*, where in each case the reference is to the North, in the first instance clearly as distinct from Judah. The only[2] passage which speaks of the restoration of Judah alone is xxxii. 36 *ff.* He looks for a return of the 597 exiles, Jehoiachin and 'the good figs', xxiv, xxvii. 22, xxix. 14, or for a return of both Israel and Judah, xxiii. 5–8, xxx. 10, xxxi. 1 *ff.*, 15 *ff.*, 27, 31, xxxiii. 7–11, 14 *ff.* Otherwise he looks for great and terrible destruction to fall on Judah, ii.,[3] iv, vi. 30, vii. 29–34, viii, ix, etc. But, as we have said, the prophet is full of words of mercy and pleas for repentance when he thinks of the old Israel of the North. Hosea's simile of the youthful marriage vows appears again in Jeremiah ii. 1–3. Again we find the plea to the erring wife to repent and return, iii. 12–15, 20. Compare Hosea xi. 8 *f.* and Jeremiah iv. 19; Hosea xi. 2 and Jeremiah xxxi. 20. Jehovah is reluctant to let His people go, even though they have forsaken and broken the Covenant.

The 'Chesed' of God in Amos

Amos was a Southerner, a Judaean from Tekoa, well away to the south, five miles south of Bethlehem. When he went to Bethel, he went to the royal sanctuary of a rival country. All his condemnations are of Ephraim-Israel. He does not condemn Judah except in vi. 1 ('Woe to them that are at ease in Zion') and in ii. 4–5. Both passages are doubtful, and may well be interpolations, the first because the introduction of 'Zion' is alien to the context, the second because the charges against Judah are so

[1] *'Asham* strictly means 'liable to pay'. It applies to compensatory offerings. The translation 'guilty' is most misleading, and the rendering 'guilt-offering' has led many astray, especially when it is also assumed that it was a sacrifice similar to the 'whole burnt-offering'.

[2] We do not regard xxx. 18–23 as from Jeremiah. See the allocations to Jeremiah and Baruch in A. S. Peake, *Jeremiah* (Century Bible), which we regard as substantially sound.

[3] We take verses 14, 26 to refer to Israel (third person pronouns), and the second person pronouns to refer to Judah.

indefinite when compared to the detailed charges against other peoples in the paragraphs in which this paragraph is embedded.[1] Even the condemnation of sacrifices which has caused so much discussion (v. 21–5), can be considered as being a condemnation of the cultus of such Northern shrines as Dan (viii. 14), Bethel (v. 5 and ? viii. 14), and Gilgal (iv. 4, v. 5). The question in v. 25 refers to the House of Israel—that is, to the Northern Kingdom only—who are to go into captivity beyond Damascus. There seems to be no difficulty in Amos's mind about Jerusalem as the centre of the worship of Jehovah, since he opens his prophecy with the sound of Jehovah roaring like a lion from Zion. Further, He roars, not against Judah, but against Israel, for 'the top of Carmel shall wither', i. 2. Our conclusion, therefore, in the case of Amos, is that whilst he looks forward to the bare possibility of the rescue of a residue of the Northern Kingdom, he does not discuss at all the state of religion in Judah. This was not his business. His call was to urge Ephraim-Israel to repentance. His national feelings are supporting his religious enthusiasms in his preaching against the wickedness of the North. We take this to be the chief reason why we miss in him those pleas and tender regrets which are so pronounced a feature of the messages of Hosea and Jeremiah. His message gives a free rein to all the sternness and hardness of those desolate lands in which he was born and bred.

The passages in Amos which speak of the certain doom of Israel are very frequent. God will not turn away the punishment, ii. 6. The warrior will not be able to stand firm, and no speed of horse or foot will provide a means of escape, ii. 15. The doom is rendered even more certain because of the Divine Election of Israel, iii. 1 *f.* Though the Lord has sent His three great disciplinary weapons, famine, pestilence, and sword (iv. 6–10), this great destructive triad which occurs again and again in the prophets, and though from all this Israel has in time past been 'as a brand snatched from the burning', yet there has been no repentance, and the end has now come. 'Prepare to meet thy God, O Israel', iv. 12. Even the smallest avenue of escape is excluded. This is

[1] Even the mention of Beersheba in v. 5, viii. 14 need not include the condemnation of a place in Judahite territory. Israel was very strong in the time of Jeroboam II, and had conquered much territory, though mostly east of Jordan. Azariah-Uzziah's victories against the Philistines (2 Chronicles xxvi. 6 *f.*) may not have extended beyond the capture of Gath, in which cases Beersheba may have belonged to Israel. See Oesterley and Robinson, *History of Israel* (1932), Vol. I, pp. 360 *f.* In any case, both cases raise textual difficulties.

clear from the three visions of chapter vii, the locusts (1–3), the fire (4–6), and the plumb line (7–9). The smallness of Jacob will not exempt him from the general destruction, and God 'will not again pass by him any more', vii. 2, 5, 8. None shall escape, and all the fugitives shall be hunted down. Not even exile and captivity will provide a means of escape, ix. 4. And the climax comes in that Israel, once the chosen people, is now no different from the Ethiopians, ix. 7, a passage which we take to involve the complete rejection of Israel.

There remains only the slenderest hope. 'It may be that the Lord, the God of Hosts, will be gracious unto the remnant of Joseph', v. 14*f.* Perhaps Israel will be rescued at last, though it be but as two legs or a piece of an ear out of the mouth of the lion, iii. 12. On the other hand, 'if there remain ten men in one house, that they shall die' (vi. 9), though 'the city that went forth (tc war) a thousand shall have an hundred left, and that which went forth a hundred shall have ten left, to the house of Israel', v. 3. But Amos is certain that Israel will go into captivity, vii. 11, 17, v. 27, vi. 7. Amos, therefore, except for a few instances, is sure of the complete doom of Israel.[1] He has little to say of that love which will not let Israel go. Her doom is writ.

The 'Chesed' of God in Micah

There is nothing to say under this head. Micah's attitude to both Samaria and Jerusalem is as condemnatory as the most sweeping of Amos's messages of doom. He is even more fierce, for there has welled up in him into an overflowing stream, all the bitterness engendered by generations of maltreatment of the peasant by city men and landowners.

The 'Chesed' of God in Isaiah

Isaiah was a Southerner, apparently a city man and *habitué* of the Temple, and, at least in adult life, in constant attendance at court. He has little fondness for Samaria and the Ephraimite kingdom, especially since he was one of Ahaz's chief supporters during the Syro-Ephraimitish war of 734 B.C., Isaiah vii. 1–9.

[1] We omit ix. 8*c*–end from the discussion. Happy endings in the prophets are suspect.

Isaiah's condemnation of the North is complete, v. 25, ix. 17, 19 (Heb. 18, 20); x. 4.[1] Also xxviii. 1–13.

When Isaiah speaks of his own people of the South, he is torn betwixt two. Jehovah of Hosts is going to be 'for a stone of stumbling and for a rock of offence to both the houses of Israel. . . . and many shall stumble thereon, and fall, and be broken, and be snared, and be taken', viii. 14 *f.* After the story of his call in chapter vi, the prophet gives a picture of wholesale and complete disaster. Even the stump that is left when the tree has been felled, even this will be destroyed, vi. 13. But on the contrary, we have xxxi and xxix. 1–14. The dilemma of the prophet is plain. On the one hand, he is fully aware of the stern retribution which is due for sin. On the other hand, he trusts in that love which will not let Judah go. This is plain even if ix. 2–7 (Heb. 1–6) should be denied to him (erroneously, we hold), and even if viii. 10, 17 should be limited in its scope to the days of hope before the great Assyrian invasion of Judah.

The National Limitations of the Prophets

We have seen that we have to distinguish between the prophets because of their national allegiances. Almost everything depends on whether the prophet is dealing with his own or the other section of the Hebrew people. Every prophet finds it more easy to speak about the ultimate punishment of rebellion against God, when he is discussing the crimes of the rival people. Every prophet finds it more easy to emphasize the wideness of God's mercy when he is speaking of his own folk. It is as well for us to recognize the intense rivalry, often amounting to bitter hatred, between the House of Israel and the House of Judah. There is no war as bitter as civil war, and no emnity as that which can exist between the nearly related. Psalm lxxviii. 67 *f.* was the firm belief of Judah after the fall of Israel: 'Moreover he refused the tent of Joseph and chose not the tribe of Ephraim; but he chose the tribe of Judah, the mount Zion which he loved.' The rejection of Ephraim appears in Southern writings as early as Amos ix. 7. The last

[1] We find a promise of better times for Galilee in ix. 1 (Heb. viii. 23). The verses which follow—namely, ix. 2–7 (1–6)—have nothing to do with what precedes. Probably nothing of viii. 19–ix. 1 (viii. 19–23) is from Isaiah. Verse 19 was said by Rabbi Simeon (*Midrash Wayyiqra' Rabba*, xv) to be one of the two surviving verses of the prophecies of Beeri, father of Hosea. All five verses seem to form a miscellaneous supplement, attached at the end of the Memoirs of Isaiah. Similarly for x. 20–27. See G. B. Gray, *Isaiah* (I.C.C.), p. 203.

editors of the Old Testament were firm in this conviction. It is perhaps debatable whether or not the first Deuteronomic writings involved the centralization of the worship in Jerusalem, but it is certain that the later Deuteronomists believed, not only in the centralization at Zion, but also in its exclusiveness. All the quarrels, from the time of Jeshua and Zerubbabel, through Nehemiah and Ezra, down to the break between Jew and Samaritan with all the subsequent bickerings, have the division between Israel and Judah as the background. The fact of the matter is that Israel and Judah were different from beginning to end. They belonged to different migrations. It is generally agreed that, whilst Ephraim came into Palestine over Jordan under Joshua, Judah was a mixed group with a Hebrew nucleus who infiltrated from the South.[1] The time of the United Kingdom was a domination of Israel by Judah. For the rest of the time Israel mostly dominated Judah. There was always rivalry, even in David's time, and often war. The bitterness deepened after the Exile, when it took on the form of a quarrel between the returned exiles and those who had never been out of the country. The picture of two happy peoples dwelling together in unity and peace is largely a Messianic dream of the future.

The prophets were children of their times, for they too were involved in the same strife. Jeremiah is most clear of prejudice, for he had affinities with both groups. Amos and Isaiah are strong in condemnation of the rival kingdom. Micah condemns them all; his antagonism is against all cities. Hosea is great in hope for his own people, whilst even Isaiah speaks of rescue when the time of greatest crisis is at hand. Ezekiel follows Jeremiah almost exactly. Our first impulse is to condemn them out of hand, until we remember John viii. 7. The prophets are but comrades with the rest of us. We all tend to look through national spectacles. The modern world is at least as firmly attached to them as any age ever was. One of the legacies of the First Great War was a tremendous revival of nationalism of the narrowest and most chauvinistic type. The prospect is no better for the aftermath of the Second Great War. What nation, then or now, does not in time of war pray to its gods for its own righteous cause?

[1] C. F. Burney, *Israel's Settlement in Canaan* (Schweich Lectures, 1917), pp. 34–6, 31 *f.* H. H. Rowley, *Israel's Sojourn in Egypt* (reprinted from the *Bulletin of the John Rylands Library*, Vol. 22, No. 1, April, 1938), pp. 23, 28–32.

The justification of this attitude varies from nation to nation, but in every case it necessitates the priority of nationalism. Inasmuch as the time is not yet when all middle walls of partition between the nations are broken down, let us judge the prophets forbearingly in this respect. The City of God takes many generations to build. Even the prophets were not emancipated from those limitations which still hold the world in thrall.

The Dilemma of the Prophets

The prophets were the first to be sure that the sins of their own people must meet with a just and terrible retribution. They were equally sure that God's love for them and His peculiar care would never let them go. They were sure that the old idea was wrong, whereby God must save them whatever they do, and yet when they thought of the love that they themselves bore to their own, they knew that there was something in the old idea, however strict the demands of Righteousness were. And so we have seen that even in the eighth-century prophets *tsedaqah* is more than ethical rectitude, and is always toppling over into a preference for the poor and helpless. How much more should the word come to mean Salvation in the fullest sense, when it is God's own people who themselves are the poor and helpless, exiles in a far land at the mercy of those that are stronger than they.

In these circumstances the double aspect of *tsedaqah* resolves itself into a definite dilemma. What is the balance of Mercy and Justice? The prophets solved it, as Rashi also said, by giving 'precedence to the rule of mercy' and joining 'it with the rule of justice'.[1] God's *chesed* for Israel is therefore seen all the more certainly to be sure, and strong and steadfast. It stands for God's eager, ardent desire for Israel, the people of His choice. There are no words to describe the depth, and strength, and certainty of this Divine Compassion. In order to appreciate its steadfastness, we must measure it by His demand for Righteousness. His demand for Right Action is so insistent that it could not be more so, but His *chesed* for the people of His choice is more insistent still. This may seem contradictory, but it is true. God's determination is that the bond between Him and Israel shall never ultimately be broken, that the Covenant shall survive, even though with the smallest remnant. The waywardness of Israel was so inborn, her

[1] See pp. 77*f.*, above.

stubbornness and her rebellion so sustained, that for the preservation even of the Remnant, God has always, in every age, had more need of mercy than of any other quality. This is why it is often possible to translate *chesed* by 'loving-kindness, mercy', and apparently to do no violence to the context. These renderings are unsatisfactory because they do not do justice to the idea of steadfastness which must always be understood. They create the impression that God cares more for Mercy than He cares for Righteousness. So He does, but not because He cares one whit less than the maximum for Righteousness. If God's mercy is to be greater than His demand for Righteousness, then how wondrous great His mercy must be, and how steadfast and insistent. We do not make His demand for Righteousness any the less. Rather we demonstrate the surpassing wonder of His unfailing covenant-love.

How God's 'Chesed' will Triumph

The prophets solved the dilemma of God's righteousness and His steadfast covenant-love, but not easily, nor at first. How can Israel, whether Ephraim or Judah, be brought to that repentance which will provide the opportunity for the exercise of God's unceasing love? The problem was faced by Jeremiah and Ezekiel. They were driven right up against the final issue, when they saw the whole national structure tumbling about their ears. Jeremiah watched the migratory birds, the swallow, the crane, the turtle-doves, and the storks. He noticed how wonderfully they return each year. They know the time of their coming. How is it, he asks, that the people of Jehovah do not know the *mishpaṭ*[1] of Jehovah?, viii. 7. The answer of Jeremiah is in the new Covenant which God will make with both North and South, xxxi. 31. In that day there will be no more only a written Law on parchment and skin, but a Law written on men's hearts, xxxi. 33. Every man himself will know God. Jeremiah has thus pointed to the solution of man's apostasy. He has solved it by his belief that even though man himself will not turn to God, yet God Himself can bring this to pass. God's sure, unswerving love will find a way by which even stubborn, unrepentant Israel can turn. It will mean new

[1] It is impossible to translate this word here by any one English word. It means (p. 76) rightful custom, ordained of God, and established by continual repetition. God's *mishpaṭ* for the swallow involves her regular return. God's *mishpaṭ* for man involves his return also.

hearts, but God will accomplish even this. Then there will be a turning to God in all sincerity, and loyal obedience to His Law. Not all Israel will be partakers in this, but only a Remnant. This too is Ezekiel's solution. The rest are doomed, Ezekiel v. 1–4, xviii. 31, xi. 19, xxxvi. 26.

Arising, then, out of this sure, unswerving love of God, we get the doctrine of the Remnant, and with it the belief that God Himself will accomplish in Israel that repentance and turning to Him without which there can never be any hope of better days, or indeed any Remnant. God will indeed find in Israel that righteousness which He demands, but it will not be of Israel's doing, even supposing that it is of Israel's desiring. It will be because God's sure love will find a way. Herein are the beginnings of those doctrines of the Christian Faith which we sons of the Reformation know assuredly to be at the root of the Gospel, in chief, Salvation by Faith alone, and through Grace, for even the first stirrings towards repentance in the human heart are the work of God Himself.

4. THE *CHESED* OF ISRAEL

We can see from Hosea's criticisms of the people what he conceived to be Israel's responsibilities towards God in respect of the covenant. The state of affairs where there is 'no truth (*'emeth*), nor *chesed*, nor knowledge of God in the land' is described in iv. 2; where he states that he finds nothing but 'swearing and breaking faith, and killing and stealing, and committing adultery; they break out, and blood toucheth blood'. This lack of *chesed* also shows itself in being 'joined to idols', iv. 17. It involves all the cults at the high places 'upon the hills, under oaks and poplars and terebinths', iv. 13.

Israel's true *chesed* to Jehovah involves, therefore, primarily Knowledge of God, and issuing from that, loyalty in true and proper worship, together with the proper behaviour in respect of the humanitarian virtues. All the prophets expect these standards, Isaiah i. 16; Jeremiah vii. 4–11; etc.

In so far as these requirements were established in a written code, they involved those ethical demands which are the background of the Book of the Covenant, Exodus xx. 22–xxiii. 33, with additional prophetic and (later) Deuteronomic influence. The content of the word *chesed* developed side by side with that of the idea of the Covenant.[1] With the establishment of the Law of Moses as the norm of daily life for the post-exilic community, *chesed* came to stand for that faithfulness to the strictness of the laws and regulations as they were enforced from the time of Ezra onwards. We find therefore in the post-exilic period the use of the adjective *chasid* to describe the man who is faithful to the Law of Moses. By this time this Law had come to be dominated by the idea of *Habdalah* (Separation), particularly of the faithful Jews from the Gentiles, and especially from those inhabitants of Palestine whom the Jews around Jerusalem alleged to be of mixed blood.

The word *chasid* is used twice of God, when it refers to that persistent, sure covenant-love of God which Hosea first realised. The two cases are Jeremiah iii. 12 and Psalm cxlv. 17. The case of Job xxxix. 13 is difficult. Probably this adjective is not found there at all, but actually a reference to the stork (*chasidah*), so-called because of her persistent and determined love for her young. But we hold that she was so called, not because of her kindliness, as the Oxford Lexicon suggests, but because that kindliness was persistent and never failing.

For the remainder, the word *chasid* is used of the loyalty of the faithful. This is the meaning which Dr. Dodd emphasizes, when he says that *chesed* means 'pious dutifulness, piety' in the sense of the Latin *pietas*.[2] We do not see any need, or indeed any justification for the suggestion made to Dr. Dodd by Professor Grensted,[3] that the use of *chasidim* by the post-exilic Jews came through an assonance with the Greek *hosios*. If there was any choice on the ground of an assonance, which we doubt since the similarity is far from marked, then it was the other way round. There was a long tradition of the word *chasid* in the sense of pious obedience to the Law, long before any Jew had ever heard a word of Greek, and certainly before the word *chasidim* came to be used of a definite party in Jewry. There is a natural development of the word *chasid* in Hebrew.

In 1 Samuel ii. 9 God's *chasid* (i.e. the man who keeps *chesed*) is contrasted with the wicked. In Proverbs ii. 8 'the way of His *chasid*' is the same as 'the paths of *mishpaṭ* (justice)'. Whether the

[1] See pp. 107 *ff.*, above.
[2] *The Bible and the Greeks*, pp. 60 *f.* See above, p. 94.
[3] *ibid.*, p. 64 (note).

chasid of Deuteronomy xxxiii. 8 refers to Moses or to Levi, it is clear that it is used with reference to observing the Covenant and teaching *mishpaṭ*. There are two other instances outside the Psalter, 2 Samuel xxii. 26 (with its parallel, Psalm xviii. 26) and Micah vii. 2. In each case the word is used in conjunction with the word *yashar* (upright). We would therefore say that in the first case the rendering 'with the merciful . . .' is neither accurate nor adequate, but that it should rather be 'with the faithful (dutiful) thou wilt show thyself faithful. . . .'

All other Old Testament instances of the word *chasid* are in the Psalter. There are seven in the First Book, three in the Second, four in the Third, one in the Fourth, and eight in the Fifth, making twenty-three in all. We are faced with the usual difficulty, in the case of the Psalter, of dating these instances. It is reasonably safe to say that the three cases in Psalm cxlix—namely, verses 1, 5, 9—refer to those Chasidim who were the chief supporters of Judas Maccabaeus in his fight for religious liberty. It is difficult to say to what extent any other cases in the Psalter should be interpreted in this way, or how far back we should trace the existence of this party of Chasidim who stood so pre-eminently for faithfulness to the Law. Our interpretation of the word *chasid* in the Psalter depends upon our solution of this historical problem.

We believe that the word *chasid* was used in the time of Nehemiah for those who supported him in his vigorous and strict enforcement of such provisions of the Deuteronomic Law as are indicated in Nehemiah xiii. 1–3, 19, 23 *f.* We have argued elsewhere,[1] and have seen no reason to change our view, that, although Psalms xlvi–xlviii are probably from the time of Isaiah of Jerusalem, yet the other earlier Korahite psalms, xlii–xliv, xlv, xlix, have clearly something to do with the North. Psalms xlii–xliii were originally one psalm in three stanzas, each with the refrain, 'Why art thou cast down. . . .' It is clear from what the Psalmist himself says that he had once been priest in Jerusalem, leading the throng to the House of God (xlii. 4) but that at the time when he was writing he was prevented from doing this (xlii. 2). He hopes and prays that one day God will enable him to return to the Temple, xliii. 3. Meanwhile, he is away in Northern Israel, in the 'land of Jordan', by the Hermons, xlii. 6. His enemies oppress him, xliii. 2. They jeer at him, and say that God

[1] *Studies in the Psalter*, (1934) pp. 19–24.

has forgotten him. They continually ask him, 'Where is thy God?' and they themselves claim to be *chasid*, xliii. 2. What is this nation which the Psalmist deliberately denies[1] to be *chasid*? 'Plead my cause', he prays, 'against a nation that is not *chasid*.' In Psalm xliv we find much the same state of affairs. The psalm opens with the story of days that are past, how God did mighty things for their fathers, and saved them from their adversaries, all because He had a favour unto them, xliv. 1–8. But at the end of the psalm there is a complete change. God has cast them off, and they are scattered among the heathen. Evidently they have been charged with 'dealing treacherously' in God's Covenant, xliv. 17. This they indignantly deny. They have not forgotten God's Name, nor have they prayed to a strange God, xliv. 20.

All this is the situation paralleled in Isaiah lxiii. 16, where we have the curious state of affairs of a people who are claiming that Jehovah is their father 'though Abraham knoweth us not, and Israel acknowledge us not'. 'We are all the work of thy hand', lxiv. 8; 'we are all thy people', lxiv. 9. There must be two groups of people involved here, in Isaiah lxiii. 16, lxiv. 8 *f.*, and equally in the Korahite psalms. One of them is in possession of the Sanctuary, denying access to the other section. They deny that the exiled group are true Jehovah worshippers, or that they are the people of God. The writer in Isaiah lxiii. 18 calls his opponents 'our adversaries', and this is the word used in the psalm for those who are preventing the Korahite psalmist from presenting himself at the Temple. In both Isaiah lxiii. 8 and Psalm xliv. 17, the writers deny that they have dealt falsely in the Covenant. See also Ezra iv. 1 and Nehemiah iv. 11. Our suggestion[2] is that here we have an early stage of the Samaritan controversy, and that the writers of both sets of passages were victims of that policy of exclusiveness and separation which began with Zerubbabel and reached its strength in Nehemiah and Ezra. We take the Korahites to have been priests exiled by Nehemiah, who had perforce to remain in the Samaritan North. What concerns our immediate purpose here is that we have an early stage of the development of the word *chasid*, of men who are faithful in keeping the Covenant in the early days when first the new ideas of the Covenant were being enforced.

We take the later Korahite psalms—namely, lxxxiv, lxxxv, and

[1] Notice the Hebrew *lo'*.

[2] *ibid.*, p. 9.

lxxxvii, to belong to a later period after the departure of Nehemiah and before the advent of Ezra, when we know North and South for once to have been on reasonably good terms.[1] We suppose the Korahites then to have returned to Jerusalem, and to have stayed on through Ezra's purge, having made terms with the powers that were, and having accepted the lower post of door-keepers, thus no longer being officiating priests.[2] These three later Korahite psalms are full of great joy and happiness at a return to Jerusalem. The sparrow has come back, and the swallow has found her a nest in the Holy Places. It is better to be a door-keeper in the House of God than to dwell in the tents of wickedness. Psalm lxxxv speaks of a glad reunion. '*Chesed* and truth (*'emeth*) are met together, righteousness and peace have kissed each other.' It is a reunion between 'His people and His *chasidim*', lxxxv. 8 (Heb., 9). We take 'His people' to mean the exiled Korahites who had been maintaining that they were indeed His people, and the *chasidim* to have been the other party, xliii. 1; 'the *chasidim* . . . who have made a covenant . . . with God . . . by sacrifice', i.e. the Asaphites who have gathered round Jerusalem, Psalm l. 5. They had prided themselves on their *chesed*, whilst the Korahite exile had maintained that they were not as *chasid* as they made themselves out to be, Psalm xliii. 1.

This, we hold, is how the word *chasid* came to be the proper word used by the post-exilic Jews to describe themselves when they referred to their pious devotion and loyalty to the Law. It was by no means a technical term in the days of Nehemiah and Ezra, but the origins of the later technical use are to be seen, as we believe, in the literature of that period—namely, the Korahite and Asaphite psalms and certain parts of Isaiah lxiii, lxiv. In Nehemiah's time it involved the rigid adherence to Deuteronomy xxiii. 3–5, with its exclusion of Ammonites and Moabites, Nehemiah xiii. 1–3. It involved strict observance of Sabbath restrictions, Nehemiah xiii. 15–22; and the condemnation of 'mixed' marriages, Nehemiah xiii. 23–7. These were the reforms on which Ezra insisted some fifty years later, and they have been sturdily maintained ever since by the faithful orthodox Jew. In course of time those who were most urgent in these matters formed themselves into a definite party under the name Chasidim. This seems to have taken place during the period when many Jews were

[1] *ibid.*, p. 13. [2] *ibid.*, pp. 39–43.

attracted by the wider life of Hellenism, and when the Hellenizing party grew so strong within Jewry that there was need for active effort if Jewry was still to survive. It was through the loyalty of the Chasidim that Jewry was saved in the second century B.C., when Judas had to fight against Hellenizers within Jewry and the Syrian-Greeks without. It was the Pharisee party, themselves the legitimate successors of the Chasidim, who saved Jewry by their devotion to the Law and their loyalty in the synagogues when the Temple was destroyed in A.D. 70.

Some of the references in the psalms may be quite early, but whatever the date *chasid* always stands for the man who seeks to do his pious, humble duty towards God. For example Psalms xii. 1 (2), xxxi. 23 (24), xxxvii. 28; but we take l. 5 and lii. 9 (11) to belong to the Nehemiah period, and to be from the hands of those who sympathized with him. It may be that Psalm cxlv. 10 is very late. Probably Psalm iv. 3 (4) originally read: 'for he hath made wonderful the *chesed* which is his'. This is the reading which the commentaries suggest, and it tells of the wonder of God's covenant-love for Israel. The suggestion is that, owing to later ideas of Separation, the original hiphil had its final consonant changed from '*aleph* to *he*', in which case the word would mean 'he hath separated', and at the same time *chesed* was understood to have other vowels and to be *chasid*.[1] The reading then becomes 'the Lord hath separated for himself the *chasid*', an admirable sentiment for the last centuries before the destruction of the Temple. For the rest of the instances in the Psalter, we do not care to be precise. Perhaps already we have sought to be more precise than the actual evidence warrants.

5. THE DIFFERENCE BETWEEN *CHESED* AND *CHEN*

The difference between these two words has been discussed at length by Dr. Lofthouse in the article which we have already quoted.[2] *Chesed* is essentially a covenant word. *Chen* is essentially not a covenant word. Both can stand for kindness, mercy, forbearance, but the first in cases where there is a definite bond between the two parties, and the second in cases where there is

[1] A few MSS. still retain the '*aleph*, as does Septuagint. The MSS. are Add. 15451 and Add. 15250 in the British Museum, and upwards of 30 in Kennicott's list.

[2] '*Chen* and *Chesed* in the Old Testament', *Z.A.T.W.*, 20 Band, Heft 1 (1933), S.S 29–35. See above, p. 100.

not such bond. There must be some recognized tie when *chesed* is used, and in this respect it is the very opposite of *chen*.

There is another great difference between the two words. In respect of *chesed*, we have seen that it is primarily that loyalty which should mutually exist between the two parties to a covenant. There is *chesed* from both sides, even if the two parties are not equals. This was the case in such a treaty as that between David and the Ammonite king Nahash: 'And David said, I will shew kindness (lit. 'make *chesed*', i.e. make a treaty and keep it) unto Hanun the son of Nahash, as his father shewed kindness ('made *chesed*') unto me', 2 Samuel x. 2. Similarly, there is the *chesed* of God towards Israel, His covenant-people, which is that of a superior to an inferior; and equally there is the *chesed* of Israel towards God, which shows itself in a humble piety and dutiful love.

But when we turn to *chen*, we find that the word is used, practically without exception, of the attitude of a superior to an inferior. Thus *chesed* works both ways, but *chen* only one way. It therefore tends to carry with it, to a greater extent than does *chesed*, the idea of unmerited favour, or of supreme graciousness and condescension on the part of the giver, who is the superior. There is not the slightest obligation on the part of the superior to show this *chen*. It is all of his generosity. There is no thought of any charge of harshness against him if he is not so gracious. The suppliant has not the slightest claim, nor is he in a position to do anything to enforce his claim beyond the actual petition itself.

The two words *chesed* and *chen* do actually approach each other in the thought of God's unswerving love. This is seen by the fact that the psalmists use both words when speaking of God's great mercy and loving-kindness. It is true in respect of the *chesed* of God towards Israel, that Israel by his continual waywardness had long since forfeited any real claim under the Covenant. To this extent God's graciousness to Israel and His persistent covenant-love were undeserved, and to this extent *chen* is used instead of *chesed*. This occurs often in the Psalms in the case of the verb *chanan*, though never of the noun, Psalm iv. 1 (2), etc., some twenty-nine times in all. Similar cases, where there is no thought of the covenant obligation, are Deuteronomy iii. 23; Psalm cxliii. 1; and especially Exodus xxxiii. 19 and Job viii. 5. Apart from such cases as these, the approach of *chesed* towards the meaning of *chen* is not very close, for after all there had been a

Covenant, and the whole secret of God's continued mercy towards Israel was that they were the people of His choice. Israel ultimately depended upon the Covenant, and her hope of salvation was in God's persistent covenant-love. Except for the psalmists in the cases we have mentioned, Israel never cast herself upon God as one who made no claim at all. She always remembered the Covenant, and that she was the chosen of the Lord. This made the difference between *chesed* and *chen* wider rather than narrower, and when post-exilic Israel based her claim on the fact that she herself was *chasid*, then the idea of undeserved favour tended to fall more and more into the background.

We do not think, however, that Dr. Lofthouse has brought out clearly enough the fact that *chen* is predominantly connected with a relationship between the superior and an inferior. He pointed this out in connection with the verb *chanan*, but he does not insist upon this in his treatment of the noun *chen*. The fact that 'the action is from the superior to the inferior'[1] is clear in the cases where Dr. Lofthouse cites the verb: Genesis xxxiii. 5, Jacob, of 'the children which God hath graciously given' him; similarly, 2 Samuel xii. 22; Job humbly beseeching his friends for mercy, Job xix. 21; and often in being gracious to the poor, the needy, the helpless, whether on the part of God or of man, both in the psalms and elsewhere. This is especially clear in the case of the use of the hithpael form of the verb, which expresses humble petition for favour by a suppliant who has no claim, nor any power beyond his helplessness to commend his request. The best examples are: the boy Joseph beseeching his brethren, Genesis xlii. 21; Job humbly entreating his own servant, Job xix. 16; the third officer appealing to Elijah, 2 Kings i. 13; and Jacob to the angel at Penuel, Hosea xii. 4 (5).

The adjective *channun* is used only of God (thirteen times), and in every case but one in conjunction with the root *r-ch-m* (mercy). Here always it is used of the graciousness and condescension of the superior. The same is true of the nouns which are derived from the verb, *techinnah*, *tachanun* (especially in the ridiculous idea of the mighty leviathan pleading with the puny Job, xli. 3 (Heb., xl. 27)), and, lastly, *chen*. This last noun, the one with which we are chiefly concerned, is never found in the plural, never with the article, and once only with the suffix, Genesis xxxix. 21, though

[1] Dr. Lofthouse, of the verb, *ibid.*, S. 30.

the 'construct' construction is found in similar circumstances in Exodus iii. 21, xi. 3, xii. 36. The word can be used as 'an elaborate way of saying "please"',[1] but this is because of the humble attitude which is thus adopted by the suppliant. It then becomes a clear case of the action being from a superior to an inferior, e.g. Laban making the request of Jacob, Genesis xxx. 27; Shechem to Dinah's people, Genesis xxxiv. 11; Joseph of Potiphar, Genesis xxxix. 4; and Joseph's brethren of Joseph, the position being now entirely reversed, Genesis xlvii. 25.

The word comes to be used of that favour which the inferior receives from the superior: the divorced wife, who finds no *chen* because she has some 'unseemly thing' in her. As Dr. Lofthouse points out, it is not because she has no *chen* (not because she has no 'charm') but because she finds no *chen* (favour). This still holds good in such a case as Psalm xlv. 2 (3), where God pours '*chen* and glory' upon the king's lips, i.e. the gracious condescension which is one of the marks of a good king, is given him by God. The instances can be multiplied indefinitely. The word *chen* never means 'charm' in the sense of beauty, and never thanks or gratitude. It is the gracious favour of the superior to the inferior, all undeserved. The inferior has not the slightest claim on the superior. There is not the slightest breath of censure possible if such good favour is not granted. From this the word can be used of the result of that good favour granted to the inferior, but it cannot mean the attitude in the suppliant which may induce the superior to grant the request.

In conclusion, *chen* is undeserved favour at the hands of a superior, where there is no bond or covenant between the parties, and no obligation on the superior to do anything at all. *Chesed*, by contrast, presupposes a covenant, and has from first to last a strong suggestion of fixedness, steadfastness, determined loyalty.

[1] Dr. Lofthouse, *ibid.*, S. 30.

Chapter VI

THE ELECTION-LOVE OF GOD

THE Hebrew verb is *'aheb*. The root seems to be peculiar to Hebrew, other Semitic languages using the root *ch-b-b*. This latter root is found in Arabic, Aramaic, Syriac, Ethiopic, and even in Mishnaic Hebrew and in Urdu. Its fundamental idea is supposed to be 'burn, kindle, be set on fire'. Possibly there is an early relationship between the Hebrew *'-h-b* and the general Semitic *ch-b-b* through an earlier biliteral root *h-b* or *ch-b* with an original significance of 'breathe after, long for'; cf. the Arabic *habba*,[1] but all this is largely speculative, and it is impossible to say anything with certainty. The root *ch-b-b* is used twice only in the Old Testament, the verb once, Deuteronomy xxxiii. 3, and the noun *chob* (bosom) once, Job xxxi. 33, as an Aramaic loan-word. The root is used frequently in the Mishnah, e.g. often in *Pirqe Aboth*.

I. THE HEBREW USE OF THE ROOT *'-H-B*

The General Use of the Root '*'-h-b*'

The root *'-h-b* is very common in Hebrew, and can be used of any and every kind of love. It is a perfectly general word, and is far from having any exclusively religious use. In a 'secular' sense it can be used of inanimate things: food, Genesis xxvii. 4 (JE); Hosea iii. 1; sleep, Proverbs xx. 13; husbandry, 2 Chronicles xxvi. 10. It can be used of wisdom, Proverbs iv. 6; knowledge, Proverbs xii. 1; the good, Amos v. 15; faithfulness and duty (*chesed*), Micah vi. 8; loving evil, Micah iii. 2; simplicity, i.e. the lack of godly sense and wisdom, Proverbs i. 22; the heavenly bodies as gods, Jeremiah viii. 2. The root is used mostly of persons, the proportion being about four to one so far as the verb is concerned, and always (thirty-three times) so far as the nouns are concerned.[2] We judge that there is no significance in the proportions, it being natural that there should be a large preponderance of the personal use.

Continuing the examination of the secular, personal use, we

[1] Cf. Gesenius, *Thesaurus*, i. 30.
[2] The total for verb and nouns is 247.

find the root used of the love of man for man, Psalm cix. 4, 5; of love for oneself, 1 Samuel xx. 17; for a neighbour as one's self, Leviticus xix. 34; for a son, Genesis xxii. 2 (JE); of the love of man for woman, often in the Song of Songs and frequently elsewhere; of adulterous love, Hosea ii. 7 (9); and of sexual desire, 2 Samuel xiii. 4, 15. Curiously, the root is never used of the love of a wife for a husband, or of a child for a parent. Apart from its general use for sexual desire, often of an illicit kind, it is used once only of a woman loving a man, 1 Samuel xviii. 20, of Michal loving David,[1] and once only of one woman loving another, Ruth and Naomi, Ruth iv. 15. There is one instance of its use of an inferior loving a superior, Deuteronomy xv. 16. This verse is the Deuteronomic law concerning the slave who refuses his right of manumission and must then continue as a slave for the rest of his life. In the JE law, Exodus xxi. 5, it is plain that the reason for such a choice is that he does not wish to leave his wife and children, who must remain slaves. The Deuteronomic form of the law extends the love to the master, 'loving thee and thine house'. The JE case is the love for inferiors, whether husband for wife or father for children; but in the D case we have the love of the slave for the master, which has to show itself in dutiful obedience. Even Ruth's love for her mother-in-law is a dutiful, obedient love.

We are led to two conclusions, both of which are of paramount importance in the understanding of the meaning of the root *'-h-b*. The first is that when the root is used of loving persons, it is used of the attitude of a superior to an inferior. Secondly, where it is used (rarely) of an inferior to a superior, it is a humble, dutiful love.

The Religious Use of the Root ''-h-b*'*

The verb is used thirty-two times of God's love. Of these two are of God's love for Jerusalem, Psalms lxxviii. 68, lxxxvii. 2. There are seven cases of Him loving righteousness, judgement, etc., and twenty-three cases of Him loving Israel, or particular individuals. On the other hand, the verb is used twenty-two times of man's love for God; nineteen of man loving God's Name, Law, precepts, etc., and twice of man loving Jerusalem. The noun is used four times of God's love for His people, and once of Jerusalem's love for God. Summing up, we get the root used twenty-

[1] It occurs also in verse 28, but the text is not original; see the commentaries.

seven times of God loving man, as against twenty-four times of man loving God, this latter including the four cases of loving God's Name, and also Jeremiah ii. 2 of Jerusalem's love for God.[1] These proportions are not what we would expect from our consideration of the secular use of the root, but the cases where the root is used of man's love for God are largely due to the special and characteristic Deuteronomic use of the root.

The Deuteronomic use of the root in the sense of man's love for God is shown by the fact that twelve of the cases occur in Deuteronomy;[2] seven others are in Deuteronomic contexts—namely, Exodus xx. 6 (D and not JE); Joshua xxii. 5, xxiii. 11; 1 Kings iii. 3; Nehemiah i. 5; Daniel ix. 4; and especially Psalm cxix. 132, since this psalm is the most Deuteronomic psalm of all.[3] In addition in Psalm xxxi. 23 (24), all the Lord's *chasidim* are bidden to love Him. This leaves only four cases[4] out of twenty-four where the Deuteronomic influence is not manifest. Further of the fifteen cases of man loving God's precepts, no less than eleven are in Psalm cxix.

The Difference between ''Aheb*' (Love) and '*Sane*'' (Hate)*

We have seen[5] that *'ahabah* is Election-love as against *chesed*, which is Covenant-love. The connection of the root *'-h-b* with the idea of Election can be seen also in the difference between *'-h-b* (love) and *sane'* (hate). The difference between these two roots can amount to a full-blooded antithesis, as can be seen in Malachi i. 2, 3: 'I have loved you, saith the Lord. Yet ye say, Wherein hast thou loved us? Was not Esau Jacob's brother? saith the Lord: yet I loved Jacob; but I hated Esau, and made his mountains a desolation.' The passage goes on to say that even though Esau-Edom should build up his waste places, yet God will throw them down again, because they are 'the people against whom the Lord hath indignation for ever', Malachi i. 4. Here God's hatred of Esau-Edom is represented as being active, even virulent, to the highest degree. But we do not find this to be the normal state of

[1] Isaiah lvi. 6; Psalms v. 11 (12), lxix, 36 (37), cxix. 132.

[2] v. 10, vi. 5, vii. 9, x. 12, xi. 1, 13, 22, xiii. 3, xix. 9, xxx. 6, 16, 20.

[3] Cf. 'The Triennial Cycle and the Psalter' in *Zeitschr. f. d. altt. Wiss.*, 10 Band, Heft 3 (1933), S. 304, where we have suggested that Psalm cxix was recited on the Sabbath when the first portion of Deuteronomy was read in Palestine.

[4] Judges v. 31; Jeremiah ii. 2; Psalms v. 11 (12), lxix, 36 (37).

[5] P. 95, above.

affairs. Malachi i. 2–5 begins perhaps with the idea of God's election love for Israel, but the enmity against Edom is not so much a consequence of God's preference for Israel, as an indication of the bitter hatred which existed between Judah and Edom. There is no hatred like that of brothers, and never has there been between peoples a hatred such as that which existed between Judah and Edom. The Jews never forgave the way in which the Edomites rushed in to make the most of the defeat of Judah at the hands of the Babylonians, Psalm cxxxvii. 7; Isaiah lxiii. 1–6; Ezekiel xxv. 12, 14; Obadiah 8–19. This bitterness lies at the root of the hatred which orthodox Jews of later times bore to Herod the Great. How much the Pharisees must have desired to get rid of the Lord Jesus, if they could bring themselves to make common cause with the Herodians in order to destroy Him, Mark iii. 6.

But whilst in the case of Esau-Edom and also in such a case as Genesis xxxvii. 4, we have a hatred that is violent and active, yet the verb *sane'* is not always used in the sense of active hatred. This can be seen from Genesis xxix. 31 (J), where the writer says that 'Leah was hated', and from a similar use in Deuteronomy xxi. 15–17. In these cases of rival wives, 'the loved one' is the one that is preferred, whilst 'the hated one' is the other. See also 1 Samuel i. 5 in the story of the birth of Samuel. This sense of 'not preferred' accounts for the phrase 'hating his mother', etc. in Luke xiv. 26. The Greek verb here is *miseo*, which is the word which Septuagint uses in Genesis xxix. 31 and also in Deuteronomy xxi. 15–17.[1] We see therefore that the root *'-h-b* is used in the sense of 'choose' even in non-religious contexts. This is the sense in which the origin of the Covenant is due to Jehovah's *'ahabah* (election-love). He loved Israel—that is, He preferred her before all other peoples. She is His elected people.

2. GOD'S LOVE FOR ISRAEL

And so we come to the position where we can lay down three main elements for the understanding of the Hebrew *'ahabah* (love). First God's love for Israel is an unconditioned sovereign love. Second, Israel's love for God is a conditioned, dutiful love, showing itself in the proper fulfilment of God's requirements as laid down in the Covenant. Third, Israel must obey, not only because he must, but also because he must 'love the Lord his God

[1] G. Abbott-Smith, *Manual Lexicon of the New Testament* (1922), p. 293.

with all his heart, and with all his will (*nephesh*, desire, self), and with all his strength'.[1]

God's love for Israel is an unconditioned love

God chose Israel, and them only did He know out of all the families of the earth, Amos iii. 2. This word 'know' means more than awareness, for the root *y-d-'* (know) in Hebrew has a personal as well as an intellectual meaning. The word is used of the sex relationship, Genesis iv. 1 (J), and often. Or again, when it is said in Psalm i. 6 that 'the Lord knoweth the way of the righteous', the Psalmist does not mean that Jehovah knows the route which the righteous man will take, as a man may know a route from a map. Neither does he mean that God knows the way so well that He is familiar with every twist and turn of it. The Psalmist means all this, but he intends very much more. He means that God is intimately and personally concerned about every step which the righteous man takes. God is concerned with the wayfarer rather than with the way. The meaning is personal, not topographical. Compare Psalm cxxxi. 2; Job xxiii. 10; Isaiah xliii. 2. And so when Amos says that Jehovah knows Israel, he is referring to the most intimate personal knowledge that is possible, something very much deeper and closer than any mere awareness or general recognition. The intellectual bias in the word 'know' is Greek; the Hebrew bias is personal.

Amos gives no reason for this choice. The Deuteronomists, themselves 'the very chiefest apostles' of the Divine Election of Israel, can say no more than 'only (*raq*) the Lord had a delight in their fathers to love them, and He chose their seed after them, yea even you above (R.V. margin, "out of") all peoples', Deuteronomy x. 15. The writer finds it amazing that the God to whom 'belongeth the heaven and the heaven of heavens, the earth, with all that therein is', x. 14, should love Israel's forefathers, and should extend this love to their descendants. This is clear from the use of the restrictive adverb *raq* (the 'only' of verse 15), which is used regularly for exceptions and for introducing what is contrary to expectation. The one thing of which all Old Testament writers are certain is that God's love for Israel was not because of anything that Israel had done or was. They say, particularly the

[1] Cf. J. Lindblom, *Profetismen i Israel* (1934), pp. 394*ff*.

Deuteronomists, that it was because of their fathers, Deuteronomy x. 15, iv. 37, or because of the promise He made to their fathers Deuteronomy vii. 8, or to David, 2 Kings xix. 34 (Isaiah xxxvii. 34).

Or, again, the Deuteronomists expressly deny that it was because of Israel's goodness, or because of Israel's greatness. 'Speak not in thine heart . . . saying, For my righteousness the Lord hath brought me in to possess the land, whereas for the wickedness of these nations the Lord doth drive them out from before thee. Not for thy righteousness, nor for the uprightness of thine heart . . . but for the wickedness of these nations . . . and that He may establish the word which the Lord sware unto thy fathers . . .' Deuteronomy ix. 4, 5. Further, 'the Lord did not set His love upon you, nor choose you, because ye were more in number than any people; for ye were the fewest of all people: but because the Lord loveth you, and because He would keep the oath which He sware unto your fathers . . .', Deuteronomy vii. 7, 8. The reason why He turned Balaam's curse to a blessing, Deuteronomy xxiii. 5, was because He loved them, but why He should love them was more than any could ever say. It was not for their righteousness, not for their greatness, and not because of anything in the Israel of the day. So they looked back, and said it was because of their fathers and His Oath of long ago. This was only pushing the problem farther away; it was not solving it. There was no solution on this side. The solution was on God's side. And so we find such statements as that it was 'for His own sake' or 'for His Name's sake': 2 Kings xix. 34 (Isaiah xxxvii. 34), xx. 6, xliii. 25, xlviii. 11; Psalms xxiii. 3, xxv. 11 (12), xxxi. 3 (4), lxxix. 9, cvi. 8, cix. 21, cxliii. 11; Jeremiah xiv. 7, 21; Ezekiel xx. 9, 41, 22, 44; Isaiah xlviii. 9. Some of these passages are perhaps to be interpreted in the old popular way, that Jehovah chose Israel because a god had to have a people of his own, or that He saved them for His own credit's sake among the gods, but such ideas as these were largely outgrown in the eighth-century prophets themselves, to whatever extent they were retained in popular thought. Often these writers say 'for His Name's sake', because they scarce know what else to say. They meant that Jehovah loved them, because that was what He was like. 'He hath loved, He hath loved us, because He would love.'

All that could be said about it was that God found Israel and loved her. He 'found Israel as grapes in the wilderness', or saw their 'fathers as the first-ripe figs in the fig-tree at her first season', Hosea ix. 10.[1] Or, again, 'He found him in a desert land, and in the waste howling wilderness; He compassed him about, He cared for him, He kept him as the apple of His eye.' He watched over him as an eagle-vulture over her nest and her young, bore him as on eagle's wings, led him about, instructed him, Deuteronomy xxxii. 10 *f.* So it is again and again, Hosea xi. 1, 3; Jeremiah iii. 4; Ezekiel xvi. 6 and 8; Jeremiah xxxi. 9, 20; etc. Jehovah's love for Israel was unconditioned by anything in Israel that was good. It was wholly unmerited. It was not in the least degree because of anything in Israel that was good, or beautiful, or desirable. This comes out very clearly in all the unpleasant details of Ezekiel xvi. 4–6. Such is the story of God's unconditioned love.

This brings us to a frequent error which men still make when they speak of the love of God for man. It is said that there must be something worth loving in the loved one before the lover can love. This is said, so far as we can judge, for two reasons. The first is that it is very difficult for us to admit that there is nothing in us which makes us worthy of God's love. The second is that it is hard to find among men a love that is wholly disinterested.[2] It may possibly be true of human love that there must first be something in the loved one worth loving. Perhaps it is true, but often only the lover can see it, and even then it is sometimes nearer the truth to say that loving makes it so. Perhaps it is that the lover sees a possibility which none other can see.[3] This last is true of God's love for Israel, but to say that it was because He saw a possibility in Israel which none other could see, is still inadequate, since there is boundless possibility in any and every nation or person, whom the great Creator God chooses. So once more we are driven back to the unmerited love of Charles Wesley's hymn, 'He hath loved, He hath loved us, because He would love.'[4]

[1] Israel was therefore very specially 'holy' to Jehovah, see pp. 35 *f.*, above.

[2] It is curious how the rationalist easily rejects the idea of a personal God because of man's tendency to personalize outside things, and yet at the same time easily accepts all such ideas as are based on man's tendency to think of himself more highly than he ought.

[3] Witness how often we say, 'I don't know what he (she) can see in her (him).'

[4] *Methodist Hymn-book,* No. 66, 'O God of all grace'.

Is God's Love Irrational?

Some say, therefore, that in this case God's love is irrational. The answer in part is, irrational or rational, such is the Bible teaching. For the rest, if 'irrational' means that man cannot find a reason, then God's love certainly is irrational. But that is not what the word means, however much some moderns may make it so. The word means contrary to reason, which is not the same thing as to say that man cannot find the reason. The fact that man cannot find the reason, by no means involves the conclusion that there is no reason in it. It is part of man's doom which he writes for himself, that he so easily comes to believe that what he himself cannot explain is therefore inexplicable. It is curious that the demand for rational explanation is not applied to science as some would apply it to religion. The quantum is accepted as the brick out of which the universe is made, but no one says that the quantum is irrational, or that the universe makes no sense, even though the why and the wherefore of the quantum is not known. The most that can be said about it, is that it is so. At root this is all that can be said concerning anything. In the last resort, we have to say it of God also.

Some say also that, in this case, God's love is arbitrary. If such a statement mean that God chooses in a way that, or for a reason that we cannot understand, then His love is certainly arbitrary. On this definition most love is arbitrary—in fact, all love in its degree. The more wonderful it is, the more arbitrary it is. But the word 'arbitrary' is capable of more than one meaning. It can mean 'not founded in the nature of things' and so 'irrational', though it is difficult to say on what grounds this or that is not founded in the nature of things, unless first it be decided whether or not it is rational. It can mean 'not according to reason'. It can mean 'absolute in power', and this in both a good and a bad sense. It can mean that it depends solely on the will of the agent. In this sense God's love is certainly arbitrary. It is not arbitrary in the sense that it is capricious. It is arbitrary in the sense that it is unconditioned by anything outside the Nature of God. Man can give no reason for it. God's thoughts are not our thoughts, neither are His ways our ways. They are 'things too wonderful for me, which I knew not', Job xlii. 3. 'How unsearchable are His judgements, and His ways past finding out', Romans xi. 33. This is this mystery of Divine Love.

But it is even more strange than this. There is an exclusiveness in God's love. This idea of exclusiveness in God's love has been part of 'the offence of the Gospel' since almost the first days. Such an idea must necessarily be involved in some degree as soon as the word 'choose' is used. We may not like this word 'choose' or its companion 'election'. They may be abhorrent to us, but they are firmly embedded in both Old and New Testaments. Either we must accept this idea of choice on the part of God with its necessary accompaniment of exclusiveness, or we have to hold to a doctrine of the Love of God other than that which is Biblical. The alternative is clear, and we do not see how it can be avoided. It may be that we cannot answer the questions which are involved in it, but the teaching is there plainly enough. Why is it, for instance, that this one is chosen, and not that one? We have no answer. Calvin tried to find the answer to both parts of the question, and his answer was Predestination. Luther said that Calvin went wrong because he sought to climb up into the majesty of God. The first part of the question can be answered. God chose this one because He loved him. To this we can add that God rejects on the ground of persistent, unrepentant wickedness, and that this rejection can apply to Israel, equally with the Ethiopians. Beyond this it is difficult and even dangerous to go, for the distinction between 'called' and 'chosen' is not everywhere maintained.[1]

God's Love is a Sovereign Love

It is of the utmost importance everywhere to remember that God is Sovereign. The idea of God as King is firmly embedded in the Biblical tradition. So much was this idea common among the Semitic peoples, of whom largely the Hebrews were born, that one of the severest battles which the prophets had to fight was to separate the idea of Jehovah as King from the general Semitic ideas, Leviticus xx. 2 *ff.* (P); 2 Kings xxiii. 10; Jeremiah xxxii. 35; Amos v. 26; etc.

God is always the superior; man is always the inferior. God always is in control. The first word and the last word are both alike with Him. The Old Testament holds strongly to this from beginning to end. God is in the heavens; man is of the earth. God

[1] Lightfoot, *Epistle to the Colossians* (1892), commenting on Colossians iii. 12. The distinction is made in the Gospels, but not in the Pauline Epistles.

is righteous, and therefore He demands right conduct from man. God has a peculiar care for the down-trodden and the oppressed, and therefore He is especially concerned to see that justice is done on the earth in respect of them. All this is determined by God alone. He conforms to no norm apart from Him Himself. There is no Justice apart from Him which (or whom) He must obey. Justice derives from Him. There is no necessity laid upon Him from outside. He decides what is to be and what is not to be. To this extent, He is arbitrary in His judgements, and arbitrary in His love. He is accountable to none. He acts in this way because it is His Nature so to act. He is the Norm by which all things must be judged, and by Him alone can the final verdict be given.

The 'Over-plus' of God's Love

Israel did not choose Jehovah. Jehovah chose Israel. This fact is dominant throughout the whole Bible; cf. John xv. 16. If God had not chosen Israel in the first place, there would never have been any Israel. It was by God's choice that Israel ever became a people in the first instance. Politically speaking, the covenant of the tribes at Sinai was the bond which bound them together into one group. Whenever it was sought to emphasize the oneness of North and South, this same covenant had to be invoked, for the nucleus of both North and South were equally parties to it. By their continued loyalty to God, and by their continued obedience to His commands, by these alone in every age has there ever been any chance of the survival of Israel. The conditions laid down in the Law are the very conditions by which Israel has preserved its identity.

But more than this, God's love for Israel was never limited by what was required in any legal or equitable sense. We saw this in our discussion of the *chesed* of God.[1] It was because God insisted on maintaining His part of the Covenant, even when Israel had broken that Covenant, that there was any continuance of it, and any hope for even a remnant. Israel's continued existence, whatever the identification of the term 'Israel', has always depended upon God doing more than was required. This is the essence of God's love. Here is that point where above all others God's love is distinctive. It is not so much the case that God rejects this one or that one, but that in some cases we can see that God does more

[1] See pp. 110–22, above.

than is required. If it had been remembered in time past that the word 'election' was involved in this over-plus of Gods' love rather than in His general love for mankind, perhaps some of the difficulties might have been avoided. God has done many things for all the sons of men, but He has done special things for Israel. He has always done that which is required on any ordinary, proper, and reasonable basis for all the sons of man, but He has done more than was required on behalf of Israel. If He had not done this, then such a small nation as Israel would never have survived all the vicissitudes of the centuries. If He had not continued to do more than was required, Israel-Judah would have slipped back, as indeed they were always trying to do, and would have become one in the midst of the nations, lost in the welter of them, just as Edom, Ammon, Babylonia, Assyria, and the rest have been lost. It was necessary, to an ever-growing extent, that God's love for Israel should show itself in that determined persistence which we have shown to be the characteristic significance of the word *chesed*. This continually increasing over-plus of God's love is exactly what makes His *chesed* so firm and so steadfast. That is why we have insisted so much on the idea of faithfulness and sureness, when we have sought to interpret the true meaning of God's *chesed* in respect of His Covenant with Israel, the people of His choice.

3. ISRAEL'S LOVE TO GOD

A Conditioned, Humble, Dutiful Love

Israel's love for God is that of an inferior to a superior. It is concerned all the time with doing His will. The opening words of the *Shema*' are typical: 'HEAR, O Israel: the Lord our God, the Lord is ONE: and thou shalt love the Lord thy God with all thine heart, and with all thy soul, and with all thy might. And these words which I command thee . . .', Deuteronomy vi. 4*ff*. Israel's *chesed* in respect of the Covenant was obedience and duty to the things which God required. On this ground, we object most strongly to Moffatt's translation of Micah vi. 8. The Hebrew does not say, 'What does the Eternal ask from you?', but 'require, demand', and it does not say, 'live in quiet fellowship', but 'walk humbly (lit., 'make humble to walk'). Men must obey, and they must be humble before Him.

Yet Israel's fulfilment of the requirements of God must be done in no spirit of enforced obedience, but in a spirit of humble and dutiful piety. 'Unto Thee do I lift up mine eyes, O Thou that sittest in the heavens. Behold, as the eyes of servants (slaves) look unto the hand of their master, as the eyes of a maiden (slave) unto the hands of her mistress; So our eyes look unto the Lord our God, until He have mercy upon us', Psalm cxxiii. 1–2. 'He will not suffer thy foot to be moved: He that keepeth thee will not slumber. Behold He that keepeth Israel will neither slumber nor sleep', Psalm cxxi. 3–4. This combination of dutiful obedience and humble love to God reached its height in such Rabbis as Hillel, Aqiba, and the teachers of the first two centuries of the Christian Era. The evidence for this shows itself in many a saying that is a monument of pious love and humble devotion, and can be seen in numerous references in the late Dr. A. Büchler's studies of that period, to which the reader is referred[1] for details.

Even in this fulfilment by Israel of the conditions of the Covenant, dutiful and humble and loving, there is something of God. In fact, there is a very great deal of God. In times of peril and apostasy, He sent His holy prophets, 'rising early to send them'—that is, sending them before the time of direst need, early in the dawn of the day of Israel's peril. In times of utter failure, He gave them new hearts and put a right spirit within them, taking away their fleshly, stony hearts. For the love of God which chose them in the first instance is also the love by which God Himselt enables them to fulfil the conditions by which alone that love can become effective in them. Never was love like this, more enduring than a mother's (Isaiah xlix. 15); the very walls of Jerusalem are graven on His hands, and their need is ever present in front of Him. He will never let Israel go, but always the conditions of the Covenant must be fulfilled. Israel must serve Him in humble, dutiful love, with true *pietas*, though, as experience has proved, this is achieved only by that new heart and spirit which God Himself implants in Israel's heart, and by that new strength which God Himself alone can give.

[1] *Studies in Sin and Atonement in the Rabbinic Literature of the First Century* (1928), No. 11 in Jew's College Publications, particularly the first part of this volume, pp. 1–119, entitled 'Obedience to the Torah, its Source and Tradition'.

Chapter VII

THE SPIRIT OF GOD

THE Hebrew word for 'spirit' is *ruach*. The root *r-w-ch*, from which the noun is derived, means primarily 'to breathe out through the nose with violence'. It is an onomatopoetic word, similar to *puach* and *naphach*, both of which mean 'to breathe out through the mouth with a certain amount of violence', or even 'to blow out . . .'.

There are three points of particular emphasis in respect of the word. It stands for Power, for Life, and it is of God as against of man.

1. THE MEANING OF *RUACH*

'Ruach' (Breath) carries the Idea of Power

There is a number of instances where spoken words are described as being *ruach* in the sense of 'empty breath, wind'. These are Job vii. 7, xvi. 3 (lit., 'words of *ruach*'), xx. 3 (probably); Isaiah xxvi. 18, xli. 29; Jeremiah v. 13; twice in Hosea xii. 1 (Heb. 2); nine times in Ecclesiastes; and perhaps Proverbs xi. 29 and Hosea viii. 7. These last two cases are more likely to mean 'trouble' than 'emptiness'.

Three cases in Job contain the suggestion of violence, viii. 2, vi. 26, xv. 2. Compare also Job xxxii. 18*f*., which also may belong to this group. This (probable) case in Elihu's speech, and two cases in Isaiah xi. 4 and xxxiii. 11, are the only cases where the word is clearly used of human breath, apart from instances where it is connected with the idea of life. Isaiah xxxiii. 11 reads, 'your *ruach* is a fire that shall devour you', whilst in Isaiah xi. 4 it is said of the Messianic King that he 'will slay the wicked with the *ruach* of his mouth', the parallel being, 'and he shall smite the earth with rod of his mouth'. It is clear that the element of violence is present and strong in these cases.

The implication of violence is generally found in the instances where the word is used of the breath of God, e.g. 2 Samuel xxii. 16 and its equivalent, Psalm xviii. 15 (Heb. 16); Job iv. 9. These cases establish a general notion of violence and power being involved in the word when it is used to mean 'breath', and this holds when we get an extension of the idea of breathing out through the nose in the phrase, 'the breath of the mouth', of the effective energy of Psalm xxxiii. 6 and Job xv. 30. The idea of violence is very marked in Isaiah xxx. 28, where, after having spoken in the previous verse of the anger of the Lord, and having said that 'His lips are full of indignation, and His tongue is as a devouring fire', the prophet continues, 'and His *ruach* is as an overflowing wady that reacheth even to the neck'. Here we have the picture of a ravine, dry and boulder-strewn in the time of drought, but suddenly transformed by the rains into a raging torrent. Such a picture as this, we remember from boyhood's days in Captain Mayne Reid's *The Scalp Hunters*, where the avenging hunters are saved from annihilation by the hands of the Navajo Indians by such a sudden and overwhelming spate of waters.

The word *ruach* stands for hard, strong, violent breathing, as against *neshamah*, which means ordinary, quiet breathing. Both nouns can be used generally without reference to any particular type of breathing. They can be used in parallel as synonyms, Job iv. 9, xxxiii. 4; Isaiah xlii. 5; and together as synonyms, 2 Samuel xxii. 16, with its equivalent Psalm xviii. 15 (16); Genesis vii. 22 (P). Such use tends to be late, though it is not exclusively so. As we have had occasion to point out earlier, words do not stand for pin-points of expression, but for large circles, and the nearer we get to the circumference, the more the particular significance gets blurred. This is why words which strictly represent completely different aspects of an action, and thus are opposites, can yet be used as synonyms when the differences between the two aspects have for the time being fallen into the background. The main point about the noun *neshamah*, in its strictest sense, is that it contains no suggestion of violence, but rather the contrary. See Isaiah ii. 22; Deuteronomy xx. 16, etc.

Curiously enough, however, in the one case in which the verb *nasham* is used, Isaiah xlii. 14; it is used of the laboured breathing of a woman in travail. Evidently the reference is to breathing that is hard and violent, but the fact that the verb is used in conjunction with the verb *sha'aph* shows that the actual significance of the word in this particular instance is breathing *out*, as against *sha'aph,* which means breathing *in* noisily. Elsewhere *sha'aph* involves the taking of long, deep, noisy breaths. It is used of the wild she-ass, seeking her mate, and snuffing up wind in the time of her heat, Jeremiah ii. 24; of the desert animals snuffing pantingly up wind for the scent of water in the time of drought, Jeremiah xiv. 6; or of the sun pictured as a runner breathing heavily in the race, Ecclesiastes i. 5. But the use of *neshamah,* the noun, in the sense of ordinary breathing is well established. Further, the use of the verb in the gentle sense is confirmed by the Arabic *nasama* (of gentle winds softly breathing), and by the use of the Ittaphel form in the Talmud (*b. Sabb.* 134 *a*) of a new-born baby breathing and thereby showing signs of life.

'Ruach' (Wind) carries the Idea of Violence and Power

The word *ruach* is frequently used of the wind; some eighty-seven times in all. Of these thirty-seven speak[1] of the wind as the agent of Jehovah, mostly destructive, and always strong and violent. In addition, Amos iv. 13 speaks of God creating the wind, and Job xxviii. 25 of Him regulating it. Five cases connect the wind with the *geshem,* the heavy downpour of the monsoon rains, that heavy rain which opens the rainy season, when the sky grows black with clouds and heavy rain, 1 Kings xviii. 45; 2 Kings iii. 17; Ezekiel xiii. 11; Proverbs xxv. 14, 23, in which last instance we are told that it is the north wind that brings rain.[2] Seventeen out of the eighty-seven cases tell of the wind, or the east wind, or the desert wind, carrying this or that away like chaff. In addition to these we have Jeremiah xxii. 22: 'the wind shall feed upon (R.V. margin) thy shepherds'. There are left twenty-five other cases where the wind (*ruach*) is mentioned. Two of these belong to the life-giving-spirit-wind-breath of Ezekiel xxxvii, where all four senses of the word are almost inextricably interwoven. We must refer to this chapter later. Seven only refer to the wind without any necessary significance of violence. These are Psalm lxxviii. 39, 'a wind that passeth and cometh not again'; Job xli. 16 (Heb. 8), of the scales on the monster's back which are so close that there is no air-space (*ruach*) between them; Zechariah v. 9; Ecclesiastes xi. 4; and especially Genesis iii. 8 of the evening

[1] See p. 152, below.

[2] This case does not seem to refer to the 'former rain', as does 1 Kings xviii. 45, for then the rain-clouds come up from the west (verses 43 and 44).

breeze.[1] The other two cases have already been mentioned, Jeremiah ii. 24, xiv. 6. We are left with nine cases, all telling of violence and destruction, or of the tremendous power of the wind in one way or another. These nine cases are Proverbs xxvii. 16, of the folly of trying to restrain the wind; Isaiah xxxii. 2 and Psalm lv. 8 (9), of the necessity of hiding from it; Ezekiel xvii. 10, xix. 12, of the east wind withering a growing vine; Isaiah vii. 2, of the trees of the forest bowing before the wind; Ezekiel i. 4, of the onset of a storm with thunder and lightnings, sweeping down through Mesopotamia from the mountains in the north towards an overheated gulf in the south.

'Ruach' as a Psychological Term to denote dominant disposition.

The idea of power involved in the word *ruach* is carried over into what we would now call psychology, to denote the dominant impulse or disposition of an individual. For instance, Genesis xxvi. 35 (P) states that the two Hittite wives of Esau were 'bitterness of spirit' (*morath ruach*) to Isaac and Rebekah. The R.V. 'grief of mind' is inadequate. The meaning is that whenever they thought of these marriages of Esau, the feeling which dominated them was one of bitterness and this to the exclusion of every other feeling. An overwhelming sense of bitterness came upon them. Another instance is that of the husband who suspects his wife's unfaithfulness. The law lays down the procedure in such a case 'if the *ruach* of jealousy come upon' the man, Numbers v. 14, 30 (P). We have the picture of a man driven, as by a power which he cannot resist, to declare the shame of his own house. The comparable classical instance is Oedipus the King, driven on to his own destruction, as if by a power of Fate that is stronger than he. There is a number of cases in the Old Testament where the word *ruach* is used in similar ways, and they cover every type of disposition; impatience, Exodus vi. 9 (P) and Proverbs xiv. 29; hardness, 1 Samuel i. 15 (E.VV., 'sorrowful'); crushed in spirit, broken, forsaken, humble, smitten, troubled, faithful, high, cool, long-enduring, excellent, and so on, some thirty-five cases in all. Two of these may especially be noted, both in Psalm li. In verse 10 (12) 'a right spirit' means a firmly established, upright disposition, whilst in verse 12 (14) 'a free spirit' means a generous disposition that gives freely and without

[1] Cf. Canticles ii. 17, iv. 6, 'until the day breathes (*puach*)', i.e. at the end of the day not at break of day. See D. W. Thomas, *Exp. Times*, XLVII, No. 9, pp. 431 *f.*

reserve. Compare the same root *nadab* in Judges v. 2: 'for the people that offered themselves willingly'.

This use of *ruach* to denote the dominant disposition is further to be illustrated in Numbers xiv. 24 (J) of the different attitude (R.V., 'another spirit') which distinguished Caleb from the rest of the people. In 2 Kings xix. 7 with its equivalent Isaiah xxxvii. 7, the prophet says that God will put such a *ruach* into the Assyrian invader that, when he hears a rumour, he will return to his own land. The word means that the Assyrian king will be in such an uneasy state of mind that as soon as he hears this rumour, he will forthwith be thrown into confusion and terror. His morale will have gone.

The idea of *ruach* standing for that in a man which so dominates him as to ensure a particular line of action is seen in the phrase, 'I will stir up the spirit of . . .'. This phrase is post-exilic, being found thrice in Haggai i. 14; four times in the Chronicler, 1 Chronicles v. 26 (*bis*); 2 Chronicles xxi. 16, xxxvi. 22, with its equivalent Ezra i. 1. See also, with a contrary result, Psalm lxxvi. 12 (13) and Isaiah xix. 3. In Job xxii. 19 Elihu says that his '*ruach* within him' (Heb., 'the *ruach* of my belly') constrains him to speak, and in the next verse he likens himself to a new wineskin that is ready to burst.[1] Exodus xxxv. 21 (P) speaks of a man 'whose spirit within him makes generous'. It is not easy for a man to control his *ruach*, for 'he that ruleth his spirit' is better 'than he that taketh a city', Proverbs xvi. 32; whereas a man 'that hath no rule over his spirit is like a city that is broken down and hath no wall', Proverbs xxv. 28. A man must therefore take heed to his spirit that he deal not treacherously, Malachi ii. 15, 16. 'The spirit of a man will sustain his infirmity', Proverbs xviii. 14; and when a man's spirit is dim (R.V. margin), then his heart melts, and his knees are weak as water, Ezekiel xxi. 7 (12). Ezekiel tells of prophets who 'follow their own spirit, and have seen nothing', xiii. 3. 'A man in whose spirit there is no guile', Psalm xxxii. 2, is a man of whom definitely it can never be said that guile dominates any of his actions. The remaining references to the 'spirit of a man' are to be found in Ecclesiastes. They are vii. 9, x. 4; and in the comparison between the spirit of a man and the spirit of a beast, iii. 18–21. In this last case the spirit is regarded as being

[1] Unless Elihu is being vulgar in the attempt to be funny, in which case the instance comes under a previous head.

the life-centre of the body, closely allied to the 'soul' in the sense in which those who believe in the immortality of the soul use the word.

This latter use of *ruach* as the spirit of the living being makes the word practically a synonym of *nephesh*, the breath-soul. God forms this *ruach* in man, Zechariah xii. 1; preserves it, Job x. 12; and it returns to Him at death, Ecclesiastes xii. 7. In Isaiah xxvi. 9 *ruach* is exactly parallel with *nephesh*, and so also in Job vii. 11. There are some twenty-five cases altogether where *ruach* is equivalent to *nephesh*.[1] But to make *nephesh* on that account the general equivalent of *ruach* is to show a complete misunderstanding of the proper significance of both words. Such an equation is wrong and can lead to nothing but error and confusion.[2] It is only in the cases where the meaning of the word *ruach* approaches the outermost fringe of the circle of its meaning that the word comes into touch with the circle of ideas represented by *nephesh*. Such instances are late. It happens only when *ruach* as controlling power in man comes to mean the man himself as a determining, active entity, and when at the same time *nephesh* comes to mean the same thing, it also being extended, this time from its truer meaning of that which makes the difference between the living and the dead. Similarly, we find the word *ruach* used occasionally where we would normally expect to find the word *leb*[3] (heart), Isaiah xxix. 24; Job xx. 3; and especially Isaiah xl. 13, where the Septuagint has *nous*[4] (intention), a rendering of which Paul makes apt use in Romans xi. 34 and 1 Corinthians ii. 16. The Hebrew *leb* or *lebab* (heart) is sometimes said to be the seat of the understanding, as against the bowels as the seat of the emotions. It may be that the predominant use favours this statement, but it is far from being exclusively the case, and it does not reveal the true state of

[1] The main meaning of *nephesh* is to be seen in Genesis ii. 7 (J): 'Jehovah Elohim shaped man, earth from the ground, and breathed into his nostrils life-breath (*neshamah*), and man became alive (*nephesh*).' It is that which makes the difference between a living being and a dead one.

[2] Cf. E. Langton, *Good and Evil Spirits* (1942), p. 170. The error here, with its even closer equation of *ruach* and *neshamah*, seems to go back to Tylor, *Primitive Culture* (1873, 2nd ed.) I, 433, though Dr. Langton's immediate source is apparently Dr. Oesterley. Tylor distinguishes plainly between *nephesh* and *ruach*, but he wrongly equates *ruach* and *neshamah*. The context, as one would expect, is Tylor's theory of the *anima* (breath-soul) as the first step in the development of religion. Such an equation as this, in our view, invalidates the whole of Tylor's position.

[3] Or *lebab*. The difference is stylistic only, unless purely accidental.

[4] Not 'intelligence' (*Encycl. Bibl.*, 4752). The author was not a Greek philosopher, and the term belongs to the realm of the will rather than to that of the mind.

affairs. The Hebrews were not nearly so exact in their psychological geography. The word *leb* (*lebab*), when used in a psychological sense, stands for that which is innermost of all, deepest down, and most important from the point of view under immediate consideration. And so it can mean mind, will, conscience moral character, and even on occasion the seat of the appetites and emotions.[1] This is how *leb* (heart), *ruach* (spirit), and *nephesh* (breath-soul) have circles which intersect, though only at one particular point. This intersection at the outmost fringe of each circle of ideas can be seen in Exodus xxxv. 21 (P), 'and they came, everyone whose heart (*leb*) stirred him up, and everyone whom his spirit (*ruach*) made willing', or, again, in 1 Chronicles xxviii. 9, 'and serve Him with a perfect heart (*leb*) and with a willing mind (*nephesh*)'. Yet again, Ezekiel xi. 5, xx. 32, where the E.VV. translate *ruach* by 'mind' and evidently mean 'memory, conscious remembrance'.

In these foregoing instances, where we have discussed the ideas of *ruach* as standing for that in a man which dominates him so as to ensure particular type of action, the *ruach* is regarded as being part of the man himself, the controlling element in him, the active and determining man. It is noteworthy that most of these instances are late, and that a high proportion of them are in the Wisdom Literature, i.e. Job, Proverbs, Ecclesiastes. The earlier use, and the more usual idea, not only for earlier times but also everywhere except in the Wisdom Literature, is of the controlling *ruach* being other than the man, as if controlling him and dominating him from outside. We find this on occasion even in the Wisdom Literature, as when, for instance, Elihu is represented as saying, 'but there is a *ruach* in man, and the breath (*neshamah*) of the Almighty giveth them understanding' (Heb., 'maketh them to understand'), Job xxxii. 8; which we take to mean that, though the *ruach* is in man, yet it comes to him from outside, from God, and is God's own breath.

The phrase '*ruach* of judgement' is found in Isaiah xxviii. 6. It refers to the power being given to 'him that sitteth in judgement', by which he is enabled to exercise his judicial functions. This power is given him by God, for 'the Lord of Hosts shall be for a *ruach* of judgement'. Similar to this we have Deuteronomy xxxiv. 9, of the spirit of wisdom by means of which Joshua will be enabled

[1] See the Oxford Lexicon (Brown, Driver and Briggs) under *leb* and *lebab*, pp. 523–5.

to govern the people in the place of Moses; Exodus xxviii. 3 (P), of the spirit of wisdom by which Aaron is enabled to perform the priestly functions; and especially Isaiah xi. 2, of 'the spirit of wisdom and understanding, the spirit of counsel and might, the spirit of knowledge and of the fear of the Lord', all of which are said to be manifestations of the spirit of the Lord which is to rest upon the Messianic King. A similar instance is Zechariah xii. 10, where it is promised that God 'will pour upon the house of David, and upon the inhabitants of Jerusalem, the spirit of grace and supplication'. An instance of similar overpowering influence, though contrary in its results, is seen in Isaiah xxix. 10: 'for the Lord hath poured out upon you the spirit of deep sleep, and hath closed your eyes the prophets . . .'. The same idea of an overpowering, dominating might is seen in Micah ii. 11 of men 'walking in a spirit of falsehood' (R.V. margin) and Hosea iv. 12, v. 4 of Israel being possessed by a 'spirit of whoredom' which impels her to continue in the idolatries and adulteries of the Canaanite cults. We have already referred to the husband who is impelled by a spirit of jealousy, Numbers v. 14, 30 (P), and to this we add Judges ix. 23, of that spirit which drives Abimelech and the men of Shechem steadily on to their doom. As we have said elsewhere, 'a man can control his *nephesh*, but it is the *ruach* which controls him'.[1]

'*Ruach*' *is not Flesh, but is of God*

Although, as we have seen, the Hebrews often spoke of the *ruach* as though it were part of the man, albeit the controlling element in him, yet they made a clear distinction between *ruach* (spirit) and *basar* (flesh).[2] Man is flesh, made from the dust of the earth, and animated by *ruach* (spirit) so that he is a *nephesh* (living being). The *ruach* is given him by God; it is God's *neshamah* (breath). When this *ruach* returns to God, then man's dust returns to the earth, Ecclesiastes xii. 7; Psalm cxlvi. 4. The division is man and flesh on the one side, God and *ruach* on the other. For

[1] *The Doctrine of the Holy Spirit* (Headingley Lectures, 1937), Lecture I, 'The Spirit of God in Hebrew Thought', p. 26.

[2] The word *basar* is from a root *b-s-r*, which means 'rub, make smooth the surface of a thing'. In one direction, it developed from 'smoothing the face' to (presumably) 'taking out the care-lines', and so to 'bringing good news', whence *besorah* ('good tidings', and 'reward for good tidings'). In another direction it came to refer to the smoothness of the skin, and so 'skin' and even 'flesh'. Whilst it can refer to 'flesh' generally, yet its strict meaning is 'the flesh near the skin' as against *she'er*, 'the flesh near the bone'.

example, 'the Egyptians are men, and not God; and their horses flesh and not spirit', Isaiah xxxi. 3. The distinction between the spirit as being of God and the flesh as being of man is to be seen in Genesis vi. 1–8 (J). Certain divine beings, 'the sons of God', intermarried with mortal women, and from them were born children half-human and half-divine. The general meaning is clear in spite of the two well-known difficulties of verse 3.[1] As children of the sons of God, it was their destiny to live for ever, since they were *ruach*. As children of mortals, they were doomed to die, since they were flesh. 'My *ruach*', says God, 'shall not strive for ever'; so He fixed the limit of this strife between deathlessness and death at 120 years.

In Ezekiel xxxvii. 1–14 we get the word *ruach* in its most effective context. The whole passage depends upon the various meanings of the word. Between verses 5 and 10—that is, in six verses—the word is used eight times, and once again in verse 14. The *ruach* is that breath by which man becomes alive (verses 5, 6, 8). This *ruach* which will animate the dead bones of the whole house of Israel is God's *ruach* (verse 14). It will come from the four winds, like the wind itself, powerful, invigorating, and strong, and thus God Himself will animate the dry bones of the House of Israel. To the group of instances where *ruach* means 'life-stuff', there belong such passages as Joshua ii. 11, v. 1; which tell of the paralysing fear which is said to have gripped the inhabitants of Canaan when they heard of the mighty deeds of the Lord on behalf of Israel against Og, King of Bashan. 'Their heart (*lebab*) melted, neither was their *ruach* in them any more.' The queen of Sheba was so amazed by the magnificence of Solomon that 'there was no more *ruach*[2] in her', 1 Kings x. 5; 2 Chronicles ix. 4. Compare also Genesis xlv. 27 (JE); Judges xv. 19; 1 Samuel xxx. 12; Psalm cxliii. 7. These verses all refer to the *ruach* as being the source of life, the 'life-spirit' of Genesis vi. 17, vii. 15 (all P), and vii. 22 (J), 'the breath (*neshamah*) of the life-spirit (*ruach chayyim*)'. See also Job xxvii. 3, xxxiii. 4, xxxiv. 14, xii. 10; Numbers xvi. 22 (P); Isaiah xxxviii. 16; and even including animals, Psalm civ. 29, 30; Ecclesiastes iii. 19, 21.

It is difficult to define precisely what is meant in Ezekiel i. 12,

[1] *Yadon* (? 'strive') and *beshaggam* ('for that he also' or 'in their going astray').

[2] It means even more than 'it took her breath away', for *ruach* means much more than 'breath'.

20 (*bis*), x. 27 in the references to the spirit of the living creature being in the wheels. It certainly means that the directive power was in the wheels, 'whithersoever the spirit was to go, they went', i. 20; the main point of the whole vision being that the chariot of the Lord has complete mobility, and can travel in any direction. Wherever God's people are in need of Him, there God can and does come. The meaning probably varies between ideas of directive and controlling power, life and perhaps even the Spirit of God.

The 'Ruach' (Wind) as the Agent of God

Returning to the thirty-seven cases which speak of the wind as the agent of God, *ruach* is the medium through which God exerts His controlling power. He brings the winds out of His treasuries, Psalm cxxxv. 7; Jeremiah x. 13, li. 16; He makes them His messengers, Psalm civ. 4; He rides upon its wings, 2 Samuel xxii. 11 and Psalms xviii. 10 (11), civ. 3. He has all power over it, for He created it, Amos iv. 13, and He regulates it, Job xxviii. 25. He can gather it in His fists, Proverbs xxx. 4. The wind fulfils His commands, Psalm cxlviii. 8; and it comes before Him as the herald of His coming, Job iv. 15; Ezekiel i. 4; 1 Kings xix. 11 (thrice). He sends the wind to assuage the Flood, Genesis viii. 1 (P), and in the J story of the Exodus the wind is His agent[1] in bringing about the plagues of Egypt, Exodus x. 13 (*bis*), xiv. 21. So also in the Song of Moses, Exodus xv. 8, 10. Further instances are Numbers xi. 31 (J); 1 Kings xviii. 45; Psalms xi. 6, xlviii. 7 (8), cvii. 25, cxlvii. 18; Isaiah xi. 15, xxvii. 8; Jeremiah li. 1; Ezekiel xiii. 11; Jonah i. 4, iv. 8; and probably Job xxxvii. 21. See especially the LXX rendering of Genesis i. 2 (*epephereto*), as in the Targum.

The proportion of cases where the idea of strength and violence is intended in all uses of *ruach* (wind) is three to one. This is counting all the twenty-two cases (nine in Ecclesiastes and seven in Job) where the meaning is 'vanity, breath, emptiness'. Apart from these cases, the proportion is fifteen to one.[2]

[1] In E the agent is Moses' rod; and in P the rod is in Aaron's hand, and he uses it at Moses' command.

[2] There is also a derived use of *ruach* to mean 'a point of the compass', e.g. 'come from the four winds'. There are twenty cases of this, of which ten are in Ezekiel, four in Jeremiah, two in Zechariah, three in Daniel, and the other in 1 Chronicles. All four cases in Jeremiah are at the end of the book, xlix. 36 (*bis*), 32, lii. 23 ('side' in E.VV.), so we see that the use is not earlier than the exile, and towards the end rather than the beginning.

Closely allied to the cases of the violent wind sent by God to execute His will in judgement is Isaiah iv. 4, where the prophet speaks of the holy remnant which will be left in Jerusalem after God has purged away the filth and the shed blood with 'the *ruach* of judgement and by the *ruach* of burning'. The E.VV. translate 'spirit', but we have more probably a metaphor drawn from the actual stormy wind from the eastern desert with all its scorching heat. The prophet may have been thinking even of the scorching wind itself.

2. *RUACH-ADONAI* (THE SPIRIT OF THE LORD)

We pass now to consider the use and meaning of the phrase *ruach-adonai*, and always against this background of power, violent, strong, overwhelming, and controlling in its nature. 'The *ruach-adonai* is the manifestation in human experience of the life-giving, energy-creating power of God.'[1]

The 'Ruach-adonai' is All-powerful

The link between the strong, overwhelming wind of the desert and the all-powerful *ruach-adonai* is provided by such passages as Hosea xiii. 15; Isaiah xl. 7, lix. 19, in all of which we should probably translate 'the wind of the Lord'. Hosea xiii. 15 refers to the east wind from the desert, with all its desiccating heat, and so also does Isaiah xl. 7. In Isaiah lix. 19 the reference is to the power that rushes with fury and speed through the narrow defile; cf. Isaiah xxx. 29. It is possible that in one or more of these cases the Sacred Name is used in order to emphasize the overpoweringness of the tempestuous wind. Compare the description of Nineveh in Jonah iii. 3, where the E.VV. have 'an exceeding great city', but the Hebrew has 'a city great to God'.[2] In some cases *ruach-adonai*, therefore, means a wind of unprecedented fury. Much therefore as we insist upon the fundamental idea of power as involved in the word *ruach*, we must look for this idea with increased emphasis in the phrase *ruach-adonai*.

Somewhat similar is 1 Kings xviii. 12, where Obadiah says that he is not very anxious to bring his master Ahab to meet Elijah, lest the *ruach-adonai* lift Elijah up and carry him Obadiah knows not where. Compare Acts viii. 39. The prophet is thinking of a

[1] *The Doctrine of the Holy Spirit* (Headingley Lectures), p. 11.

[2] The vulgar English equivalent is obvious.

miraculous whirlwind, but at the same time he is thinking of the *ruach-adonai* as that power of God which is mighty and effective in the affairs of men. 2 Kings ii. 16 is another instance of the same set of ideas. Other examples are Ezekiel iii. 14, xi. 1, xliii. 5. Such passages as Ezekiel viii. 3 and xi. 24 show how intimately interwoven are the ideas of an actual wind and of the direct activity of God. In viii. 3 we read, 'and he put forth the form of a hand, and took me by a lock of mine head; and the spirit lifted me up between the earth and the heaven, and brought me in the visions of God to Jerusalem'. In xi. 24 we have a parallel to the latter part only: 'the spirit lifted me up, and brought me in the vision by the spirit of God into Chaldea'. Another variation is xxxvii. 1, 'and the hand of the Lord was upon me, and he brought me out in the spirit of the Lord, and set me down in the midst of the valley'.

The 'Ruach-adonai' controls the Prophets

Other passages in the Book of the Prophet Ezekiel form a bridge to the idea of the *ruach-adonai* as that power which enters into and controls the prophets. Ezekiel ii. 2 reads, 'and the spirit entered into me when he spake unto me, and set me upon my feet', and then we find immediately following, the message which was delivered to the prophet. So also Ezekiel iii. 24, and especially xi. 5, where the spirit which enables the prophet to speak the word of prophecy is called the *ruach-adonai*. This identification is clear in Nehemiah ix. 30, but it reaches its classical expression in Micah iii. 8: 'but I truly am full of power by the spirit of the Lord (the *ruach-adonai*), and of judgement, and of might, to declare unto Jacob his transgressions, and to Israel his sin'. Other instances are Numbers xxiv. 2 (JE), of Balaam; Zechariah vii, 12, of the former prophets; 2 Chronicles xx. 14 of the Asaphite choir who sang their way to victory in the time of Jehoshaphat; and the two cases in 2 Chronicles xv. 1, xxiv. 20, where we have the variation *ruach-elohim*, without any change of meaning.

The 'Ruach-adonai' is More-than-human

The idea of a more-than-human power runs through the whole of the use of the phrase *ruach-adonai*. As a result of this special endowment of divine power men are able to do that which, in the ordinary way and relying upon purely human resources, they are quite unable to do. It shows itself in the power by which the judges rescued Israel from the oppressor and 'judged' the people, Judges iii. 10, vi. 34, xi. 29; it shows itself in its crudest form in the power which came mightily[1] upon Samson, Judges xiii. 25, xiv. 6, 19, xv. 14, enabled him to perform such extraordinary feats of strength, and made him the Trickster[2] of Hebrew lore. Those sudden seizures of ungovernable behaviour to which Saul was subject are described as the effect of the *ruach-adonai* leaping upon him. He became another man, and he 'prophesied', i.e. he was seized with the ecstatic dervish-like frenzy which was regarded as being the sure test of spirit possession in those early days, 1 Samuel x. 6, 10, xi. 6. Between this crude stage and that of true prophecy in Nehemiah ix. 30 and Micah iii. 8 there is a long development, of which an intermediate stage is represented by Numbers xi. 25–9 (JE). The sixty-eight elders who were gathered to the Tent of Meeting outside the camp, and the two who were detained in the camp, all 'prophesied' when the spirit first rested upon them, 'but they did so no more'. The power of judging and governing the people nevertheless remained with them as an abiding ability.

We are here bordering on the realm of *mana*, that strange personal-impersonal power which we have previously[3] discussed. The same idea occurs in the case of Elisha and the double[4] portion of *mana* which he received from the departing Elijah. We have seen it in the sudden strength which came to Samson, and in the guerrilla skill of Gideon. It appears in the skill of the craftsman which came upon Bezalel, Exodus xxxi. 3 (P), and in the skill of the women who made the priestly garments, Exodus xxviii. 3 (P).[5] We have something of the same type, though in a developed stage, of the skill of the Messianic King, Isaiah xi. 2, which is of the same type as that Wisdom by whom (which) 'princes rule, and nobles, and all the judges of the earth', Proverbs

[1] The Hebrew is 'leapt'.

[2] Cf. Qat of the Melanesians, Mawi of the Maoris, and the Transformer of general native lore, especially in respect of his irresponsibility and puckishness. See P. Radin, *Monotheism among Primitive Peoples* (1924), pp. 22–9.

[3] See pp. 38 *f.*, above.

[4] Probably the elder sons's inheritance, Deuteronomy xxi. 17. Elisha is to be Elijah's heir.

[5] Compare the similar occupation in 2 Kings xxiii. 7.

viii. 16. It is the '*ruach-Stoff*' of which Paul Volz writes,[1] when he says, 'it is not anything personal, but a stuff, a fluid'. Here again we have the old[2] error of trying to force undeveloped ideas into modern categories. It cannot be said that *mana* is either personal or impersonal, but in any case it is divine power, and the man who possesses it, is 'a man of God', Deuteronomy xxxiii. 1; Joshua xiv. 6; and very often of Elisha. Whatever it is that he does, he does it superbly, and all because he is possessed of[3] more-than-human power.

The Idea is Ethicized

At first superhumanness and abnormality is all that is required of the *ruach-adonai*, but gradually the idea is ethicized as well as personalized. The ethicizing process can best be seen in the story of the transference of the kingdom from Saul to David. In the first part of that story, that part which deals with the choice of Saul, the two phrases *ruach-adonai* and *ruach-elohim* are used without any difference of interpretation in the variation, 1 Samuel x. 6, 10, xi. 6. But with the choice of David a change appears. In 1 Samuel xvi. 13 it says that 'the *ruach-adonai* leapt upon David from that day forward'. According to the next verse, 'the *ruach-adonai* had departed from Saul, and an evil *ruach* from *adonai* (the Lord) terrified[4] him'. Henceforward we get the phrases *ruach-elohim* and 'an evil *ruach-elohim*' used of Saul and his servants, 1 Samuel xvi. 15, 16, 23, xviii. 10, xix. 20, 23. The writers seem to have been guided by two fixed principles. They were determined to retain the phrase *ruach-adonai* for the king whom the Lord had chosen, i.e. for the Messianic King. They wished to avoid saying that the *ruach-adonai* was evil. They permitted themselves to say that the *ruach-elohim* was evil, doubtless intending *elohim* to be understood in the profane sense.[5] On the change-over from Saul

[1] *Der Geist Gottes* (1912), S. 23.

[2] See pp. 38 *ff.*, above.

[3] When we say 'possessed of', we mean that the more-than-human power possessed him rather than he it.

[4] The root is frequently used of the awful terror occasioned by the onset of Deity, resulting in a dismay and desolation which is beyond expression.

[5] See Genesis xxxi. 53, where *elohim* is used of the god(s) of Nahor. The Massoretic text has the note *chol* (profane) to show that whereas the *elohim* of Abraham refers to Jehovah, the *elohim* of Nahor does not. R.V. preserves the intention of the Massoretes with the word 'gods' in the margin. The phrase *ruach-elohim* has this invidious meaning attached to it only in these particular chapters of 1 Samuel.

to David, they used the phrase 'an evil *ruach* from *adonai*'. The case of 1 Samuel xix. 9 is peculiarly informative as to this editorial process. The Hebrew Text reads, 'the *ruach-adonai* was evil to Saul', as in the R.V. margin. It is strange that the Massoretes let this pass, for whilst they allowed to pass 'an evil *ruach* from *adonai*', they have avoided saying that the *ruach-adonai* was evil. The Septuagint has completed the pious editorial work which here the Massoretes left unfinished by reading *theou* (*elohim*) instead of *kuriou* (*adonai*).[1] Lucian omitted the word *adonai* altogether,[2] but Rahlfs quotes one minuscule as adding 'from God' after 'Saul'. The English Versions, including the Douai, have not gone quite so far as this, but repeat the phrase of 1 Samuel xvi. 14: 'an evil *ruach* from *adonai*'. This is found in Luther also. We thus see that the turning point is 1 Samuel xvi. 13, the verse where it is stated that David has been anointed by Samuel. After this, Saul still 'prophesies', i.e. he is still seized with fits of ungovernable behaviour, but the *ruach-adonai* is that power of Jehovah by which the true Messianic King is inspired. It is therefore this spirit which clothed Amasai,[3] and caused him to affirm his allegiance to the true king whom Jehovah had chosen. In 2 Samuel xxiii. 2 we find a link between the idea of inspired utterance and the power of the Messianic King.

The climax, as we have said, is the *ruach-adonai* by which the prophets are inspired. It comes from on high, Isaiah xxxii. 15; it is good, Nehemiah ix. 20; Psalm cxliii. 10. The spirit of Jehovah was upon the Servant of the Lord, Isaiah xlii. 1; upon Israel's seed (?), Isaiah xliv. 3; and upon the redeemed who were to come to Zion, Isaiah lix. 21. It is that spirit which will engender in the revived Israel a new heart and a new spirit, Ezekiel xxxvi. 26, 27, xxxvii. 14. It inspired the prophet of the Lord who was anointed to preach good tidings to the meek, Isaiah lxi. 1, etc., and in the latter days God will pour out His spirit upon all flesh, Joel ii. 28 *f.* (iii. 1 *f.*). The *ruach-adonai* cannot be hindered (is not 'straitened'), but is like His word, which shall not return unto Him void, but will accomplish that which He pleases, Isaiah lv. 11.

[1] So Codex Vaticanus, but not Codex Alexandrinus, which follows the Hebrew Text, as does Origen.

[2] So also one Hebrew MS. (Kenn., 128).

[3] Either Abiathar or Amasa. See the commentaries.

Ruach as a Synonym for God

There is a tendency to use the word *ruach* with a suffix as an equivalent of the Sacred Name, just as the phrases 'Thy Name' and 'Thy Presence' are used, Haggai ii. 5; Zechariah iv. 6, vi. 8; Psalms cvi. 33, cxxxix. 7; Isaiah xxx. 1, xxxiv. 16. Such use tends to be late rather than early. The most difficult case is Isaiah xlviii. 16, 'The Lord hath sent me and his spirit'. If 'His spirit' is the object, then we have to choose between the explanation of Rabbi Sa'adya, 'the Lord God hath sent me with His Holy Spirit (the spirit of prophecy)', and the separation of the spirit from God, an idea wholly unacceptable in Jewish circles. It may be that the end of the verse is missing, in which case *rucho* (His spirit) could be treated as being in parallel with 'the Lord God'.

Conclusion

The word *ruach* stands for power, strength, life, and all is of God, and from God. The phrase *ruach-adonai* stands for that special power by which God inspires the individual man, enabling him to do the will of God, and thus to do those things which in his own strength he is wholly unable to do.

Chapter VIII

THE DISTINCTIVE IDEAS OF THE OLD TESTAMENT AS THEY APPEAR IN THE NEW TESTAMENT

We have discussed the distinctive ideas of the Old Testament, those ideas which make the Old Testament what it is, and, as being what it is, distinct from any other book whatsoever. These ideas are (1) Righteousness, always more than ethical, with a steady bias on behalf of the poor and weak, tending towards Salvation or to a benevolence that is far beyond strict justice, and at last opposed to it; (2) the Love of God for man, (*a*) His election-love for Israel, unconditioned, sovereign, and undeserved, (*b*) His covenant-love for Israel, conditioned by the existence of the covenant, sovereign, steadfast, and undeserved, going far beyond the measure of what is required; (3) the love of Israel (Man) for God, humble, dutiful, and issuing in *pietas*; (4) the *ruach-adonai* (spirit of the Lord) as the life-giving, energy-giving power of God in the lives of individual men, enabling them to do what otherwise, and in their normal strength, they would be quite unable to do.

Our object in the present chapter is to examine the extent to which these distinctive ideas of the Old Testament are the basis of the New Testament also. We believe that this is the case. There are transformations because of the Incarnation, the language is Greek and not Hebrew, but the Old Testament is the foundation of the New. The message of the New Testament is in the Hebrew tradition as against the Greek tradition. Our tutors to Christ are Moses and the Prophets, and not Plato and the Academies.

The Septuagint is the Bridge between the Two Testaments

The generally accepted approach to the New Testament is to insist in the first place that the New Testament is written in the common (*Koine*) Greek of the period, and forthwith to interpret much as any other Hellenistic book. This allowed for Aramaisms, Latinisms, and the like, for Hellenistic Greek varied to this extent from place to place. But mainly it involved the study of Hellenistic Greek in the inscriptions, the papyri, and in such Hellenistic writers as Polybius and Josephus. It has not involved, to any marked extent, the study of the Greek Bible, the Septuagint, which for 400 years was the Bible of the Christian Church.[1]

This procedure has been sound so far as syntax and grammar are concerned, and a great step forward from the old approach whereby New Testament Greek was compared with classical Greek, weighed in the balances, and found wanting. To have studied the grammar and the syntax of Septuagint would have been worse than useless, since Septuagint is largely translation Greek. But the neglect of the Septuagint from the point of view of the meaning of the words has been serious. It is becoming more and more clear, thanks to such studies as Dr. C. H. Dodd's *The Bible and the Greeks* that considerable attention must be paid to the way in which the Septuagint translators rendered the Hebrew words. The Greek word in the Septuagint tends to carry the meaning of the original Hebrew word, and not its own meaning as a normal Greek word. In many cases, perhaps in most cases, the neglect of this distinction is of little account, and entails no serious error. But the cases where it does make a very great deal of difference are precisely those cases where we are dealing with the distinctive ideas of the Old Testament. These ultimately are the only cases that matter. Dr. Dodd gives a diagram[2] which is most instructive from this point of view, showing how the Septuagint *nomos* (law) is exactly equivalent to the Hebrew *torah*. So also is the *nomos* of John. On the other hand, surprisingly for those who pin their faith to the essential Judaism of the General Epistle of James, the use there is entirely Greek. Paul covers the whole range, both Hebrew and Greek, with the varied meanings of Teaching (Hebrew), Principle (Greek), and Law (both). Such a study as this makes it clear that the old procedure, whereby the study of a word in the Greek New Testament began with Plato and Aristotle or even with Homer and the tragedians,[3] could be entirely misleading, and might be even erroneous. It is essential, especially if the word in question is a religious word, to begin with Septuagint, and to notice to what extent Septuagint used the word

[1] Compare the number of references to inscriptions and papyri with those to the Septuagint in J. H. Moulton, *Grammar of New Testament Greek* (3rd ed., 1908), Vol. I, pp. 257, 291, and 259–62, 291 *f.*

[2] *The Bible and the Greeks*, p. 41.

[3] E.g. Sanday and Headlam, *Romans* (I.C.C.), on *dikaiosune*, pp. 28 *f.*

as the equivalent of the original Hebrew, and next to see to what extent the New Testament usage in any writer is covered by this Septuagint use, and then to examine to what extent, as e.g. Paul in the case of *nomos-torah*, the Greek usage also is involved.

The extent to which the Greek of the Septuagint is really Hebrew-Greek has not been recognized in time past as it ought to have been recognized. Particularly is this so, since the medium through which Old Testament ideas came to the Christians in the first place was Greek. We are of the opinion that incalculable harm has been done by this neglect. It began very early. The confusion appears as early as Clement of Alexandria and Origen,[1] and it arose from the fact that these scholars were Hellenists first and Christians second. It was furthered by the fact that all men until Jerome, tended to read the Greek Bible as a Greek book, and with Hellenistic eyes. This lasted till the fifth century, and both learned and unlearned were equally at fault. They interpreted the words as Greek words, just as if Greek had been the original tongue. Later this was done for centuries with the Latin Bible, and it has been the fate of the Bible in every language into which it has been translated. The result of this has been that from a very early stage, Christianity itself has tended to suffer from a translation out of the Prophets and into Plato. Later the master was Cicero, and with the Renaissance, Aristotle. Plato has indeed been made to be 'divine', and Aristotle 'the master of them that know'. The tragedy of Christian theology through the years is the extent to which these statements are true in the matter of 'knowing Christ'. The Reformation was an attempt to restore the original Hebrew setting of the Gospel, and, theologically, to break the shackles of the Greeks. The Revival of classical learning was a reshackling of the Faith, to which many of the Reformers themselves succumbed.

1. RIGHTEOUSNESS IN THE NEW TESTAMENT

The Greek 'Dikaiosune' is the Hebrew 'Tsedaqah'

The verb is *dikaioun, dikaiousthai*; the adjective, *dikaios*; the noun *dikaiosune*. Our contention is that the meaning of these words is governed in the New Testament almost entirely by the meaning of the root *ts-d-q* in the Old Testament. This involves the plea

[1] A. Nygren, *Agape and Eros*, Part. II, Vol. I (tr. by P. S. Watson), pp. 137 *ff*.

that the New Testament owes, in respect of this group of words, practically nothing to the Greek philosophers.

The interpretation of Chrysostom was that *dikaioun* meant 'to make righteous'.[1] This equation held the field for centuries, but is now generally agreed to be wrong. In its place there is offered the rendering 'to declare righteous'. This is said to remove the difficulty of the phrase '*dikaioun* the ungodly', Romans iv. 5; so that it does not mean 'to make righteous the ungodly', but 'to declare righteous the ungodly'. It does not appear to us that the new rendering is any great improvement on the old. It is certainly true that not even God can make the ungodly righteous. He can forgive the ungodly if he comes in faith, repentant and believing; and He does this. But that is not making the ungodly righteous. All moderns are agreed on this. But we cannot see that there is any greater wisdom in the phrase 'declare righteous'. Why should God declare anything, and to whom does He declare it? Is He answerable to anything or to any one outside Himself? Must He justify His ways to men? And if He must do this, why declare the ungodly to be anything? Surely the action of forgiving him and saving him is sufficient and a far more adequate demonstration. Or has God to satisfy some Righteousness, some Necessity outside Himself? Is Righteousness (*dikaiosune*) supreme over God and man? Or does God divide Himself into some perilously united binity of Justice and Mercy, of which the one must be satisfied before the other can come into operation? Such a solution avoids Scylla only to fall into Charybdis.

In non-Biblical Greek, as Dr. Dodd says,[2] *dikaioun ton asebe* ('to justify the ungodly', Romans iv. 5) would mean 'to condemn the ungodly'. Dr. Dodd continues by pointing out that there are two differences between the Septuagint and the non-Biblical use of the verb *dikaioun*[3]. One is that in Septuagint the sense is always favourable, as against the almost entirely unfavourable use in non-Biblical Greek. The other is that Septuagint gives the verb a personal object. These two differences, we would point out, are

[1] *Hom. in Rom.*, VIII (VII), p. 485 E. The passage is quoted at length in Dodd, *The Bible and the Greeks*, p. 58. Compare the discussion in Sanday and Headlam, *ibid.*, pp. 30 *ff*.

[2] *The Bible and the Greeks*, p. 52. The whole section is most important in this connection, and should be contrasted with the treatment in Sanday and Headlam, *Romans*, pp. 30 *ff*. See also p. 167, below.

[3] But see p. 167, below.

both due to the fact that Septuagint is translation Greek, for both are due to the original Hebrew. We doubt whether, in view of these differences and the reason for them, the non-Biblical meaning of *dikaioun* should enter into the discussion at all. The differences are radical, certainly in the one case, and almost certainly in the other. A non-Biblical approach limits the word from the start to the narrower sense of justice which is inseparable from the word in ordinary[1] non-Biblical Greek, and ensures an ethical approach which we have seen to be secondary so far as the Old Testament is concerned. In Hebrew the idea of 'justice' was never paramount, and ultimately *tsedaqah* can be contrasted with 'righteousness' (strict justice). It is therefore best to assume that where there is an original Hebrew, the Septuagint *dikaioun* carries the meanings of the Hebrew *tsadaq*, and that *dikaiosune* (righteousness, justification) means *tsedaqah*.

In Septuagint, the Hebrew root *ts-d-q* in all its forms (noun, verb, etc.) is represented by the *dikaios*-words 452 times out of 476. Of the twenty-four cases where *dikaios*-etc. is not found, eleven are pity (*eleos*, *eleemosune*), one is joy, and four are juridical in the narrowest sense, though in two of these four the MSS. disagree. This means that the Greek group varies almost exactly as the Hebrew group varies. Septuagint never translates 'salvation', though there are many cases where this meaning is certain and plain in the Hebrew. That Septuagint was fully aware that *tsedaqah* meant 'benevolence' going beyond the strict measure of justice is plain from the eleven cases where the rendering is 'mercy, pity', and especially in both the Septuagint and Theodotion of Daniel iv. 27 (24); also in Ezekiel xviii. 19, 21; and perhaps Psalms xxxiii. (LXX, xxxii) 5. In these cases 'the pull away from the idea of "justice" has been strong enough to bring *ts-d-q* out of the field of *dikaiosune* altogether'.[2] Septuagint was evidently fully aware of the tendency always inherent in *ts-d-q*, and knew that 'the idea is far broader than what we usually mean by right and justice'.[3]

We return to the modern rendering of *dikaioun* (to declare righteous). This involves us in holding that God pronounces a

[1] I.e. the more common use as against that in Aristotle and Plato; see Sanday and Headlam, *ibid.*, p. 29 (top).

[2] Dodd, *ibid.*, p. 46.

[3] Skinner, Art. 'Righteousnessin the Old Testament', in *H.D.B.*, iv, p. 274.

man righteous, or declares him to be righteous, when in reality he is nothing of the sort. Sanday and Headlam therefore rightly[1] say that 'the Christian life is made to have its beginning in a fiction'. They continue: 'No wonder that the fact is questioned, and that another sense is given to the words . . . not the attribution of righteousness in idea, but an imparting of actual righteousness.' We cordially agree that it is no wonder. We see no reason why God should indulge in the fiction of declaring the sinner righteous. The sinner is not righteous. Why declare him so? Still less do we see any reason why God should impart righteousness to the sinner. The only reason why such suggestions are made is that righteousness is conceived as being a necessary condition of Salvation. Since it is obvious that actual righteousness is out of the question, it is suggested that righteousness must be either imparted or imputed. That is, a man must have some sort of righteousness before he can be saved, even if either at the price of a fiction, or belonging to some one else. There are two errors here. One is that we have not emancipated ourselves from that very doctrine which Paul spent most of his life in combatting—namely, that salvation is by righteousness. The other is that *dikaiosune* is interpreted as though there were never any Old Testament, either Hebrew or Greek. It cannot be maintained that a man can offer unto God any true righteousness of his own, so he is regarded as offering a fictional righteousness, or some one else's righteousness. The fact which is regarded as fixed is that God must have some sort of righteousness before He saves.

Righteousness is not a Condition of Salvation

The fact of the matter is that God does not require righteousness at all, in any shape or shadow, as a condition of salvation. He requires faith. This involves primarily an utter and complete trust in God, a full recumbency on Him. It involves such repentance as the sinner is capable of at the time, and in that sense it involves a 'full repentance'. True repentance is something which grows with the years of Christian experience, and the truest saint most shows godly sorrow for sin. Righteousness is a result of salvation, and not a condition of it. It is one of the fruits. This is the Gospel according to Paul. We believe it to be the plain teach-

[1] *ibid.*, p. 36.

ing of the Lord Jesus Himself, the Gospel of the New Testament; and we are convinced that the rudiments of it are to be found in the Old Testament also.

As long as we insist upon righteousness, in whatever way, as a condition of salvation, we do not recognize God as Sovereign Lord. Though we honour Him as such with our lips, we still tend in our theology to insist that He must satisfy Righteousness before He can be Mercy. Even a fictional Righteousness will do, but He must satisfy some Righteousness. Either it is a Righteousness to which God and man alike must bow, or it is one half of God which must first be satisfied before the other half can accomplish its (His) saving work. In the first case our theology is based on Aristotle, and *dikaiosune* is the final virtue, an Absolute beyond God.[1] In the other, we have divided the Godhead more surely than any tritheist. We hold therefore most strongly that, according to both Old and New Testaments, God does not require righteousness as a condition of salvation, neither actual, nor imputed, nor imparted. He requires faith, and faith alone. Any other doctrine may be the orthodox doctrine of a part (or parts) of the Christian Church. In that case it ought to be recognized that it arises from the interpretation of the Greek *dikaiosune* and the Latin *justitia* in a non-Biblical way. It is a non-Biblical theology. This is why there appears to be a fiction at the beginning of the Christian life. The fiction is due to wrong assumptions on the part of the interpreter. He is forcing the Biblical teaching into a non-Biblical framework. There is no fiction in the Biblical teaching.

The Juridical Sense is Limited

We would make another criticism of the general modern interpretation of this *dikaios*-group of Greek words. It is said that they have a juridical sense. For instance, Sanday and Headlam assert[2] that 'the constant usage of the Septuagint (O.T. and Apoc.), where the word (i.e. *dikaioun*) occurs some forty-five times' is 'always or almost always with a forensic or judicial sense'. Our objection to this is a double one. In the first place, we do not agree that this statement ought to stand at all as a primary statement. The main statement should be that the Greek verb almost always

[1] *Eth. Nic.*, V, i. 3; V, i. 15. [2] *ibid.*, p. 31.

stands for the Hebrew verb *tsadaq*. In the second place, supposing it to be correct that both verbs have a 'forensic or a judicial sense', this sense is sometimes very attentuated, and can include even such a case as Ecclesiasticus i. 22, 'unjust wrath can never be justified'. The juridical sense here is slight, and it means 'shown to be right' according to common behaviour and standards, or by its results in ordinary life. This latter is the usual 'judicial' sense of the Hebrew verb, as we have seen previously.[1]

The evidence that the Greek *dikaioun* stands in the main for the Hebrew *tsadaq* is as follows. In the twenty-nine cases where the Greek *dikaioun* has a Hebrew equivalent, that equivalent, with six exceptions, is the root *ts-d-q*. The six cases carry the meaning 'to show to be pure' or 'to be pure'. They are: 'vindicate' by successful pleading, 1 Samuel xii. 7; Isaiah i. 17; Micah vii. 9; 'vindicate' by testing successfully, Ezekiel xxi. 13 (18); 'to be pure, make pure', Micah vi. 11; Psalm lxxiii. (LXX, lxxii), 13. The two last cases are comparable to the six cases where Septuagint has translated the Hebrew *tsadaq* by *amemptos* (blameless, Job xxii. 3), or by *katharos* (clean, Genesis xxiv. 8; Isaiah lxv. 5; Job iv. 17) and *katharizein* (Daniel viii. 14: LXX and Theod.). The forensic sense is most to be looked for in the hiphil form *hitsdiq*. This is unfailingly rendered by *dikaioun*. The forensic sense does not appear to have been as obvious to the Septuagint translator of Proverbs xvii. 15 as it is to the moderns, for there the Greek rendering is *dikaion krinein*, i.e. the actual verb 'judge' is inserted in order to make clear the forensic sense.

The evidence for the judicial sense of *dikaioun* in the Septuagint is much slighter than is generally assumed. The instances are quite general and varied, and include the idea of a man or action being pure, just, upright, or of a man justifying his conduct, either in the courts or in the sight of men. The sixteen cases where *dikaioun* in the Septuagint has no Hebrew equivalent are indicative of the general Septuagint use, though there is possibly[2] one exception. In four cases the meaning is 'legal right', Tobit vi. 11, 12, xii. 4; Esther x. 3. The other cases are Ezekiel xliv. 24 and the rest in Ecclesiasticus i. 22, vii. 5, ix. 12, x. 29, xiii. 22, xviii. 2, xviii. 22, xxiii. 20, xxvi. 29, xxxix. 5. The possible exceptional

[1] See pp. 69 *f.*, above, and pp. 167 *f.*, below.

[2] If this is actually an exception, it is of the utmost importance. It is Ecclesiasticus xlii. 2. See below.

case is xlii. 2, where the verb is probably used in the condemnatory sense which is usual in non-Biblical Greek. The phrase *dikaiosai ton asebe* here probably means 'to condemn the ungodly' and not 'to save (justify) the ungodly' as in Romans iv. 5. Both meanings can be made to fit, but firstly, proper punishment is the plain meaning of some of the lines in the context, and, secondly, we doubt whether any one would ever have doubted the condemnatory sense if it has not been for the general Septuagint sense. If the sense is indeed condemnatory, then we have here evidence that the Septuagint sense is not always favourable, and that actually there are two Septuagints, that which has a Hebrew original and that which is in its original Greek.[1] In the former we must expect the word to tend to carry the original Hebrew sense; in the latter, we must expect Greek usage also.

We have said that the juridical sense of *dikaioun* in the Septuagint is much less pronounced than is generally assumed. Here we revert again to the Hebrew *ts-d-q*. It is true that this word is used of procedure in the courts, and that the same occurs in the case of the root *sh-ph-ṭ* to an even greater degree.[2] Generally, however, the place of judgement is not so much a court of law as the whole wide world, the general affairs of men, custom and history. *Mishpaṭ*, as we have seen, can mean 'custom, habit, manner'. Something of the same applies to *tsedaqah*. This word does not often mean justice and right as maintained in the courts, but rather righteousness as it is shown in the affairs of men, but most of all in God's dealings with the Israel of His choice during Israel's long history. Inasmuch, then, as the Hebrew picture did not generally involve a court of law, we suggest that it would be better if we could largely abandon the idea that the Pauline 'justification'-terminology is primarily, or even mainly, 'forensic and judicial'. With Paul also the court is mostly the whole world of human affairs, and the jury is the whole world of man.

We maintain, therefore, that it is a mistaken procedure to commence the study of the Greek verb *dikaioun* from the Greek point of view. It is better to start from the position that *dikaioun* stands for the Hebrew *tsadaq*, and then to carry over into Septuagint the meanings of the Hebrew verb. The same procedure is to be adopted for the Greek *dikaiosune* (righteousness, justification)

[1] Or perhaps is such a free translation that it is equivalent to the original tongue.

[2] See pp. 76*f*,, above.

as standing for the Hebrew *tsedaqah*. These same meanings must be carried over into the New Testament, and all the varied meanings of the Hebrew must be at our disposal for the interpretation of the New Testament words. The judicial meaning of the word, therefore, may sometimes be strong, but usually it is so attentuated as to be without importance. Further, and much more importantly, the ethical meaning is definitely secondary, and *dikaiosune* becomes primarily a salvation-word and not an ethical word.

Paul's Use of 'Dikaiosune' in an Ethical Sense

We do not deny that Paul uses the noun *dikaiosune* (righteousness) in an ethical sense, for anything that is of God must necessarily have such a meaning as part of its content. Paul actually uses the word in a double sense, sometimes in a truly ethical sense, and sometimes in the full sense of salvation, exactly in both respects as the Hebrew *tsedaqah* is used in the Old Testament. The distinction between the two uses is in the main as follows. When Paul speaks of *dikaiosune* in connection with the Law, he means ethical righteousness, as any good scribe would do. Also when he uses *dikaiosune* to stand for one of the results of faith (i.e. as one of the 'fruits of the spirit'), he means ethical righteousness, but with that overplus of more than is required which constitutes one of the differences between ordinary ethics and Christian ethics. But when Paul writes of the *dikaiosune* of God, he means nothing less than Salvation, 'the divine activity in which God gives effect to His redeeming work in Christ'.[1] He never meant *dikaiosune* in any purely Greek sense of the word whatever. Still less did he mean *justitia* in any ordinary Roman sense of the word. This is an example of the way in which the Hebrew Old Testament is essential for the understanding of the New Testament. Without this basis, a knowledge of Hellenistic Greek, and of classical Greek and Latin may be a snare.

The effect of the general assumption that *dikaiosune* in the New Testament means primary ethical rightness (i.e. we must start with the meaning in classical Greek and make it an ethical term first and then fit it into the salvation scheme) is seen in Dr. Vincent Taylor's careful study of the relation between 'justifying faith and

[1] V. Taylor, *Forgiveness and Reconciliation* (1941), p. 79.

righteousness'.[1] Dr. Taylor finds 'neither the Catholic nor the traditionally Protestant explanation . . . satisfactory to the modern mind, although each emphasizes important aspects of the truth'.[2] He believes that 'Reformation teaching is much nearer the Pauline doctrine than the Catholic theology', but that 'it cannot be said to have been successful in surmounting the ethical difficulties of justification'.[3] Dr. Taylor is soundly Protestant in his threefold objection to the Catholic position that 'man is made righteous by the infusion of divine grace'. The word *dikaioun* does not mean 'to make just', and justification is not sanctification. But, on the other hand, he will have nothing to do with any imputed righteousness. He is certain that there is a necessary 'ethical condition for reconciliation',[4] but has to stop short of a righteousness of 'actual holiness and achieved excellence'.[5] The Greek *dikaioun* demands this last, apart from the whole body of Pauline and Reformation theology. There must be, so Dr. Taylor holds, a real righteousness of some kind before a man can have fellowship with God, but he avoids the Catholic position by saying that 'the believer is pronounced righteous because, in virtue of his faith resting upon the work of Christ, he really is righteous in mind and purpose, though not yet in achievement'.[6] Or, again, he refers to 'that righteous mind necessary to communion' with God.[7] Dr. Taylor has insisted upon doing away with every kind of fictional righteousness. He has insisted upon a true ethical condition for reconciliation. In effect, however, he concludes with a righteous intention—that is, a changed heart, changed from sinful thoughts and ways. We quote Dr. Taylor's conclusion: 'Our conclusion, then, is that justification is rightly distinguished from forgiveness, reconciliation, regeneration, conversion, adoption, and sanctification, and that it describes a vital element in the story of man's return to fellowship with God. It is the divine activity in which God gives effect to His redeeming work in Christ by making

[1] *Forgiveness and Reconciliation* (1941), pp. 65–72. The whole subject of Justification is most carefully and precisely treated in pp. 34–82, including a careful survey of the New Testament use of the *dikaioun*-group of words.

[2] *ibid.*, p. 65.

[3] *ibid.*, pp. 67 *f.*

[4] *ibid.*, p. 77.

[5] *ibid.*, p. 70.

[6] *ibid.*, p. 69.

[7] *ibid.*, p. 79.

possible that righteous mind necessary to communion with Himself.'[1] The phrase in which we are chiefly interested here is 'making possible that righteous mind'. This apparently means 'changing his attitude' from his previous state of sin, turning him towards God, giving him a new heart and mind so that by the power of the Spirit he can become righteous in achievement. Justification therefore is the first stage in Salvation, and is actually what the Evangelical Protestant means by 'being saved'. It is followed by Sanctification. Its only condition is faith in Christ and His redeeming work. It is not primarily an ethical term at all, but a salvation term. It is ethical in a secondary sense because it is the preliminary step to those works of righteousness which follow faith. We too, like Dr. Taylor, would distinguish it from forgiveness, reconciliation, and so forth, and exactly on the same grounds as Dr. Taylor sets forth in pp. 77 *f.*, the exception being that we think he has not entirely emancipated himself from the confusion of which he rightly complains, but that he would have done so, if he had not been misled by the Greek meaning of *dikaiosune* into insisting primarily upon an ethical content in justification.

'*Righteousness*' *in the Epistle to the Romans*

We turn to the Epistle to the Romans in order to illustrate our statements as to the way in which Paul uses the word *dikaiosune*.

Romans iii. 21 makes it clear that there is a 'righteousness of God' apart from the Law. When we make the Law a way of salvation, the ethical problem becomes paramount (verse 20). The awareness of sin takes the foremost place. The sin of man, his inability to do what is right (vii. 21) make it impossible that a man should be saved (justified). But there is another way of salvation (a righteousness of God) which is revealed in the Old Testament (the law and the prophets), and this is 'through faith in Jesus Christ', and it is open 'to all who believe'. There is no distinction here. God shows His salvation (righteousness, iii. 25) by 'the passing over of sins done aforetime, in the forbearance of God'. This is the way in which God is *dikaios* (i.e. *tsaddiq*) and the *dikaion* (justifier, i.e. Saviour) 'of him that hath faith in Jesus'. The whole point of the passage is that the fulfilment of the ethical

[1] *ibid.*, p. 79.

demands of the Law is not a condition of salvation. The one condition is faith. This does not mean that God is not concerned about sin. He is concerned about it, and that in part is why He is Saviour. He is most concerned that men should not sin. Therefore He forgives the sinner who comes to Him in faith. Thereafter He enables the sinner to accomplish that righteousness which in his own strength he was unable to do. This 'salvation' is the 'righteousness of God from faith to faith', and that is why the Gospel is 'the power of God unto salvation', i. 16*f*.

In Romans iv. 3 Paul quotes the Septuagint of Genesis xv. 6 that Abraham's faith was reckoned to him *eis*[1] *dikaiosunen* (as righteousness). The context nowhere says that Abraham's conduct was ethically sound; indeed the whole point of the passage is that it was not ethically sound. The most that is said of his ethical purity by Paul is that his sins were not counted against him. In Genesis xv there is nothing at all about his conduct. There his prosperity followed his trust in the promises of God. In Paul, he was forgiven on the basis of his faith. There is nothing about any good action. We hold therefore that it is quite wrong to say that 'these words, he (Paul) argues, "counted as righteous", imply that he (Abraham) had no actual righteousness, but was credited with that which he did not himself possess'.[2] We fail to see that he was credited with anything. He came to God in faith (i.e. in full trust in God, repentant and believing), and because he came thus, he was regarded as having fulfilled the condition for salvation. Paul's whole argument is that this condition is not righteousness at all, but faith. No faith, no salvation. The order is Faith, Salvation, Righteousness. To assume that ethical righteousness, whether actual, imputed, or imparted (infused), is a necessary condition of salvation, is a travesty of Paul's teaching. This assumption is not made by Paul, but by his interpreters. The reason the assumption is 'imputed' to Paul is because the interpreters are still dominated by Greek ideas of *dikaiosune*.

In Romans v. 17 Paul speaks of the 'overplus of grace and of the free gift of salvation'. To insist upon even a fictional righteousness is to deny that it is a free gift. It is making Salvation an exchange,

[1] The construction *eis* is due to the Hebrew use of *le* with the root *c-sh-b*; cf. Winer, *Grammar of New Testament Greek* (3rd ed., by W. F. Moulton, 1882), p. 229.

[2] Dr. Dodd's paraphrase in *The Epistle to the Romans* (Moffatt N.T. Commentary, 1932), p. 68.

a *quid pro quo*, for righteousness, and the exchange is insisted upon even at the price of a fictional transaction. If the righteousness is imparted, then there is no free gift in salvation, but a gift is made in the first place in order that Salvation may not be a free gift.

In Romans v. 21 the contrast is between 'sin' and *dikaiosune*, which we would translate 'salvation', but insisting that it will ultimately issue in ethical righteousness as contrasted with the former sin. This applies also to Romans vi. 13. We find Romans vi. 16 to be most instructive. The R.V. reads 'whether of sin unto death, or of obedience unto *dikaiosune*'. Here the contrast is between sin and obedience, as in the Old Testament prophets, and between death and *dikaiosune*. Evidently *dikaiosune* here is something akin to life, i.e. it means 'salvation'. In the remainder of the chapter *dikaiosune* varies between 'salvation' and that ethical righteousness which is a necessary outcome of it. But in viii. 10 *dikaiosune* is that which gives life to the spirit of man, i.e. it is that power of God which works salvation and issues in right action.

In Romans ix. 30 *f.* we read that 'the Gentiles, which followed not after righteousness (i.e. they did not seek to be ethically righteous according to the Law), attained to "righteousness, even the righteousness which is by faith" (i.e. that salvation which is of faith, the other "righteousness of God"), but Israel, following after a law of righteousness (i.e. seeking to fulfil the ethical demands of the Law as a means of salvation) did not arrive at that Law'. They fell short, as Paul believed that men must always do, and never found salvation. The reason is that the order is faith, salvation, works of righteousness, and not works of righteousness, salvation. In Romans x. 10 the phrase 'belief unto righteousness' means 'faith unto salvation'.

Other passages worthy of consideration are 2 Corinthians iii. 9, where 'righteousness' is the opposite of condemnation; Galatians ii. 15–21, iii. 21; Ephesians iv. 24, v. 9; Philippians iii. 6, 9; Hebrews v. 13, where 'the word of righteousness' is something which is beyond the 'rudiments of the first principles of the gospel'; Titus iii. 5; Hebrews xii. 11, where 'righteousness' and not 'the fruit of righteousness' is the 'peaceable fruit'. See also 1 John i. 9: 'If we confess our sins, he is faithful and *dikaios* to forgive us our sins, and to cleanse us from all unrighteousness'; John xvi. 8–10, where 'righteousness' means the completed Work of Christ.

An illustration of the use of the verb *dikaioun* can be seen in Romans v. 9, 'being "justified" by his blood when we were yet sinners', where we would translate 'saved'. Another case is Galatians ii. 17, where Paul is actually combatting the idea that 'justified' is to be interpreted as having to do with ethics. There is, on the other hand, one clear instance where Paul is strictly ethical in his use of *dikaios*—namely, in the distinction which he draws between the 'just' (*dikaios*) man and the 'good' (*agathos*) man. Here *dikaios* is the man who is correct in his conduct and no more, whereas *agathos* includes those kindlier feelings which are more than the strict measure of ethics requires.

2. THE LOVE OF GOD TO MAN

In the Old Testament the Love of God is manifested in two ways: firstly, in His choice of Israel, and, secondly, in His continued love for Israel. The first is *'ahabah,* that election-love with which He chose Israel out of all the families of the earth. The second is *chesed*, that persistent, determined, unfailing covenant-love, by which He showed His great mercy to Israel, His covenant-people, in spite of all their rebellion and waywardness. What do these two words become when they are transferred into their new environment? What are their New Testament Greek equivalents? And what effect has God's redeeming activity in Christ upon these Old Testament idcas?

(*a*) *God's Election-love*

The Hebrew ''Ahabah' and the Greek 'Agape'. There was never any doubt concerning the first, for the Septuagint had already invented a Greek word to stand for the Hebrew *'ahabah.* That word is *agape*. It is not found before Septuagint,[1] though the verb *agapao* and its derivatives are common enough in Greek of all periods.[2] The New Testament writers therefore found a word already to hand, with a specialized meaning already involved.

The word *agape* is not common in the Septuagint, sixteen times only where there is a Hebrew equivalent, and always for *'ahabah.* This latter occurs some thirty times altogether, and, apart from *agape* (sixteen times), it is represented by the verb *agapao*

[1] J. H. Moulton, *Exp. Times*, XXVI, 3 (December, 1914), p. 139.

[2] Notably *agapao* in Plato, and *agapazo* in Homer and Pindar.

(one), the classical *agapesis* (seven), *euphrosune*, 'joy' (one), and, to complete the list, *philia* (five, all in Proverbs). The word *philia* is frequent in the Apocrypha (twenty-eight times), and twice more in Proverbs. Where, therefore, we get Greek influence rather than Hebrew influence, i.e. in the Apocrypha and in the freely-translated Proverbs, we get *philia* and not *agape*. No noun for 'love' occurs very often in the Old Testament, either Hebrew or Greek. This is because Hebrew has very few abstract nouns, and they are mostly late. Where we do actually find a noun for 'love' it is *'ahabah* in the Hebrew, and *agape* in the Greek.

The Hebrews did not think of love as an idea or as an abstraction, they thought of it as an activity. Here, as always, their emphasis was on what happens. This is why the Hebrew verb *'aheb* occurs in overwhelming proportions as against the noun. The verb is rarely translated by anything else than *agapao*.

Paul therefore takes over the Greek Old Testament *agape*, when he speaks of the Love of God for man. He gives it the full meaning of *'ahabah*, that free election-love of God for man. He chose it definitely in preference to *philia*, and the verb *agapao* in preference to *phileo*. Grimm-Thayer gives[1] the distinction between *agapao* and *phileo*—the former 'properly denotes a love founded in admiration, veneration, esteem, like the Latin *diligere*', whereas *phileo* 'denotes an inclination prompted by sense and emotion'. This distinction cannot hold for the Septuagint when it is expressed in this form, for the one thing that is certain about God's *'ahabah* for Israel is that it is not founded upon admiration and esteem for Israel. But the distinction between the two verbs can be cast into another form, namely *agapao* denotes a deliberate love, a love that chooses, whereas *phileo* denotes a love that is unpremeditated, an emotional, spontaneous love. This we hold to be a sounder definition than that offered by Grimm-Thayer, for the real point of departure in the discussion of the difference between the two verbs is that *phileo* is an emotional, sudden uprising which has no reason in it anywhere, either in the lover or the loved one, whilst *agapao* denotes a love that is deliberate on the part of the lover. This is true of God's *agape* for man. It is a deliberate love, a selective love, a love that chooses. *Agape* is 'uncaused' in the sense that no reason for it can be found in the loved one. *Philia* is an emotional love for which there is no proper

[1] *Greek-English Lexicon of the New Testament*, (4th ed., 1898), p. 653.

reason anywhere; it might happen to anybody for anybody. There is no element of deliberate choice in it. We presume that the Septuagint translators knew very well what they were doing when they used *agapao* in preference to *phileo*, and *agape* in preference to *philia*.

The Christian 'Agape'. But there is a difference in the New Testament, for the middle wall of partition is broken down. The Old Covenant has gone, and in its place is the New Covenant, sealed in the blood of Christ. *Agape* therefore is no longer God's election-love for 'Israel after the flesh'. It is wider and includes men of every nation and tongue, even as many as the Lord our God shall call. It opens the new way for fellowship between God and man, the new way of 'righteousness', i.e. Salvation.

Further, *agape* is used also of the Christian's love for his fellows. It is described in 1 Corinthians xiii. This is not man's love for man, for which by that time *philia* would be used. It is the love of a man who is 'in Christ', and therefore of one who loves his fellows with the sort of love wherewith Christ first loved him. It is not self-love (*eros*), neither is it general humanitarian love (*philia*). It is love like the love of God for man. That is why it 'seeketh not its own, . . . taketh no account of evil, . . . beareth all things, believeth all things, hopeth all things, endureth all things'. This is why '*agape* never faileth'. It is not dependent to the least degree upon the worth or the actions of the loved one, but only on the lover. This is exactly what we have seen to be the case with God's love for man. The fatal compromise of Augustine in *caritas* (charity) is one of the great calamities of the history of Christian theology.[1] It is rivalled only by the present-day notion that Justice must come first. It is true that Justice must come before *philia*, but not before *agape*.

(*b*) *God's Covenant-love*

But what was to be done with reference to God's covenant-love, His *chesed* for Israel? This was gone, in so far as it was confined to the people of His choice, 'Israel after the flesh'. There was now no such thing. In any case *chesed*, when used of God, had come to mean 'mercy, loving-kindness, pity', being represented by the Greek *eleos*, or *eleemosune*. Paul uses *eleos*, for the most part, to

[1] A. Nygren, *Agape and Eros*, especially Part II, Vol. II, pp. 231–344.

mean pity for man's misery. But what of God's covenant-love for those whom He has chosen? Here Paul uses *charis* (grace), the Septuagint equivalent for the Hebrew *chen*, which describes favour where there is no recognized tie between the two parties, and where there is no obligation upon the part of the superior to do anything at all. The word *charis* stands for the free gift of God's favour and love. Nothing impressed Paul more than the fact that God's love for man was a free gift from God, entirely undeserved on man's part, depending only upon God's own Will.

We have spoken of God's election-love and God's covenant-love separately, as though they were two different loves. This, of course, is not the case. The love which chose Israel in the first place is also the love which preserved the Israel that had been chosen. God's *chesed* for chosen Israel is also His *'ahabah* through which He chose Israel. *Chesed* is God's love as Israel experienced it, whilst *'ahabah* is God's love which first enabled Israel to experience it. In the same way God's *agape*, His election-love for the New Israel, is also His Grace (*charis*). Paul tends to use the two words interchangeably. God's love (*agape*) is that love which God continuously manifests towards the sons of men. It is also His Grace (*charis*) in the sense that it is wholly and entirely God's free gift to man. *Charis* is therefore prevenient Grace and covenanted Grace. It is the basis of the first stirring in the human heart by which we are brought to God—that is, it is effectual election-love. It is also that free gift of God by which we find daily strength in every time of need. It is post-election-love in the sense that no man realizes anything of it at all, unless first he be chosen in the love of God. The Christian knows God's love as God's supreme gift to Him, undeserved and in abundance. He knows it as a redemptive Power in the world, because he first knows it as this in his own personal experience. It is not correct to say that Grace is God's love in action, for there is no love of God that is not active. Grace is God's boundless and undeserved love for man as it is realized in man's experience of it, particularly in its aspect of undeserved favour. This latter idea of undeserved favour is essential to the New Testament meaning of Grace (*charis*). Contrast Wisdom iii. 14: 'there shall be given him for his faithfulness (*pistis*) chosen grace (*charis eklekte*)'.

3. MAN'S LOVE TO GOD

Here once more we get a difference, though not this time such a transformation. We have seen that in the Old Testament the Hebrew *'aheb* and the Greek *agapao* are used of man's love to God equally as well as of God's love to man. The same is true of the Hebrew *'ahabah* and the Greek *agape*, though the noun is used once only of man's love to God, and then in a simile, Jeremiah ii. 2.

Not 'Agape'

Paul, however, rarely speaks of *agape* in the sense of man's love for God. This curious fact was noticed with surprise long ago by Augustine, who realized that when Paul uses *caritas* (so the Vulgate), he generally means man's love for his neighbour, and very rarely man's love for God. It is not quite accurate to say that it means man's love for his neighbour, rather it means the Christian's love for his neighbour. This we have seen to be because the Christian is 'in Christ'. Therefore his love for his neighbour is of the same type as Christ's love for him, that is, it is *agape* and not *philia*. This curious absence has to be coupled with the fact that in spite of the statement of the Lord Jesus that love to God is the greatest Commandment of all,[1] Paul apparently exalts the second commandment into being the summary of the whole Law, 'Thou shalt love thy neighbour as thyself', Romans xiii. 9.

Why does not Paul use *agape* of man's love to God? As Professor Nygren says, this 'can indeed be no accident', 'the matter must be one of principle'.[2] His explanation is that *agape* is spontaneous and creative. 'In relation to God, man is never fully "spontaneous". Man's self-giving to God is no more than a response; . . . It lacks all the essential marks of Agape.'[3] And that, says he, is why it requires a different name. This explanation certainly provided a good reason why *agape* is not used of man's love to God, but it provides no reason for Paul's use of *pistis* (the noun) and *pisteuo* (the verb) to describe man's relation to God, i.e. Faith, to have faith in (believe).

[1] Matthew xxii. 37; Mark xii. 30, 33; Luke x. 27.

[2] *Agape and Eros*, Part I (Eng. tr. by A. G. Hebert), pp. 91, 92; cf. the whole section, pp. 90–3.

[3] *ibid.*, p. 92.

Paul uses 'Pistis'

Our explanation is that the characteristic feature of man's love to God in the Old Testament is that it is a humble, dutiful, and obedient love. It issues in humble godliness, that filial love (*pietas*) which is shown in humble and dutiful, loving obedience to God's Will.[1] It involves a humble confidence, a deeply rooted trust, completely loving and utterly devoted. The relations between the New Testament words *pistis* (faith) and *pisteuo* (have faith in, believe in), and the uses of the same words in ordinary Greek and in Septuagint, are discussed by Dr. C. H. Dodd.[2] He shows that there was already in Greek a use of the verb to express 'confidence in God', in the sense of accepting His revelation as true.[3] This is the basis of the main Pauline use of both verb and noun. The use of the Greek verb *pisteuo* with the dative is, in such cases, comparable with the Hebrew use of the hiphil form of the verb *'aman* with the preposition *be*. Compare especially Psalm cvi (LXX, cv), 12, where 'trusting in God' involves trusting in His words. In as much as these words, *pistis* and *pisteuo*, stand in the Septuagint regularly for the Hebrew root *'-m-n*, it is safe to say that in Septuagint they always involve to some extent the idea of 'trust'. Paul therefore has followed Hebrew usage through the Septuagint use of *pistis-pisteuo* as equivalents of the Hebrew root *'-m-n*. This he developed into loving trust and active confidence in a specifically Christian sense. *Pistis* (faith, confidence, complete reliance) thus comes to be used as the outstanding term for the Christian's attitude to God, just as *agape* (love) is the outstanding term for God's attitude to the Christian. The interpretation of 'faith' to mean 'belief' arises from the Greek associations of *pistis* and later from the Latin association of *fides*. The meaning 'belief' is found in the General Epistle of James. He used *pistis* in its Greek sense, and not in its Septuagint-Hebrew sense. He did exactly the same thing with *nomos* (law).[4] It is not surprising, therefore, that he finds himself at variance with the Apostle Paul in the oft-quoted James ii. 17. James and Paul are talking about different things when they use the words *pistis* and *nomos*. Paul uses both words in the Hebrew as well as in the Greek sense, but

[1] Pp. 94, 123.
[2] *The Bible and the Greeks*, pp. 65–70.
[3] Xenophon, *Mem.*, I, i. 1–5.
[4] C. H. Dodd, *The Bible and the Greeks*, p. 41

in the Hebrew sense when he is doctrinal and theological. James used both words in the Greek sense.

4. THE *RUACH-ADONAI:* THE SPIRIT OF GOD: THE HOLY SPIRIT

The New Testament *pneuma* (spirit) is used in all the ways in which the Hebrew *ruach* (breath, wind, spirit) is used. It is used of the wind (John iii. 8), of human breath, both ordinarily (2 Thessalonians ii. 8) and of the breath which means life (Revelation xi. 11). It is used of the vital principle in man (Luke viii. 55, etc.); as opposed to 'flesh' (*sarx*, 'flesh', thus being in Paul equivalent to the Hebrew *basar*) of disposition (Luke i. 17, etc.). In addition we find it used of incorporeal spirits of every type, angels and evil spirits, and of disembodied human beings, that is of both 'spirits' and 'ghosts'. This actually is an extension of such ideas as that of the evil spirit which troubled Saul (1 Samuel xvi. 14, xviii. 10), though by this time it is fully recognized that no such evil spirit could come from God, but from Beelzebub[1] the prince of devils, Matthew xii. 24. It is a use of *pneuma* as exactly equivalent to the Hebrew use of *ruach* as an outside power which comes upon a man, sometimes quite suddenly, and controls him. Just as the jealous husband is dominated and driven by a '*ruach* of jealousy' (Numbers v. 14, 30: P), so a spirit can take a child, tear 'him that he foameth', and with difficulty depart from him, Luke ix. 39. The very phrase 'possessed of an evil (unclean) spirit' shows that *pneuma*, like *ruach*, is regarded in these cases as the controlling power.

But we are concerned chiefly with the development in the New Testament of the Old Testament *ruach-adonai* (spirit of the Lord). In the Synoptic Gospels, the phrase *pneuma kuriou* (spirit of the Lord) and its equivalent *pneuma theou* (spirit of God) is chiefly Old Testament in its significance. Even when it is applied to the Lord Jesus Christ it still is either the life-creating spirit of Genesis i. 2 (LXX) and Ezekiel xxxvii or that same *ruach-adonai* by which the prophets were inspired. The former finds expression in the birth stories of Matthew and Luke, and both in the account of the Baptism common to all three Gospels.[2] It is true that the Spirit of God descended uniquely upon Him, but the use of the phrase *pneuma theou* (spirit of God) is closely allied to Old Testament usage.

[1] Cf. 2 Samuel xxiv. 1 and 1 Chronicles xxi. 1.

[2] Notice the reference to the dove in Rashi's comment on Genesis i. 2.

The Gospel According to St. John

The same general position is seen in the Fourth Gospel. In iii. 8 *pneuma* is used of the wind, though immediately it is compared with 'the spirit' of God, which itself determines whither it shall go and whom it shall inspire and control. The psychological use is also found, and again with the same idea of dominating emotion, e.g. xi. 33, 'moved with indignation in spirit' (R.V. margin), and xiii. 21, 'troubled in spirit'. But in this Gospel the special Christian use becomes clear. Here *to pneuma* (the Spirit), *to hagion pneuma* (the Holy Spirit), and *to pneuma tes aletheias* (the spirit of truth), are used to denote that convincing, convicting Power of God which will be given after the Lord Jesus has been glorified.

This life-giving Spirit is spoken of in vi. 63, but it is plain that the writer refers to that Spirit which bursts into full activity after the Lord Jesus is glorified, vii. 39. He is the Paraclete, the 'Comforter'. By the power of this Spirit a man is born 'from above' (iii. 7: R.V. margin). This is that birth 'of water (i.e. baptism) and of spirit' by which a man enters into the Kingdom of God, iii. 5. The contrast is made between those who are born of the flesh, and those who are born of the spirit, iii. 6. The former is a birth into ordinary human life (*bios*), which ceases with what we call death. The latter is a birth into eternal life (*zoe*), life in the spirit, and this does not cease with what we call death. This Spirit is of God, and God is *pneuma* (Spirit). Because it is a birth of *pneuma*, we hold it to be better to follow the R.V. margin in iii. 7 and translate (as we have done immediately above) 'from above' in preference to 'anew'. The Spirit is of God, and is quite distinct from anything which is from below, of flesh (*sarx*). This is the old Hebrew contrast between *ruach* (spirit) and *basar* (flesh). It is noticeable that nowhere is this 'heavenly *pneuma*', this *pneuma* which survives mortality, spoken of as belonging to man. It is of God, and it is God's gift to man. 'No man can come unto Me' says the Lord Jesus, 'except it be given him of the Father.'

Paraclete means Convictor

There are two important matters to be pointed out in connection with the words and phrases used of the Holy Spirit in the Fourth Gospel. The first is that the word Paraclete means Convictor rather than Comforter. The Greek verb *parakaleo* is in this respect the equivalent of the Hebrew *nacham*, of which it is one of the general equivalents in Septuagint. This Hebrew root does not mean 'comfort' in the ordinary English sense of that word. It means 'comfort *out of* sorrow', and not 'comfort *in* sorrow'. It involves the cessation of sorrow. The root is associated again and again in the Old Testament with the idea of change of mind, heart, intention. It is therefore not without reason that it is often translated in the Old Testament by 'repent'. Indeed, in A.V. the English word 'repent' occurs forty-six times,[1] and in forty-three cases the Hebrew root is *nacham*, against thrice *shub* (return, turn back, repent). Similarly the English word 'comfort' and kindred forms of the same word stands for the Hebrew *nacham* some sixty-four times. The Hebrew word *nacham* is therefore a conversion word, and the same applies to *parakaleo*, even in the majority of cases where the reference is to tears and sorrow. It should be recognized as being a conversion word in the Fourth Gospel also. The Holy Spirit is not that Spirit which comforts the disciples after the Lord Jesus has been glorified, but rather that Spirit which convinces them of the truth of the things of Christ.

'Aletheia' sometimes means 'Faith'

The second matter concerns the phrase *to pneuma tes aletheias* (the Spirit of Truth), xv. 26. If this phrase is translated into Hebrew, it is *ruach 'emeth*, i.e. 'spirit of confidence, reliance, faith'. In Septuagint, the Hebrew word *'emeth* (or its equivalent, *'emunah*) is represented by *pistis* and by *aletheia*. We have seen[2] that Paul uses *pistis* to describe the attitude of the Christian to God, and that this word in Paul has the meaning of 'full reliance, complete trust, recumbency' because of this Septuagint association with the Hebrew *'emeth*. We suggest that the author of the Fourth Gospel tends to use *aletheia* in a similar way, and also because of the use of this Greek word in Septuagint as an equivalent of the Hebrew *'emeth*. We would therefore translate *to pneuma tes aletheias* not by 'spirit of truth', but by 'spirit of reliability, faith', or even by 'spirit which creates faith'. This involves translating *aletheia* in its Septuagint sense as equivalent to *'emeth*, and not in its Greek sense of truth as against a lie, or of reality as against appearance. Thus

[1] Including 'repentance' once, and 'repentings' twice.

[2] P. 178, above.

aletheia in the Fourth Gospel has sometimes a meaning closely akin to Paul's *pistis*. This might well explain why *pistis* is not in the vocabulary of the Fourth Gospel, even though *pisteuo*, the verb is found so often. We do not hold that *aletheia* always has this tendency to mean 'faith', in the Pauline sense, in this Gospel, but, rather, that it tends to vary between the true Greek and the true Septuagint meanings, just as indeed *pisteuo* varies between 'have faith in' and 'believe'.

The Acts of the Apostles

In the Acts of the Apostles the gift of (the) Holy Spirit crystallizes in the experience of Pentecost, when first the Apostles received 'power from on high', Luke xxiv. 49; Acts i. 8. They are enabled 'to speak with other tongues, as the Spirit gave them utterance', ii. 4. It is a gift of God. It is associated with baptism (ii. 38), as in John iii. 5 ('water and spirit'). By this power, Peter speaks with authority to rulers and elders, iv. 8. The company of Christians, as they came later to be called, are 'filled with the Holy Ghost' and they speak 'the word of God with boldness', iv. 31. And so throughout the book, the gift of Holy Spirit is given to individuals, just as in the Old Testament, but here they are bound together into 'one heart and soul', iv. 32. It is characteristic of the working of the Holy Spirit that this fellowship is created, a new Messianic community, of which the test is not Abraham's sons after the flesh, but Abraham's sons according to the Spirit. The Word of God is spoken in and through this fellowship, by those who believe, and by them in the power of the Holy Spirit. This same Holy Spirit also works in the hearts of individuals, bringing them to conviction and change of heart and mind, and uniting them into the fellowship of those that believe. The Church, that is, is the channel of the Word, though not of Grace.

The Pauline Writings

In the writings of Paul the doctrine of the Holy Spirit is central. Everything depends upon His effective working. Herein is the full and effective working of *agape* (the love of God to man). He convicts men of sin; He sows in men's hearts the seed of true repentance; He turns men to God. Here is the Old Testament *ruach-adonai* (the Spirit of the Lord) in fullest activity. He takes hold of a man, controls him, gives to him a power that is not his own. Here we have no longer an activity of God. He is God Himself, manifest once in the flesh in the Lord Jesus, and now manifest in human lives. The identification both with the realization of the ancient *ruach-adonai* as a 'mystery' now revealed to the initiated, and with the Lord Jesus (2 Corinthians iii. 17), is complete and clear.

It is generally agreed that in his antithesis between *pneuma* (spirit) and *sarx* (flesh), Paul is dependent upon Old Testament ideas, as also for his whole concept of the constitution of man.[1] Paul makes a sharp contrast between the things of God and the the things of man. In this distinction he is true to the Old Testament tradition of the *ruach-adonai* as that Power of God which descends upon a man, changes his heart and spirit, gives him new life and, in New Testament phrase, makes him a child of God. We do not propose to enter into a detailed discussion of the use and meaning of the term 'Holy Spirit' in the writings of Paul, but only with reference to the particular point of the relation between the 'soul' (*psyche*) and the *pneuma* (spirit) of man on the one hand, and the Spirit of God on the other. Here mostly we find, during the centuries of Christian interpretation, a marked tendency erroneously to interpret the Pauline material in a Greek rather than in a Hebrew framework.

The Spirit of Man

Paul certainly uses the word *pneuma* of the spirit of a man, e.g. Romans i. 9, 'whom I serve in my spirit . . .', and Galatians vi. 18, 'The grace of our Lord Jesus Christ be with your spirit, brethren.' Parallel to these cases, and more significant, since these two cases concern converted men, is 1 Corinthians ii. 11: 'For who among men knoweth the things of a man, save the spirit of a man, which is in him?' Origen held[2] that the word *pneuma* (spirit) here includes both intellect and conscience, but it is better not to define the precise meaning more than to say that Paul is referring to the controlling, directive power in man. Particularly we regard it as unfortunate that the conscience should be introduced here, since the conscience is a human faculty, included in the *psyche* ('soul') and not in *pneuma* (spirit). We therefore deprecate such an inter-

[1] Sanday and Headlam, *Romans* (I.C.C.), p. 181.

[2] *Comm. in Rom.* ii. 15.

pretation as 'man's entire intellectual and moral nature',[1] since Paul is thinking in terms of the Hebrew *ruach* (spirit) rather than of Plato's *ho entos anthropos* (the inner man).

Paul's main use of the word *pneuma* as the spirit of man is in definite contrast to the Spirit of God, this being, as we have indicated, an inheritance from the Old Testament. The distinction is very clear in 1 Corinthians ii. Here it is the Spirit of God who reveals the true wisdom of God to men. These things of God are received by the spiritual (*pneumatikos*) man, and not by the 'natural' (*psychikos*) man—that is, not by the human faculties. Man as man cannot know these things. They are not within the sphere of the 'soul' (*psyche*). It is clear from this that Paul does not use the word *psyche* either in the Homeric sense of that which survives death or the sense of the Greek philosophers as the immortal soul or spirit of man. That which is 'psychic' is earthy, doomed to death; that which is raised up is 'pneumatic'. The whole matter is made clear by Dr. H. Wheeler Robinson, both in his article, 'Hebrew Psychology in Relation to Pauline Anthropology',[2] and in his *The Christian Doctrine of Man* (1913), pp. 104–36.

It is, we hold, of the utmost importance to realize what actually is the New Testament teaching concerning the work of the Spirit of God. By Him, and by Him alone, is a man convicted of sin, and convinced of the things of God. This is the case, not only according to St. Paul, but also in the Fourth Gospel. By the Holy Spirit alone is a man born into that new life which is eternal. No man apart from the Spirit is raised from the dead. 'The Christian life is essentially the product of the new conditions, the spiritual atmosphere into which the believer has been transferred.'[3]

5. CONCLUSION

In the New Testament teaching as to the effective working of the Spirit of God (the Holy Spirit), we see most clearly the difference between the Hebrew and the Greek attitudes to life. They are fundamentally different. The object and aim of the Hebrew system is *da'ath elohim* (Knowledge of God). The object and aim

[1] T. C. Edwards, *A Commentary on the First Epistle to the Corinthians* (1897), p. 59.

[2] *Mansfield College Essays*, pp. 267–86.

[3] H. Wheeler Robinson, *The Christian Doctrine of Man*, p. 131.

of the Greek system is *gnothi seauton* (Know thyself). Between these two there is the widest possible difference. There is no compromise between the two on anything like equal terms. They are poles apart in attitude and method. The Hebrew system starts with God. The only true wisdom is Knowledge of God. 'The fear of God is the beginning of wisdom.' The corollary is that man can never know himself, what he is and what is his relation to the world, unless first he learn of God and be submissive to God's sovereign will. The Greek system, on the contrary, starts from the knowledge of man, and seeks to rise to an understanding of the ways and Nature of God through the knowledge of what is called 'man's higher nature'. According to the Bible, man has no higher nature except he be born of the Spirit.

We find this approach of the Greeks no where in the Bible. The whole Bible, the New Testament as well as the Old Testament, is based on the Hebrew attitude and approach. We are of the firm opinion that this ought to be recognized on all hands to a greater extent. It is clear to us, and we hope that we have made it clear in these pages to others, that there is often a great difference between Christian theology and Biblical theology. Throughout the centuries the Bible has been interpreted in a Greek context, and even the New Testament has been interpreted on the basis of Plato and Aristotle. This may be justifiable, but we hold that those who adopt this method of interpretation should realize what it is that they are doing, and should cease to maintain that they are basing their theology on the Bible.

We find this tendency to interpret the New Testament in Greek terms almost everywhere. To give one instance out of very many, Sanday and Headlam say,[1] in commenting on Romans viii. 9, 'he (Paul) rises almost imperceptibly through the *pneuma* of man to the *Pneuma* of God'. But this surely is precisely what Paul does not do. Paul starts, after the Hebrew fashion, with the *Pneuma* of God when he is discussing the life in the Spirit. The passage continues, 'from thinking of the way in which the *pneuma* in its best moods acts upon the character, he passes on to that influence from without which keeps it in its best moods'. Again we find an interpretation quite contrary to what we believe to be the Pauline attitude. It is true that Paul uses *pneuma* on occasion to mean the controlling element in man's nature, but it is not the case that the

[1] *Romans* (I.C.C.) p. 196.

Pneuma from without 'keeps it in its best moods'. On the contrary, it transforms it and changes it. Paul's whole position rests on the conviction that before the invasion of this heavenly *Pneuma* (the Spirit of God), man is *psychikos* ('psychic', natural) by nature, and not *pneumatikos* ('pneumatic', spiritual) at all. Whilst Paul, as we have said immediately above, uses *pneuma* in the ordinary way of 'the spirit of man', yet when he uses the word in connection with the effective working of the Spirit of God, he means a new *pneuma* which is born of the Spirit of God, and which points in its fullness to the resurrection life. The word *pneuma*, used of the 'natural man', is not the same thing at all as the *pneuma* of the 'spiritual man'. According to Greek ideas, doubtless the identification can be made. This is actually what Sanday and Headlam have done. But they are not interpreting Paul. They are re-interpreting him according to the Greek model, and, we believe, therefore misunderstanding him. We therefore disagree entirely with Sanday and Headlam when they continue still further to speak of the Spirit of God in the Pauline writings as 'a settled, permanent, penetrative influence'. It is not a penetrative influence at all, according to Paul. It is a transforming Power.

The true development from the Pauline theology is to be found in Luther and in John Wesley. This Reformation theology is certainly based on Biblical theology. It speaks of Salvation by Faith alone, i.e. by Faith in Christ alone. It involves a complete and utter trust in God, a recumbency upon Him. It does not, as some allege, deprecate the value of good works, neither does it decry ethical values, but it denies that good works are themselves the avenue to salvation. It emphasizes good works as a consequence of the working in the human heart of the Holy Spirit. In John Wesley's sermons, the whole matter is set forth. This is Scriptural Christianity. It comprises what is distinctive in the Bible, those doctrines which make the Bible what it is, unique and different from any other book whatever.

If we are to maintain that the distinctive ideas of the Bible, both of the Old and the New Testaments, are the distinctive ideas of Christianity, then let us be faithful to them, and let us hold to them. On the other hand, if we are going to start from the Greek point of view, enhanced and brought to new life by our modern evolutionary theories, then let us say so boldly, and realize what it is that we are doing. It is high time that we made our position clear, not only to ourselves, but also to others. What is the Christian Faith? Is it a Faith which is founded on the Bible, with the distinctive ideas of the Bible as its determining factors? Or is Christianity in truth the greatest eclectic system the world has ever known, with the ideas of the Greek philosophers as the determining factors? Are Sanday and Headlam right, for instance, in the re-interpretation of Romans viii. 9?

Is there still, in these days, such a thing as Revealed Religion? Or is all religion Natural Religion? When the Christian seeks to reply to Dr. Julian Huxley, who makes articulate the 'religious' beliefs of great numbers of people to-day, on what does his reply rest? Do we also begin from speculations as to the good in man, or the proper development of man's 'better nature' or man's 'true self'? Or do we look to the transforming Power of the Holy Spirit working in man, and bringing him to God? This latter is what the Bible says, and we do not see that it admits of any compromise. To agree to some sort of statement to the effect that a man's better nature is influenced by the Spirit of God, may sound to be a good compromise between the two points of view, but it is no compromise at all. The Bible teaches that a man must be dominated by the Spirit of God, transformed, born again into a new life.

'Thy sons, O Zion, against thy sons, O Greece' (Zechariah ix. 13) arose first as a rallying cry in days long ago when some Jews sought to re-interpret Judaism in order to make it more acceptable to Greek ways of thought and life. There have always been Jews who have sought to make terms with the Gentile world, and it has in time meant the death of Judaism for all such. There have been Christians from the beginning who have sought to do this. Often it has been done unconsciously, but, whether consciously or unconsciously, the question needs to be faced as to whether it is right. Our position is that the re-interpretation of Biblical theology in terms of the ideas of the Greek philosophers has been both widespread throughout the centuries and everywhere destructive to the essence of the Christian faith. Dr. A. Nygren has dealt[1] with the matter in connection with what his earlier translator, Father A. G. Hebert, has called 'the fatal confusion between Agape and Eros which now obscures the meaning of Christianity'.[2] We commend this remark of Father Hebert's because, whilst we our-

[1] *Agape and Eros.*

[2] Translator's preface to *Agape and Eros*, Part I, pp. xi *f.*

selves may be accused of having a Protestant or even an Evangelical Methodist bias, these charges cannot ever be laid against Father Hebert, much less to any degree substantiated. Father Hebert rightly sees in the Catholic system a conception of salvation conceived in Aristotelian terms, and an 'idea of Beatitude . . . closely related to the Neoplatonic idea of the Vision of the One, and (bearing) little relation to the Beatitudes of the Gospel'.[1] On the other hand, equally rightly he sees a marked tendency in contemporary Protestantism 'to lay emphasis on the development of personality, and a human movement towards the realization of ethical ideals. The Kingdom of God is regarded as something . . . which is achieved by human effort.'[2] If these judgements are sound, and we believe that they are sound, then neither Catholic nor Protestant theology is based on Biblical theology. In each case we have a domination of Christian theology by Greek thought.

What, then, is to be done with the Bible? Is it to be regarded as the norm, and its distinctive ideas as the determining factors of Christian theology? Or are we to continue to regard Plato and Aristotle with their pagan successors as contributing the norm, and the main ideas of Greek philosophy as the determining factors of Christian theology, with the Bible as illustrative and confirmatory when and where it is suitable? Father Hebert holds[3] that 'there can be no right answer to the question, "What is Christianity?" except by a clear view of the real meaning of the *Agape* of the New Testament, and its difference from the pagan Eros'. We go further. We hold that there can be no right answer until we have come to a clear view of the distinctive ideas of both Old and New Testaments and their difference from the pagan ideas which so largely have dominated 'Christian' thought.

[1] Translator's preface to *Agape and Eros*, Part I, p. xi.
[2] *ibid.*, p. xii. [3] *ibid.*, pp. xi *f.*

INDEX OF PROPER NAMES

INDEX OF OLD TESTAMENT PASSAGES

INDEX OF NEW TESTAMENT PASSAGES

INDEX OF EXTRA-BIBLICAL PASSAGES